Globalism Versus Realism

Also of Interest from Westview Press

† *Change in the International System,* edited by Ole R. Holsti, Randolph M. Siverson, and Alexander L. George

† *The Theory and Structure of International Political Economy,* edited by Todd Sandler

† *The Challenge of the New International Economic Order,* edited by Edwin P. Reubens

Self-Determination: National, Regional, and Global Dimensions, edited by Yonah Alexander and Robert A. Friedlander

† *Politics, Values, and Public Policy: The Problem of Methodology,* Frank Fischer

† *Studies on a Just World Order: Volume 1 — Toward a Just World Order,* edited by Richard Falk, Samuel S. Kim, and Saul H. Mendlovitz

† *Nations and States: An Enquiry into the Origins of Nations and the Politics of Nationalism,* Hugh Seton-Watson

† *Transnational Enterprises: Their Impact on Third World Societies and Cultures,* edited by Krishna Kumar

Managing Transnationalism in Northern Europe, Bengt Sundelius

† *The Foreign Policy Priorities of Third World States,* edited by John J. Stremlau

† *Nonstate Actors in International Politics: From Transnational to Substate Organizations,* Phillip Taylor

Global Human Rights: Public Policies, Comparative Measures, and NGO Strategies, edited by Ved P. Nanda, James R. Scarritt, and George W. Shepherd, Jr.

† *Psychological Models in International Politics,* edited by Lawrence S. Falkowski

† Available in hardcover and paperback.

About the Book and Editors

Globalism Versus Realism:
International Relations' Third Debate
edited by Ray Maghroori and Bennett Ramberg

Since World War I, when the movement toward a comprehensive and systematic examination of international relations began, two intensive debates about the nature and methodology of the discipline have helped shape the field. The first was between the realist and the idealist schools; the second, between the traditionalists and the behavioralists. Now, a third debate has emerged, pitting state-centric conceptualizations against the globalist focus on interdependence. At issue is the nature of the international system. Is it still one in which the sovereign nation-state constitutes the dominant actor? Or has a process of global political, economic, and even social integration transformed the world into a "global village"?

This text presents seminal works that define and illuminate the third debate, focused by the editors' comments prefacing each chapter and their synthesizing introductory and concluding chapters. It is designed to allow students and scholars to compare and contrast the contending approaches in order to better understand and develop the discipline of international relations. Given the consensus among both realists and globalists that our assumptions about world affairs affect how we construct theories to explain events and that the model we impose on the world directly affects the policies we prescribe, it is difficult to overemphasize the importance of the subject.

Ray Maghroori is a lecturer in political science at the University of California in Riverside and has also lectured at the University of California in Santa Cruz. He is the coauthor of *The Yom Kippur War: A Case Study in Crisis Decision-Making in American Foreign Policy* (1981). **Bennett Ramberg** is a research associate at the Center for International and Strategic Affairs at the University of California in Los Angeles. He was a congressional foreign policy consultant in 1970 and 1972, and he served as a member of President Carter's Nuclear Disarmament Task Force in 1976. His most recent book is *Destruction of Nuclear Energy Facilities in War: The Problem and the Implications* (1980).

Globalism Versus Realism: International Relations' Third Debate

edited by Ray Maghroori
and Bennett Ramberg

Westview Press / Boulder, Colorado

Copyright © 1982 by Westview Press, Inc.

Published in 1982 in the United States of America by
Westview Press, Inc.
5500 Central Avenue
Boulder, Colorado 80301
Frederick A. Praeger, President and Publisher

Library of Congress Cataloging in Publication Data
Main entry under title:
Globalism versus realism.
    Includes bibliographic references and index.
    1. International relations—Addresses, essays, lectures. I. Maghroori, Ray.
II. Ramberg, Bennett.
JX1391.G53   327.1   82-2770
ISBN 0-86531-346-6   AACR2
ISBN 0-86531-347-4 (pbk.)

Printed and bound in the United States of America

Contents

Globalism Versus Realism

JAMES N. ROSENAU

Order and Disorder in the Study of World Politics: Ten Essays in Search of Perspective

Although the observations of the editors and the analyses of the authors that follow do not actually constitute a debate, in that they are not responding directly to each other, they certainly reflect different perspectives on the dynamics of present-day world politics. And the differences among them are not trivial or picayune. They spring, rather, from conflicting assumptions about the structure of international systems, the nature of the order that underlies them, the operation of the causal processes that give rise to recognizable outcomes, the identity of the central actors, and the degree to which change and continuity are likely to mark the course of events. To an important extent, moreover, these differences are both a source and a consequence of diverse methodological premises.

Let us be clear about what the differences amount to. They are not different "schools of thought," because in some instances the underlying philosophical foundations are taken for granted and are not examined or justified. Nor can the differences be viewed as constituting "analytic frameworks," inasmuch as more often than not the premises and procedures governing inquiry are implicit and inchoate, and thus lack the degree of articulation and coherence necessary to frame and guide analysis. Likewise, the differences can hardly be treated as summing to competitive theories, since integrated propositions about the interaction of key variables are conspicuously absent from most formulations. Notwithstanding their lack of theory, structure, and coherence, however, the aforementioned differences are sufficiently important to justify differentiation among students of world politics today in terms of their general approach to—or perspective on—the phenomena of the field. An ap-

1

proach or perspective is much looser and broader than a school of thought, a framework, or a theory, but it does derive from some organizing assumptions about the nature and dynamics of international relations.

Exactly how many general approaches to the field can be distinguished in the work of its practitioners depends, of course, on how the differences among them are conceptualized. As the editors point out in Chapter 1, the past is marked by a tendency to dichotomize all differences and to consider the field as evolving through tensions between two broad perspectives—first (in the decades preceding World War II) between the realists and the idealists, then (in the early decades after World War II) between the realists and the behavioralists, and more recently between the realists and the globalists. The essays in this book are confined largely to these last two approaches. However, the editors show in their concluding chapter that they believe that important differences can be lost through dichotomization and that debate in the field should move on to competition among a greater variety of perspectives. To alert the reader to the limits of a set of dichotomized perspectives, in this foreword I have deliberately anticipated the editors' conclusions by allowing for a third approach (the last column of Table 1)—one that is peripheral to the main work in the field but that does attract some adherents by virtue of its stress on economic variables.

It is perhaps useful to note that the labels attached to the various approaches fall far short of designating a central tendency and can therefore be highly misleading. Most notably, they tend either to exaggerate or to understate what those who proceed under each label actually do or believe. Surely, for example, realists are not the only analysts who feel confident they are focusing on the realities of world politics. Doubtless those who employ each approach see themselves as realistically assessing and interpreting the course of events. Similarly, the behavioralist label connotes a focus on action and interaction that is hardly the exclusive concern of behavioralists. Realists and globalists also see themselves as preoccupied with the flow of behaviors that sustain international life. To confound matters further, at least one of the labels (behavioralist) also suggests a methodological orientation, whereas the others seem exclusively confined to substantive concerns. In short, one is well advised to beware of the labels used in the field and, instead, to think of the various approaches in terms of the central assumptions on which they rest.

In recent years I have found it useful to think of the study of world affairs as marked by three main approaches, each differentiated by its core assumptions about the structure of the global system. To get as close as possible to the central tendency underlying each approach, I have

TABLE 1   THREE MAJOR APPROACHES TO WORLD POLITICS:
SOME CONNECTIONS BETWEEN SUBSTANTIVE PREMISES AND METHODOLOGICAL IMPULSES IN INTERNATIONAL STUDIES

	State-Centric	Multi-Centric	Global-Centric
Structure of the global system	Fragmented, with power distributed among nation-states	Interdependent, with power distributed among nation-states and a variety of nonstate actors, such as multinational corporations, international regimes, ethnic groups, etc.	Integrated, with power distributed in terms of centuries-long patterns that are global in scope
Nature of underlying order	Anarchic, because all actors respond to different stimuli	Mostly orderly, because most actors are performing functions necessary to system maintenance or transformation	Very orderly, because a capitalist world economy locks actors into their circumstances
Essential manifestation of underlying order	Predominance of nation-states	Complexity, because old patterns of interdependence become obsolete and new ones become salient	Production, trade and distribution patterns of goods and services
Status of knowledge about underlying order	Basic dynamics known	Basic dynamics not yet uncovered	Basic dynamics known
Causes underlying observed effects	National interests that change with changing times	Perceptions, motives, role conflicts, etc., at the microlevel and resource capabilities, power balances, technological developments, etc. at the macrolevel, all of which are both rooted in past practices and responsive to new conditions	Deep structures, such as division of labor, class conflicts, and bureaucratization
Time frame in which relevant phenomena unfold	Limited, such as an era, a regime, an administration, a lifetime	Varied, depending on whether microphenomena or macrophenomena are under examination	Extensive, crossing decades and centuries
Degree to which changes can prevail over continuities	Considerable, because national capabilities and definitions of interests change	Variable, depending on whether new conditions transform past practices	Minimal, because the capitalist world economy is capable of absorbing any challenge to its structure
Phenomena to be clarified through inquiry	Time-and place-bound events, situations, issues, policies, conflicts, crises	Recurring patterns, their shifts and their breakpoints, within and among systems, issue-areas, and structures of authority	Long-time continuities, deep structures
Methods of inquiry most suitable to the phenomena to be clarified	Careful analysis, historical examples, case studies	Quantitative analysis, theory development, hypothesis testing	Comparison of long-term historical analyses (using both quantitative and qualitative data) with each other
Openness to new data supporting alternative approaches and resulting readiness to change approaches	Virtually nil	Virtually nil	Virtually nil

labeled them the state-centric, the multi-centric, and the global-centric approaches. As can be seen in the first row of Table 1, the initial distinction among these three approaches involves the distribution of power within the global system. The state-centric analysts presume a fragmented structure in which power is located in nation-states; those who adhere to a multi-centric approach picture an interdependent structure with power distributed among a variety of types of actors; and those who subscribe to a global-centric perspective view the system as having an integrated structure deriving from patterns of power distribution that have been in place for centuries.

Associated with these differences are a series of further distinctions that are indicated in the remaining rows of Table 1. Comparisons across the rows of the table thus reveal the thoroughgoing extent to which the three approaches are substantively and methodologically differentiated, while analyses down the columns highlight how each approach is founded on a set of coherent and interconnected premises and procedures.

I do not wish to imply, however, that a person's basic approach to world politics necessarily originates in how he or she views power as structured within the global system. That dimension certainly constitutes a central feature of each approach, but it does not necessarily give rise in a causal sense to the other differences among the three approaches. Initially you might just as easily be drawn to a particular approach by the kind of assumption it makes about orderliness in human affairs (row 2) or by the time frame you are most comfortable with (row 6). On the other hand, I would argue that the several premises of each approach are sufficiently interconnected and differentiated to lead one to accept all of its assumptions, whatever the reason for being drawn to it in the first place.

Stated differently, the way in which analysts become adherents of one or another approach is not necessarily based on intellectual or rational calculation. One does not simply look at the course of events and conclude that its structure more nearly conforms to, say, the state-centric pattern than the other two. Empirical developments may have some bearing on our fondness for a particular approach, but it seems to me that the choice is more a matter of temperament than of observation. The meaning of events on the global scene is not self-evident. They have to be interpreted in some kind of context, and the context (i.e., approach) we employ determines how we will interpret the events and attach significance to them. Thus, faced with the *same* sequence of events or data pattern, adherents of the three approaches would interpret them in three fundamentally different ways. But, one might ask, what about the empirical reality inherent in the sequence or pattern? How could, say, state-centric and multi-centric analysts differ on whether a series of events were shaped primarily by the foreign policies of states or by the decisions of other actors? The answer is, of course, that the two types of analysts would assess that series of events on the basis of widely differing assumptions and thus come to very different, even conflicting, conclusions as to what actually happened. This is why I argue that our temperaments – our tolerance of uncertainty and variability, our inclination to focus on situations as evidence of constancy or of change, our tendency to look for causation in microphenomena or macroprocesses, our readiness to accept ambiguous evidence or demand concrete proof, and so on – are the central determinants of which approach we will find most suitable. Such temperamental factors serve as filters through which we perceive, structure, and evaluate the empirical realities of world politics.

Let us consider a specific example. The proliferation of multinational corporations and international organizations after World War II was interpreted by some as portending a significant alteration in the structure of the global system. For them the emergence of these new actors on the world scene, along with the advent of oil shortages, fiscal crises, and terrorism on a global scale, justified reconsidering their state-centric approach and, eventually, the adoption of a multi-centric perspective. Other analysts, however, assessed the evolution of new types of actors as nothing more than a ripple in the stream of history, a minor perturbation within a global structure they perceived as essentially unchanged. Which approach is more accurate? Neither; both depend on how you define change and what kind of evidence of change you are prepared to accept.

This is not the place to elaborate on each of the entries in Table 1. Although they use somewhat different labels, the following chapters fully amplify the differences between the first two approaches and touch on some of the factors out of which the stress on global economics has emerged as a third possible approach. To facilitate assessment of the discussions that follow, however, I would like to highlight several aspects of the formulation set forth in Table 1.

Perhaps the most complex issue that divides the three approaches involves the orderliness presumed to underlie and sustain the global system. We can hardly have a conception of any system without also having some notion of the order on which it rests and the degree to which that order is subject to distortion and upheaval as a result of capriciousness on the part of any of its components. To posit an underlying order, in other words, is to presume that events have a logic of their own, that they do not occur spontaneously, that there is a cause for every effect. Since the three approaches differ in their view of the coherence of the global system's structure, it follows that they also subscribe to disparate presumptions about the nature and degree of orderliness in the universe from which the system derives. For state-centric analysts the dynamics that sustain the underlying order are quite obvious: since power is located primarily in nation-states and since each state acts in terms of its own national interests, there are few general rules governing international behavior and the result is an order that is essentially anarchic. This is not to say that there are no patterns whatsoever, but rather that the underlying patterns are disparate, diffuse, and knowable only through understanding why each state is motivated to act as it does. Similarly, those who adhere to a global-centric approach also presume to know the underlying order of the system: it derives from the structure of the centuries-long capitalist world economy and is highly integrated and coherent because all actors seem to act within the parameters set by the global economy. Multi-centric analysts, on the other hand, do not presume to have discovered the dynamics of the underlying order, inasmuch as the parameters of action within their system are not seen to be as uniform as those set by national interests or the requirements of capitalism. Yet, since the multi-centric approach sees all actors, national or otherwise, as acting on the basis of such common sources as the microrequirements of roles and the macroimperatives of technology, the underlying order it posits is more interdependent and much greater than the anarchy that results when all states act in terms of idiosyncratic conceptions of their national interests.

An interesting and often unrecognized consequence of these different assumptions about the order underlying world politics is that they tend to lead to different methodologies especially suitable to carrying forward the inquiries that the practitioners of the different approaches deem important. As can be seen in rows 8 and 9 of Table 1, there is a close connection between the substantive premises and methodological impulses that differentiate the various approaches to the field. Thus, the state-centric analysts' presumption of an anarchic structure underlying the system predisposes them to eschew quantitative analysis and to rely instead on a looser, more interpretive methodology that allows them to probe more fully the time- and place-bound vagaries of anarchic situations. Multi-centric researchers, on the other hand, are more inclined toward quantitative inquiries because their underlying conception of an interdependent order suggests the existence of recurring micro- and macropatterns that are not easily traced or verified through studies of specific situations. In a similar manner the presumption of a highly ordered world integrated by a capitalist economy leads global-centric investigators to employ still another methodology, one founded on the development and comparison of case histories that stretch across periods of time long enough to reveal and elaborate the dynamics of the global political economy.

The last row of Table 1 points up the important question of whether convergence is possible among any or all of the three approaches. Is it not possible, those who believe in the unity of knowledge might ask, that somewhere down the line, after many creative and successful inquiries yield many new insights and data, the adherents of the various approaches will conclude that reality lies somewhere between them and that a synthesis of their perspectives is both possible and desirable? Or, at least, might not state-centric and multi-centric analysts gather enough data on the global system to converge around a common understanding of its underlying dynamics? In my judgment the answer must be very negative indeed. For, as already implied, temperaments tend to remain too fixed and resistant to new evidence for most adherents of any approach to abandon their fundamental premises.

Such a conclusion highlights the importance of this book. It suggests that the differences described in the ensuing pages are likely to mark the field well into the foreseeable future and that the reader is thus well advised to ponder them seriously. Happily, the editors have brought together a collection of essays that facilitate this task and render it manageable.

1
Introduction: Major Debates in International Relations

In this chapter, Maghroori explores three definitional debates that have shaped the field of international relations since it emerged as a distinct discipline over sixty years ago. The realist-idealist debate of the interwar period focused on the means of maintaining world order—power politics versus collective security. The traditionalist-behavioralist dialogue of the 1950s and 1960s addressed methodological questions, but in the late 1960s a third debate arose that continues this day. It involves "realists"—those who conceptualize world affairs in terms of power politics—and "globalists"—those who argue that political and economic interdependence and integration are transforming international politics.

The study of international relations as a distinct discipline is a relatively recent development, although such antecedents as diplomatic history and international law have long traditions. Movement toward a comprehensive and systematic examination of international relations began only with World War I.[1] The war shook many of the dominant ideals about the correct conduct of global politics, and the discipline of international relations took shape during a period of profound change in attitudes about world affairs. This undoubtedly contributed to the introspection and controversy that have marked the growth of the field. Since the close of World War I, two extensive debates have taken place. The first was evidenced by the clash between the realists and the idealists. The second involved the traditionalists and the behavioralists.

The realist outlook rested on the simple proposition that the pursuit of national power was a natural drive and that those who neglected to cultivate power actually invited war. The realists further assumed that the community of states, composed of individual actors attempting to maximize their own power, influence, and fundamental security, would be naturally drawn into transitory alliances that would in turn tend to impose a certain balance of power among opposing blocs of states. Thus, the realists upheld the sovereign nation-state's right to pursue power and relied on a balance-of-power system to constrain the competition among states. The scope, duration, and social costs of World War I rendered most, if not all, of the realists' arguments unacceptable. In particular, the notion that sovereign states were entitled to unrestrained independence lost popularity, and the balance-of-power system was rejected as unserviceable. A new school of thought arose that called for the renunciation of war as a national policy, the institutionalization of an international order, and the replacement of balance-of-power politics by collective security.

The idealist approach dominated the study of international politics between World War I and World War II, even though some realists continued to cling stubbornly to their own view of the world. The first assumption of the idealists was that national self-determination within Europe would remove one of the major sources of war. Each nationality, as far as possible, was to be organized as an independent state. A second assumption was that war often resulted from secret agreements between states, and that if citizens of these states were aware of such agreements they would not be tolerated. The idealists called for an end to secret diplomacy and urged greater public participation in the conduct of foreign policy. They also argued that the creation of an international political organization would provide a forum in which states could negotiate their differences. This movement led to the founding of the League of Nations. Finally, and most importantly, the idealist program advocated abandoning the balance of power in favor of a system of international collective security that would require states to reduce their military preparedness to the lowest possible level and to rely on the combined military capability of the world community for their security against armed aggression. It also presupposed (1) that a world governing body would exist to determine whether aggression had occurred and to coordinate a global response, and (2) that states would automatically join in collective responses to aggression anywhere in the world.[2]

The debate between the realists and the idealists centered on the issue of collective security.[3] The realists argued that collective security depended on altruistic behavior and was therefore unreliable. They criticized the idealists for assuming that states would automatically put aside their own interests to assist an aggrieved nation even when the particular act of aggression posed no immediate or imminent danger to them. The idealists argued that peace was indivisible – that aggression anywhere, at any time, against any state was a threat to all states. The realists ridiculed this view as inconsistent with national motivation. They argued that only a balance-of-power system, in which each state guarded its own security and compensated for the aggressive tendencies of other states through defensive alliances, could promote the cause of peace.

The debate, then, involved a fundamental disagreement about the nature of the international political system and the motivations behind state behavior. The idealists rejected the realist depiction of the world because they considered its consequences unacceptable. The realists countered that, like it or not, the pursuit of state power was an inescapable fact and the theory and practice of international relations must adjust to that reality. The idealists, they argued, were actually endangering peace by relying on utopian measures to control aggression. As with most debates, the conflict was not decided by the merits of the arguments, but rather by the course of events. The inability of the League of Nations to check Japanese aggression in Manchuria, the Italians' assault on Ethiopia, and Russia's attempted subjugation of Finland strengthened the position of the realists. The outbreak of World War II was attributed to the naiveté of idealism, much as World War I had been ascribed to the fallacies of realism.

The creation of the United Nations, along with its various mechanisms for dealing with international disputes, demonstrates that aspects of the idealist outlook had influence even after World War II. But the realist perspective became the dominant outlook, especially with the breakdown in U.S.-Soviet relations and the rise of the Cold War. As Theodore Couloumbis and James Wolfe have noted, "In the 1950s the realists became the prevalent school of thought in international relations. Using the argument that only policies based on power could afford a semblance of global security, they had comparatively little difficulty in overcoming the remnants of the idealistic tradition."[4]

The revival of the realist school was reflected in the leading work of the period, Hans J. Morgenthau's *Politics Among Nations: The Struggle for Power and Peace.* As the subtitle indicates, the pursuit of state power was once again accepted as consistent with the goal of international peace. Indeed, retrospective analysis of the origins of World War II led to a belief that the appeasement of aggressive demands and the military weakness of the democracies were the primary causes of the war. In the postwar period most states returned to the realist prescription of meeting threats to peace with strength, not appeasement. Although such attitudes softened somewhat with the emergence of U.S.-Soviet détente, the realist view continues to strongly influence our understanding of the international political system.

The second important debate arose during the 1950s, when the dispute between realism and idealism was fading into the background. Unlike the disagreement between realists and idealists, which centered on the nature of the international system and the most viable approaches to the conduct of international politics, the debate between the traditionalists and the behavioralists focused on the best method of studying international relations. The realist-idealist clash had remained largely confined to the field of international relations, but the traditional-behavioral controversy involved nearly the entire discipline of political science (and some other disciplines as well). At the heart of the issue was the desire of a new generation of scholars to develop a more systematic or "scientific" study of political phenomena.

The movement to make the study of politics more rigorous so that it would meet the standards of scientific procedure developed in other fields (and thereby gain prestige as a discipline) took the form of behavioralism. As one text explains, "Behavioralism can be defined as the systematic search for political patterns through the formulation of empirical theory and the technical analysis and verification thereof. Behavioralism involves two basic emphases: 'the formulation of concepts, hypotheses, and explanations in systematic terms' and 'empirical methods of research.'"[5] By contrast, the more widespread traditionalist approach relied on a variety of factors, including history, personal experience, legal formulations, and intuition, to provide the foundations for generalizing about world politics. Many traditionalist works on international relations were based on immeasurable single variables, such as the assumed universal drive for power that served as the starting point of Morgenthau's work. Behavioralists rejected the literary and philosophical approaches of the traditionalists and demanded the construction of formal models with testable hypotheses.

One of the first important behavioral works written in the field of international relations was Richard C. Snyder, H. W. Bruck, and Burton Sapin's *Decision-Making as an Approach to the Study of International Politics.* [6] It advanced an extensive set of measurable variables by which foreign policy actions could be studied. Traditionalist critics argued that the number and complexity of the variables would make the model's application infeasible. However, later studies of the United States' decision to intervene in Korea that used the decision-making framework demonstrated quite convincingly that the model could be employed economically in case research.[7] The decision-making approach, which never gained very wide acceptance, was followed by even more rigorous empirical frameworks. They included game theory, using mathematical models of probability; transnational analysis, using quantified indexes of interaction between nation-states; and linkage theory, which focused on observable relationships between intrastate variables and interstate behavior. The most enduring contribution of behavioralism to the study of international relations has been the application of statistical analysis to international phenomena. The major limitation of the approach is that significant variables in world politics do not readily lend themselves to quantification or mathematical manipulation.

In the 1950s the behavioralists expected that cumulative studies would gradually reveal general patterns of international politics and lead to a general theory. By the late 1960s, however, they increasingly recognized that although the behavioral approach had made great contributions, the insights it provided were limited and were not superior to those resulting from the traditional approach. This realization led behavioralists to conclude by 1969 that, in the words of Charles McClelland, "it is necessary to utilize both techniques and both approaches. It would be unwise to neglect the meaningful products of experience and history."[8] By the early 1970s the traditionalist-behavioralist debate began to mellow. As James Rosenau has remarked, "Where the differences between the scientific and traditional approaches to the subject once appeared to pose a fateful choice among mutually exclusive premises and procedures, they are now seen to be complementary as well as conflictual and, accordingly, the existence of several viable routes to knowledge has come to be accepted."[9] The controversy tapered off within the field of international relations and within the discipline of political science as a whole. As a 1970 text on politics noted, "While the 'battle' is not over, the harshness of the split within departments has begun to soften. This has happened as the validity of a division of labor based on the existence of enough work for all has been recognized."[10]

Advocates of realism and idealism, traditionalism and behavioralism remain in the field, but these issues themselves no longer constitute the main launch point for current debate. What is emerging in the professional journals is conflict over the validity of the state-centric approach as compared to a focus on a presumedly emerging global interdependence. This debate is not entirely independent of the two earlier controversies. The realists (who also prove very often to be traditionalists) generally uphold the state-centric view, whereas many idealists and behavioralists are attracted to the notion of global interdependence, either for the usual reasons or because this focus affords a better opportunity to apply empirical methods. The controversy revolves around fundamental assumptions about international relations. As Michael Sullivan explains, "The framework for understanding international politics, and the underlying assumptions concerning the basic structure of the international system, are once again coming under scrutiny."[11] At issue is the nature of the international system. Is it still one in which the sovereign nation-state is the dominant actor, or has a process of global political and even social integration transformed it into an interdependent community?

A growing body of literature is beginning to question the continued usefulness of the realists' state-centric outlook. For instance, one source argues that "the assumptions of political realists, whose theories dominated the post-war period, are often an inadequate basis for analyzing the politics of interdependence."[12] The literature suggests that a globalist or transnationalist paradigm would provide a more accurate picture of the structure, dynamics, and operation of the contemporary international system. The realists, for their part, dismiss these arguments. They assert that the independent state remains the decisive actor in world politics and warn that "the international system may not be moving in the direction most globalists seem to think."[13] While the advocates of the state-centric perspective acknowledge the transformation that is occurring within the international system, they maintain that "the argument for the existence of a drastically altered new international system is not yet convincing."[14]

Although realists and globalists disagree on the essential character of the international system, they both accept one point: models do count. They agree that "one's assumptions about world politics profoundly affect what one sees and how one constructs theories to explain events."[15] Even more important, they believe that "the model we impose on the world affects directly the policies we prescribe."[16] Hence, it is easy to appreciate that the outcome of the unfolding debate could well determine the direction of the field, its priorities, and its research agenda, if either school of thought prevails completely. For this reason, it is important to differentiate clearly between these competing perspectives.

THE STATE-CENTRIC (REALIST) VIEW

The realist model of international politics is based upon a number of assumptions. The basic postulate is that "the state in its modern form is the fundamental political unit in the world system and that, therefore, it is possible to analyze world politics largely in terms of interstate relations."[17] Although realists admit that considerable changes have occurred in the international system since World War II, they believe that the state remains the primary actor in world politics.[18] The state-centric model defines the state as a "relatively hard-shelled unit,"[19] and often views it in terms of concretely defined geographical areas. Furthermore, realists believe that "most human activities (both political and non-political) can be defined with reference to the boundaries of states."[20] Because they view the state as the basic component of the international system, many realists approach international politics through the analysis of foreign policy.[21]

Realists dismiss the notion of interdependence. Most of them argue that interdependence among nations has not increased; one analyst claims that it is "on the decrease."[22] Referring to the increasing body of literature on interdependence, Kenneth Waltz writes, "The American rhetoric of interdependence has taken on some of the qualities of an ideology."[23] In his view, interdependence has become an emotional issue devoid of objective significance. The word "interdependence," according to Waltz, "subtly obscures the inequalities of national capability, pleasingly points to a reciprocal dependence, and strongly suggests that all states are playing the same game."[24]

The state-centric paradigm puts considerable emphasis on the notion of military security.[25] Power, often defined in military terms, is an essential ingredient of realist throught. Realists assume that statesmen think and act in terms of power.[26] Many realists accept some or all of the assumptions of the balance-of-power theory. Hans J. Morgenthau, a leading realist proponent, has argued that "the international balance of power is only a particular manifestation of a general social principle to which all societies composed of a number of autonomous units owe the autonomy of their component parts; that the balance of power and policies aiming at this preservation are not only inevitable but are an essential stabilizing factor in a society of sovereign nations."[27]

International organizations are of limited worth in the state-centric model. "Experience has shown that the attempt to use the United Nations for the purpose of forcing agreement upon either of the superpowers is futile and only aggravates the disagreement."[28] Although realists recognize the United Nations' accomplishments in certain areas, they maintain that "there is no evidence to show that [it] has prevented any war."[29] Realists seem similarly skeptical about the centrality of the multinational corporation (MNC) in shaping world politics. They acknowledge the economic significance of the MNC but often disregard its political impact. According to Robert Gilpin, "Under certain circumstances and in relation to particular states there can be little doubt that the multinational corporation has, and can exercise, considerable influence over domestic and international relations. . . . But in general there is little evidence to substantiate the argument that the multinational corporation as an independent actor has had a significant impact on international politics."[30] In realist thought the state still dominates international politics.

Realists believe in the separation between domestic and foreign policy, and they use different criteria to judge the soundness of each. They accept the need to integrate moral concerns into domestic policy, because, as Morgenthau has argued, "The moral law is not a utilitarian instrument aiming at the protection of society, even though its observance has this effect, but its commands are absolute and must be obeyed for their own sake."[31] However, the state-centric perspective shows little concern with moral issues in foreign policy. The realists' main criterion for judging foreign policy is how it affects "national interest."[32]

The foregoing paragraphs summarize the major tenets of the realist model, which dominated major academic and policymaking circles in the United States immediately after World War II. In recent years, however, the realist model has come under scrutiny, and some have argued that it is no longer a valid paradigm for understanding international politics. They suggest that today's international system should be viewed in terms of a new model—the globalist paradigm.

THE GLOBALIST (TRANSNATIONALIST) VIEW

According to the globalist model, the present international system differs sharply from the one that existed prior to World War II. The most important change has been the decline in the role and significance of the nation-state. There are several explanations for this phenomenon. Seyom Brown has argued that "the alignments and antagonisms of the recent past are shifting ground, and structures premised on their stability appear to be crumbling. Even the bedrock of the international system, the sovereignty of nation-states, is subject to severe erosion."[33] Although Brown views the end of the Cold War as a turning point, other analysts regard technological advancement and its impact on interstate relations as the main source of system transformation. Oran Young believes that "rapid and continuing developments in a variety of areas such as communications, transportation, and military technology have caused an effective shrinking of the world and have led to a situation in which the state, nation-state, and state system are increasingly obsolescent and ineffective structures for the achievement of human security and welfare."[34]

The "shrinking of the world" has been caused by the emergence of interdependence. There are various definitions of this concept and analysts disagree about how it should be put into operation.[35] However, an important characteristic of the globalist view is the premise that recent decades have seen a growing degree of interdependence among nations in both political and economic spheres.[36] The globalist sees this increase in interdependence as incongruent with the traditional assumptions of the state-centric model. The state is no longer the effective agent of political and economic security. Furthermore, technological development, particularly nuclear power, has made the state even less viable, for it can no longer protect its citizens.[37]

Globalists view the proliferation of international organizations as a significant development in world politics. They believe that "many of the international organizations function effectively to influence the lives and welfare of people in almost every country of the world" and that "international interaction via international organizations is rapidly becoming an even more important feature of world politics today."[38] The result of this development is that the system can no longer be characterized by anarchy. According to Donald J. Puchala and Stuart I. Fagan, "What is interesting and what may be new about international organizations in our time is that their existence and functioning have introduced a certain amount of bureaucratization, routinization, continuity, and predictability into international politics, so that we may be presently taking at least small steps away from the anarchy of the traditional state system."[39] Thus, for the globalist, "national governments are but some actors among many on the international scene."[40]

In the globalist model, all organizations that cross boundaries are important, whether they are governmental or private. In particular, the emergence of the multinational corporation is regarded as a significant development in world politics.[41] The globalist believes that internationalization requires, and eventually will result in, the decline of the nation-state. In part, speculation on this point is prompted by "the search of big business for the ultimate in freedom for international movement of capital, profits, and goods."[42]

Another assumption of the globalist view relates to war. The globalists believe that nuclear weapons have made war increasingly dysfunctional as a tool of diplomacy. They suggest that "we are moving [into] an era in which war between major states may virtually disappear."[43] The disutility of force, coupled with the proliferation of international organizations and the emergence of interdependence, suggests to the globalists that states will no longer be preoccupied by the security concerns that dominated international politics through the 1960s. Accordingly, they view the realist paradigm as outmoded.

These assumptions and hypotheses form the basic tenets of the globalist paradigm. At least some are shared by all globalists. But it would be erroneous to suggest that the globalists are an intellectually unified group. Fundamental disagreements exist among them, not so much over how to characterize the international system as over the consequences of change. One group of analysts views the changes in the international system with considerable optimism; the other recognizes the changes but seems alarmed about their impact on world politics. These two groups can be called "optimist-globalist" and "pessimist-globalist." The optimist-globalist believes that "if the level of interdependence in the system continues to rise, this will eventually precipitate the emergence of a world 'community' or a world 'culture' which will in turn lead to the development of a world 'state' capable of managing the rising level of interdependence."[44] A pessimist-globalist, however, would argue that "there is no *a priori* reason to suppose that a rising level of interdependence will precipitate the emergence of a world community."[45] On the contrary, the emergence of interdependence could result in an increasing level of conflict, because "the rise of systematic interdependence generally creates new opportunities for conflict as well as increased scope for cooperation in world politics."[46]

Pessimist-globalists do recognize the emergence of interdependence in the economic realm. But they view this development with apprehension because of the problems associated with it. According to Richard N. Cooper:

> Broadly speaking, increasing interdependence complicates the successful pursuit of national economic objectives in three ways. First, it increases the number and magnitude of the disturbances to which each country's balance of payment is subjected, and this in turn diverts policy attention and instruments of policy to the restoration of external balance. Second, it slows down the process by which national authorities, each acting on its own, are able to reach domestic objectives. Third, the response to greater interaction can involve the community of nations in counteracting motions which leave all countries worse off than they need be. These difficulties are in turn complicated by the fact that the objective of greater economic integration involves international agreements which reduce the number of policy instruments available to national authorities for pursuit of their economic objectives.[47]

Optimist-globalists, however, are hopeful about economic interdependence because of their assumption regarding the spillover effects. Peter G. Peterson argues that

> Closer economic ties bear both cause and effect relationships to relaxation of political tension. Improvement in political relationships is a prerequisite for improved economic relationships but, once in place, economic ties create a community of interest which in turn improves the environment for further progress on the political side. Once set in motion, the cause-and-effect process can portend a downward spiral in political tension.[48]

Similarly, an optimist-globalist would view the proliferation of the MNC with considerable hope. "The idea that this kind of business enterprise can be a strong force toward world peace is not so farfetched. Beyond the human values involved, the multinational firm has a direct, measurable, and potent interest in helping prevent wars and other

serious upheavals that cut off its resources, interrupt its communications, and kill its employees and customers."⁴⁹ According to this argument,
the MNC has a unifying property that will work toward transnational
integration. George Ball once predicted before the Canadian House of
Commons that "the logic of economics would lead inevitably to the
integration of the United States and Canada. Parochial territorial
loyalties give way to economic rationality."⁵⁰ Aurelio Peccei, a director of
Fiat and organizer of the Club of Rome, expressed a similar view when
he stated that the MNC "is the most powerful agent for internationalization of human society."⁵¹

Pessimist-globalists recognize the increasing importance of the MNC in
the international system but observe this development with concern. In
their view, the MNC's drive for higher profits forces it to go overseas,
thus taking away employment from the mother country. In the host
country, particularly if it is in the Third World, the MNC serves as an
agent of foreign domination; and regardless of the benefits they may
bring, multinational operations in the Third World also "result in a net
flow of capital from the underdeveloped to developed nations."⁵²

An optimist-globalist believes that "international organization has
given us a set of procedures for international conflict control applicable
(and proven effective) in a variety of conflict situations."⁵³ A pessimist-
globalist reserves judgment. Robert O. Keohane and Joseph S. Nye, two
globalists, have argued that "not all types of transnational organizations
have increased in importance."⁵⁴ They see a decline in the importance of
political organizations but a growth in the significance of institutions
with social and economic functions. However, even Keohane and Nye
postulate that "the increase in the functional importance of the economic
and social organizations may have very significant political consequences."⁵⁵

This chapter has briefly summarized international relations' third
debate. The essays that follow provide a better understanding of the controversy. They are written from four perspectives. Brown, Puchala and
Fagan, and Young represent the globalist view. They argue that since the
height of the Cold War in the 1950s and early 1960s, the international
system has undergone a significant transformation: new actors, new
issues, and new ways of looking at the world have come forth. The
superpower contest no longer dominates global politics. Rather, the
decay of Cold War alliances coupled with the growth of new transnational institutions and technologies compel cosmopolitanism. By contrast, Waltz, Gilpin, and Sullivan contend that the present is not fundamentally different from the past. To be sure, there are new actors; still,
the nation-state remains the most important global fixture and national
security is of paramount concern. Although, to a limited extent, interde-

pendence does exist, it may not be increasing and may even be declining. Richard Rosecrance and his colleagues take a third path. Asserting that interdependence has been historically cyclical, they view the world today as poised between nationalism and transnationalism. In the concluding chapter Bennett Ramberg and I suggest that the world is more complex than either realists or globalists acknowledge and put forward a reconceptualization.

NOTES

Thanks go to Stephen M. Gorman for his review of this article.

1. For a review of the field, its development, and its controversies, see Chadwick F. Alger, "International Relations," *International Encyclopedia of the Social Sciences* (New York: Macmillan, 1968), pp. 61–68; Norman D. Palmer and Howard C. Perkins, *International Relations: The World Community in Transition*, 3rd ed. (New York: Houghton Mifflin, 1969), pp. xi–xxxiii; and Quincy Wright, *The Study of International Relations* (New York: Appleton-Century-Crofts, 1955).

2. One of the best discussions of this debate is in Edward Hallett Carr, *The Twenty Years' Crisis, 1919–1939* (London: Macmillan, 1939).

3. One of the better discussions of the requirements of collective security can be found in Inis L. Claude, Jr., *Swords into Plowshares*, 4th ed. (New York: Random House, 1971), chap. 12.

4. Theodore A. Couloumbis and James H. Wolfe, *Introduction to International Relations: Power and Justice* (Englewood Cliffs, NJ: Prentice-Hall, 1978), p. 4.

5. James A. Bill and Robert L. Hardgrave, Jr., *Comparative Politics: The Quest for Theory* (Columbus, OH: Merrill, 1973), p. 15.

6. For a discussion of the decision-making approach, see James N. Rosenau, "The Premises and Promises of Decision-Making Analysis," in James C. Charlesworth, ed., *Contemporary Political Analysis* (New York: Free Press, 1967), pp. 189–211.

7. See Richard C. Snyder and Glenn D. Paige, "The United States' Decision to Resist Aggression in Korea: The Application of an Analytical Scheme," *Administrative Science Quarterly* 3 (December 1978), pp. 341–378.

8. Charles A. McClelland, "International Relations: Wisdom or Science?" in James N. Rosenau, ed., *International Politics and Foreign Policy* (New York: Free Press, 1969), p. 5.

9. James Rosenau, "International Politics and Foreign Policy as a Subject of Study – Introductory Note," in Rosenau, *Ibid.*, p. 1.

10. Stephen L. Wasby, *Political Science: The Discipline and Its Dimensions* (New York: Scribner's, 1970), p. 230.

11. Michael P. Sullivan, "Competing Frameworks and the Study of Contemporary International Studies," *Millennium: Journal of International Studies* 7 (Autumn 1978), p. 93.

12. Robert O. Keohane and Joseph S. Nye, Jr., *Power and Interdependence: World Politics in Transition* (Cambridge: Harvard University Press, 1977), p. 23.

13. Sullivan, p. 108.

14. *Ibid.*, p. 106.

15. Keohane and Nye, p. 23.

16. Sullivan, p. 108.

17. Oran Young, "The Actors in World Politics," in James N. Rosenau, Vincent Davis, and Maurice A. East, eds., *The Analysis of International Politics* (New York: Free Press, 1972), p. 125.

18. Sullivan, pp. 99–100.

19. Young, p. 131.

20. *Ibid.*

21. Edward L. Morse, "The Politics of Interdependence," *International Organization* 23 (Spring 1969), p. 312.

22. Kenneth Waltz, "The Myth of National Interdependence," in Charles P. Kindleberger, ed., *The International Corporation* (Cambridge: MIT Press, 1970), p. 206.

23. *Ibid.*, p. 220.

24. *Ibid.*

25. Donald J. Puchala and Stuart I. Fagan, "International Politics in the 1970s: The Search for a Perspective," *International Organization* 28 (Spring 1974), p. 248.

26. Hans J. Morgenthau, *Politics Among Nations: The Struggle for Power and Peace*, 5th ed. (New York: Knopf, 1972), p. 4.

27. *Ibid.*, p. 167.

28. *Ibid.*, p. 475.

29. *Ibid.*, p. 473.

30. Robert Gilpin, "The Politics of Transnational Economic Relations," in Robert O. Keohane and Joseph A. Nye, eds., *Transnational Relations and World Politics* (Cambridge: Harvard University Press, 1970), p. 68.

31. Hans Morgenthau, *The Purpose of American Politics* (New York: Alfred A. Knopf, 1960), p. 354.

32. Morgenthau, *Politics Among Nations.*

33. Seyom Brown, *New Forces in World Politics* (Washington, DC: Brookings Institution, 1974), p. 1.

34. Young, p. 128.

35. See for example Alex Inkeles, "The Emerging Social Structure of the World," *World Politics* 27 (July 1975), pp. 467–495; Richard Rosecrance and Arthur Stein, "Interdependence: Myth or Reality," *World Politics* 26 (October 1973), pp. 1–27; Oran Young, "Interdependencies in World Politics," *International Journal* 24 (Autumn 1969), pp. 726–750; and Waltz.

36. Rosecrance and Stein, pp. 1–27.

37. Young, "The Actors in World Politics," p. 130.

38. Puchala and Fagan, p. 252.

39. *Ibid.*

40. *Ibid.*, p. 350.

41. Lester Brown, *World Without Borders* (New York: Vintage Books, 1973), pp. 209–229.

42. Harry Magdoff, "The Multinational Corporation and Development – A Contradiction?" in David E. Apter and Louis Wolf Goodman, eds., *The Multinational Corporation and Social Change* (New York: Praeger, 1976), p. 210.

43. Robert E. Hunter, "Power and Peace," *Foreign Policy* 9 (Winter 1972–1973), p. 381.

44. Young, "Interdependencies in World Politics," p. 728.

45. *Ibid.*, p. 729.

46. *Ibid.*, p. 728.

47. Richard N. Cooper, *The Economics of Interdependence: Economic Policy in the Atlantic Community* (New York: McGraw-Hill, 1968), p. 148.

48. Peter G. Peterson, *U.S.-Soviet Commercial Relations in a New Era* (Washington, DC: Department of Commerce, August, 1972), p. 3.

49. David H. Blake and Robert S. Walters, *The Politics of Global Economic Relations* (Englewood Cliffs, NJ: Prentice-Hall, 1976), p. 116.

50. Richard J. Barnet and Ronald E. Muller, *Global Reach* (New York: Simon and Schuster, 1974), p. 77.

51. *Ibid.*, p. 13.

52. Magdoff, p. 217.

53. Puchala and Fagan, p. 252.

54. Keohane and Nye, *Transnational Relations and World Politics*, p. 376.

55. *Ibid.*, p. 377.

2
The Changing Essence of Power

By the mid to late 1960s, the rigid bipolar system that emerged in the aftermath of World War II was undergoing a transformation. Vietnam seemed to be a benchmark suggesting the limits of force and its realist theory underpinnings. Brown identifies and discusses aspects of the emerging international system. He argues that the end of the Cold War, the rise of nonsecurity issues, and the diversification of friendships and adversary relations altered the essence of world politics. He then elaborates on the consequences and concludes by prescribing how the United States should address this changing set of circumstances. Brown's chapter summarizes the essence of the globalist argument.

Today's political flux features on its diplomatic surface three interacting trends: a disintegration of the cold-war coalitions, the rise of nonsecurity issues to the top of diplomatic agendas, and a diversification of friendships and adversary relations. These surface movements are the expression of deeper currents, which, if appropriately exploited by providential statesmanship, could fundamentally alter the essence of world politics, changing the structures and ingredients of power itself.

Let us examine each trend in turn, accepting the risks of oversimplification that are inescapable in any broad projection of the future.

First, the United States and the Soviet Union are today less anxious than they were in the 1950s and 1960s that shifts by smaller countries toward nonalignment, neutralism or even the other's coalition will fundamentally affect either of their vital security interests. Changes in military technology have reduced the value of forward bases not only for strategic deterrence but also for combat and reconnaissance in large-scale conventional war. An exception is Eastern Europe, where the Soviets still insist upon a security belt made up of completely loyal allies. Elsewhere, superpower protection, having become less credible, loses some of its value, while at the same time the price of securing that protection rises. This generates high incentives for the smaller countries to strike postures of independence in the hope of creating more opportunity for diplomatic maneuver against both superpowers. In turn, the superpowers find the fidelity of their allies less reliable. New geopolitical doctrines that assert a reduced security requirement for allies are given greater play in military planning and foreign policy generally. Ideologies which make it imperative to defend on a global basis the good people against the bad are pushed aside in favor of more "pragmatic" considerations.

Second, the loosening of the hierarchical relationship between the superpowers and their smaller allies within each of the grand cold-war coalitions gives freer play to conflicts over nonsecurity issues – economic primarily – while the relative emergence of the nonsecurity issues reinforces the fragmentation of these coalitions. When protection against a threatening enemy coalition was the most pressing concern, the subordination of special economic, political and cultural interests to the requirements of the common defense was more readily accepted as was the hegemony over one's coalition by the country with the most powerful military capabilities. Today, questions concerning the best means of providing for the common defense of the coalition – strategies toward the opposing coalition, the allocation of roles and burdens among the members – are still prominent. But the ability of the United States on the one side, and the Soviet Union on the other, to prevail over their respective allies in intra-coalition politics has been decreasing, in considerable measure because of the increasing ability of lesser members, when nonmilitary matters are at issue, to form coalitions with one another or with nonaligned countries, and even with members of the other cold-war coalition. This aspect of the process of coalition disintegration is beginning to play a role even among the Warsaw Pact countries. Thus, some countries have an incentive to push nonsecurity issues to the top of international agendas partly for the purpose of increasing their bargaining power vis-à-vis the coalition superpower; and to the extent that the rise in nonsecurity issues and the construction of multiple coalitions are the results of East-West détente, these countries develop a vested interest in the evaporation of cold-war issues. In this way the disintegration of the cold-war coalitions, once begun, sets in motion other forces that tend to accelerate the pace and force of the erosion.

Next, the disintegration of global bipolarity and the rise of nonsecurity issues open new opportunities, and provide greater incentives, for countries to cultivate a wider and more diverse range of international friends than was possible previously. In the heyday of the cold-war coalitions each superpower, while competing for allies all around the globe, made firm distinctions between its coalition partners and members of the enemy camp. Rarely would lesser members of either alliance deal bilaterally with members of the opposing alliance unless the exchanges were stage-managed by the alliance leader. Even for transactions within the camp, when important political or economic issues were being negotiated, the superpower was usually heavily involved and bilateral or multilateral dealings among a subset of members were discouraged—unless, of course, the superpower was one of the parties. To be sure, "nonaligned" countries (notably India, Egypt and Indonesia) played the field, but many statesmen and analysts assumed this international stance was untenable over the long run. Now it is precisely such a flexible posture, in many respects resembling nonalignment, that seems to be serving as the model for realistic diplomacy.

Thus, more and more, divergences in world view or differences in social systems are insufficient causes to bar cordial relations among countries. Economic intercourse, technological cooperation and scientific and cultural exchanges are considered legitimate among virtually all possible combinations of countries; and increasingly, organizations and forums for these purposes are using functional or geographic rather than ideological criteria for participation. Multilateral groupings established for cooperation in various fields have crosscutting memberships—for example: some members of a given security grouping find themselves co-members of a regional environmental control grouping with countries which are in the adversary security grouping, and a different subset of members of each of these groupings are participants in a space-communications system. This means that rival international coalitions also vary in membership according to the issues in dispute.

II

If the dominant tendencies continue to mature as indicated above, an international system whose essential characteristics are grossly different not only from the bipolar cold-war system but also from previous "balance-of-power" systems could emerge full-blown, very likely by the 1980s. We can only conjecture as to what these essential characteristics will be, and even then only in broadest outline. But, admitting the guesswork inherent in such an exercise, and recognizing the possibility that unpredictable contingencies—such as rapprochement between Russia and the People's Republic of China plus a renewal of belligerent expansionism by either or both – could halt or reverse the disintegration of the cold-war coalitions, it is not too early to try a sketch of the emerging system.

First and foremost, the new system would feature a change in the nature of international power itself. If the international power of a country is defined as the capacity to influence other countries to accede to its objectives, then in a system characterized by multiple and cross-cutting coalitions formed around a variety of issues, the properties of power would be significantly different than in the predominantly bipolar system. In the new system, those with the most influence are likely to be those which are major constructive participants in the widest variety of coalitions and partnerships, since such countries would have the largest supply of usable political currency – in effect, promissory notes that say: "We will support you on this issue, if you support us on that issue." Conversely, threats to withdraw support would serve as negative sanctions.

The power-maximizing country would want to have its own pledges of support universally honored and highly valued; frequently, these would be in the form of financial assets or economic and technical inputs it can make available to the projects desired by others. Such a country also would want to be able to convert pledges it has collected from others into currency for its own use. When these are from poorer countries which lack surplus material assets, they may be in the form of votes in the various multinational forums whose endorsement is important to projects desired by the richer country.

Power in the form of promises to apply or withhold military capabilities – the dominant form of power during the cold war – would still be of ultimate decisive importance in conflicts over vital security interests. But it would have little utility compared with other forms of power, and sometimes even a negative effect, in bargaining over the non-security issues around which coalitions would be forming and reforming. For the threat to apply military power carries a high risk of devaluing the other bargaining chips in one's possession, since it is almost certain so to alienate the involved societies from one another that they dismantle their cooperative projects and withdraw from mutual coalition partnerships in virtually all fields. Pairs of countries that have few interlocking relationships to start with (as used to be the case with East-West relations in the cold war) can afford to be indifferent to such a falling out between them. But active participants in the emerging international system, with elaborate overlapping of interests and coalitions, ought to be highly constrained by the knowledge that their opponents in one area are often their supporters in another.

If coercive bargaining strategies must be resorted to, the prudent statesman will conserve his overall store of influence by proffering, withholding and withdrawing assets well below the level of military force and avoiding the development of total nation-to-nation or coalition-to-coalition hostility. Rarely should a specific dispute warrant the costs, in loss of influence, that would accompany escalation to war threats, the mobilization of military alliances or the polarization of international politics.

What, then, becomes of today's great powers, especially the two super-powers? How would they stand under new criteria of power? America and Russia could continue to be the most influential in the emerging system by virtue of their command over economic resources, technological skills and military capabilities. But if they were to rely primarily on the coercive leverage of their first-ranking material positions instead of exploiting the opportunities in the new system for participating in multiple coalitions, they might find themselves falling behind other actors in usable power. Moreover, in competition with each other for global influence, the United States and the Soviet Union would find that constructive cooperation with smaller countries gains more votes in global and regional forums than coercive or denial strategies.

The nine or more members of the European Economic Community (EEC), when acting as a unit on particular international issues, could well emerge as an equally powerful unit in world politics – especially if the United States and the Soviet Union continue to act as if the obsolete bipolar confrontation of security communities still were the essence of international relations. The usable power of the West European group in any case would not stem from its military capability. It would derive principally from techno-economic capabilities, cultural ties, geography and diplomatic skill. The EEC countries are well situated for coalition-building with the countries of Eastern Europe, being partners or competitors in a larger all-European market and over the use of common all-European resources: river basins, seas, energy supplies, air space and the atmosphere. Moreover, the West Europeans can be expected to be especially active in maintaining and constructing North-South interdependencies, building particularly upon the intimate connections France maintains with most of her former colonies in Africa and upon British Commonwealth ties.

Japan, though envisioned as equal to or surpassing the Soviet Union in gross national product by the end of the century, is nevertheless likely to rank lower in overall power (as defined here), and possibly will remain somewhat behind the EEC. While having the high technological and financial assets to assure that other countries desire her cooperation, Japan herself, because of extensive reliance on others for raw materials, will continue to be vitally dependent on the good will of others, and on the absence of regional or global conflicts that could interrupt her supply lines. She has neither the potential for self-sufficiency of the United States or the Soviet Union, nor the historic community ties of EEC countries to Third-World partners, to insulate this vulnerable dependency. As such she must please as well as be pleased. A hefty military capability will be of practically no use to her in day-to-day bargaining relationships, and, in light of recent history, even the slightest suggestion that she might attempt to escalate a dispute over economic matters to the military level would surely alienate a large number of her suppliers, and revive a broad international coalition against her.

The fifth great power, China, must rely almost entirely upon skillful diplomacy, rather than exchangeable material assets, to exert any great influence beyond her borders. The only wide swath she can hope to cut in international coalition politics is as a champion of the Third-World countries, among whom she may continue to be the only nuclear-armed nation for some time. But China's nuclear capability, even if useful to deter military attacks upon herself, is unlikely to be pertinent as a bargaining counter on behalf of other members of any Third-World coalition. Her diplomatic leadership opportunities in the Third World will depend rather on the degree and quality of the Third-World policies of the United States, the Soviet Union, the EEC countries and Japan. If the industrialized great powers, either as a result of preoccupation with their own rivalries or a moral indifference to Third-World concerns, appear to be treating the less-developed countries as pawns, the way will be open for China to strike heroic poses in international forums as an aggressive spokesman for the world's poor.

China also can be expected to exploit any opportunities for driving wedges between the Soviet Union and the East European countries, as a part of her continuing effort to be an alternative pole of attraction in the world Communist movement. As either a major market or source of specialized products, China will be of growing importance to many countries, but not of decisively greater importance than major countries or regional groupings in Africa, Latin America, the Middle East, South Asia or Southeast Asia.

III

Yet, though one may thus seek to assess the present great powers, it would be misleading to characterize the relationships among the five most powerful actors in the emerging system as a five-sided balance of power, since this conveys rough equality of weight among the five in their intramural competition. Most of the usable kinds of power at the disposal of each are incommensurate; and in specific categories some of the countries are clearly more powerful than others.

Wars between Europe and the United States, between the United States and Japan, or between Japan and Europe are too implausible for the respective military balances between these pairs to have any important effects on disputes likely to arise among them. Even between the United States (or Europe) and the Soviet Union (or China), Japan and the Soviet Union or Japan and China, the rapid escalation of any particular dispute to the war-threat level would be rarely if ever warranted, given the costs and risks of this pattern of interaction and the availability (in the system we have postulated) of nonmilitary means of exerting pressure. The only pair for which the military equation may yet be immediately relevant is China and Russia – given a continuation of their border dispute.

In the nonmilitary categories of power, the relationships among the five often lack any common denominator for measurement; and to the extent that there are comparable categories, they tend to exhibit imbalance more than symmetry. Thus, the Soviet Union and members of COMECON probably would be more in need of commerce with the West than vice versa. On the other hand, being state-controlled economies, the Socialist countries could more easily subject their commercial negotiations to the requirements of their international political maneuvers. Japan, as suggested above, would be more vulnerable to economic pressures involving a potential cut-off or increase in price in essential raw material sources, particularly petroleum products, than the United States, Russia or China. Western Europe would also be weak in this respect. But the power of each of the major actors to influence the flow and price of raw materials could come to depend most of all on its overall relationship with producer countries in the Third World.

On the increasingly important issues of terms of access to and privileges in the space and ocean environments, and international ecological standards and controls, who gets what, when and how would be highly dependent upon (1) international structures set up to allocate benefits and costs and to resolve disputes, and (2) the configuration of coalitions in each of these fields. These institutional structures and coalitions are unlikely to be congruent with the hierarchy of power based upon either standard military or economic indicators. The relevant "balance of power" in such areas would take in a much wider set of critical actors and interdependent relationships than is contemplated in most visions of a five-power world.

Moreover, the emerging international system would not be congenial with the concept of "multipolarity," if this term is used to connote a magnetic pull by certain powerful countries, presumably over the other nations in their respective regions, and the resulting creation of spheres of (hegemonial) influence – jurisdictions of domination marked out for themselves by each powerful country, and respected by the others. Such a carving up of the globe, even if ostensibly agreed to by the major actors, would not be sustainable, given the condition of multiple interdependence and crosscutting coalitions. Smaller countries within a region would actively seek extra-regional partners for commerce or other functions in order to retain bargaining leverage against the dominant regional country. Rather than being a pole of attraction, a dominant regional country with pretensions to hegemony is likely to reinforce the centrifugal tendencies already present in the system. It might appear to succeed in the short run, but would tend to produce in time a subregional coalition in opposition. The existence of this coalition would tempt other big powers, or other coalitions outside of the region, to subvert the sphere of influence of the dominating regional power by establishing special ties with the aggrieved nations and publicly championing their causes.

Just here one sees readily a principal threat to the new system. As in the Czechoslovakian and Dominican episodes, it may be very hard for a regionally hegemonial power to choose to relax its overbearing control when challenged, instead of applying physical force to keep extra-regional influence out of its would-be satellites. The coercive option, even when applied to a smaller power within one's region, is likely to revive the salience of power in international politics, and rather rapidly destroy the underlying preconditions of the postulated system.

Indeed, if countries with nuclear weapons and other powerful military capabilities invoked their military superiority for purposes of facing down opponents in any type of conflict situation, then military force and militarized diplomacy—although bad currency—in a kind of Gresham's law of international politics, would tend to drive out the good currency of cooperative and limited coalition-building. Inevitably, many prestige-seeking countries would refuse to rely on their own material resources and diplomatic skill for protecting their interests. Instead, they would want their own weapons of mass destruction, and a dangerous nuclear "Nth-country" pattern could become a fundamental feature of international politics.

Thus a few instances of escalation to high-level military coercion by one or some of the most powerful actors could engender a retrogressive chain-reaction of coercive diplomacy, throwing most countries back into the classic mode of attempting to balance one another's power by military means, which now, for any adversary of a nuclear-armed country, would require some sort of devastating second-strike capability. The system of multiple interdependence would soon contain multiple arms races and multiple paranoia. And there would be strong temptations to resort to the drastic Hobbesian alternative of a global "Leviathan": a centralized authoritarian law-and-order system imposed on the world by those with sufficient coercive power to overwhelm all opponents. It takes little imagination to recognize that any attempt to impose such a system probably could not be undertaken without provoking a world war.

IV

Obviously, the maturing of a full-blown system of multiple interdependence where power would be exercised largely in the form of constructive exchanges of valued resources rather than threats of physical destruction cannot be forecast with confidence. In Washington and Moscow, the habit of calculating power primarily in terms of military capabilities and of displaying these capabilities, as a tiger displays his teeth, in conflicting situations still appears to be strong. The United States, though pledged to liquidate its participation in the Southeast Asian war, has for most of the last decade applied major military force against a smaller adversary in that region. The Soviet Union, having just a few years ago enforced a régime change in Czechoslovakia with tanks and bullets, does not yet appear ready to abandon the use of brute force as a control mechanism in Eastern Europe or to withdraw the 450,000 troops it has there. The NATO countries in Western Europe still view the 300,000 U.S. troops deployed in Germany as a critical bargaining chip in East-West negotiations. The Sino-Soviet border issues continue to be prosecuted in the classic mode of exhibiting menacing deployments of force on each side. The balance of military power between the Arab nations and Israel is buttressed on each side by equipment from the Soviet Union and the United States. And in many areas of the globe more removed from great-power rivalries, smaller powers often seem even further behind in accepting the new disutility of physical coercion.

What, then, are the requirements of a providential statesmanship that will increase the likelihood of the world's political development toward a more peaceful and just world order?

First of all, a special responsibility falls on the existing nuclear-armed countries, particularly the two military superpowers, not to utilize their military superiority, even as an implicit bargaining chip, in order to influence weaker military actors to comply with their demands. If such self-restraint is not exercised, other countries – most prominently Japan, but also India, Brazil and others – will be compelled to conclude that an essential factor in one's bargaining position is status as a nuclear-armed country.

Second, the largest, strongest and wealthiest countries will have to refrain from attempting to maintain or establish spheres of dominance, or even to maintain permanent extended alliance systems. Such "hegemonial multipolarity" is inherently unstable given the trends we have postulated. Moreover, there are certain to be overlapping, and thus contested, areas in the would-be spheres – a situation making for dangerous miscalculation in the bipolar system, which would be compounded in a multipolar system.

Third, the leading economic and technological nations not only will have to allow substantial lines of interdependence to run between countries within their geographic regions and extra-regional countries, but should actively encourage the elaboration of multiple and intersecting webs of interdependence between countries formerly in rival ideological blocs and between pairs of nations that have had historic rivalries. The objective should be to create on the world scene the dense interlinking and crosscutting of communities that prevent extreme polarization and civil war within the more stable domestic societies.

Fourth, in order to counter a bitter polarization between the more affluent and mobile elements of world society, and those elements which because of their relative poverty and vulnerability to competition are susceptible to exploitation, a global system of open access and interdependence will have to be regulated by institutions and policies designed to redress this kind of imbalance. If political borders are to become significantly more porous on a North-South basis without in effect reinstituting new forms of colonial dependence by the world's poor on the world's rich, then the world's political economy will have to be structured to implement redistributive interferences in the global market analogous to those that now obtain within the advanced democracies.

Finally, to prevent the misuse of and conflicts over the world's common resources, and a new stage of dangerously competitive empire-building in newly exploitable environments – the oceans, the atmosphere and outer space – new sets of representative institutions will need to be elaborated and empowered on regional and global bases to ensure that all the communities affected have a fair say over how these common goods of mankind are used.

V

The stark alternatives are becoming increasingly evident to peoples all around the globe. But few societies have a secure enough material base and physical insularity to maintain the well-being of their own people and still devote substantial energies to world community tasks. Yet without some societies willing to take the initiative in sloughing off the anachronistic habits of 300 years of international politics, the new pattern of relationships required to avoid world anarchy is probably not going to emerge.

Is the United States likely to be one of those societies that constructively comes to grips with the new forces? Could its people become ready and willing to support this kind of statesmanship?

The apparent obsolescence of the cold war, which for most Americans has a special sting of despair associated with the tragedy of Vietnam, has disposed even those segments of the policy community and the public which have been most internationalist to doubt that their country has any business trying to look after the well-being of others. There appears to be growing support for policies that would reduce the foreign commitments of the United States, bring American military personnel home, trim the defense budget and cut foreign military and economic assistance.[1]

Yet it would be unfair to the essential character of American society to infer a long-term trend toward isolationism from the current fatigue and frustration associated with recent foreign policy failures. There is a deep strain of idealism in the American political ethos which is continually seeking expression on a universal scale. The country in its best image of itself is a place of domicile and shared power for peoples of all cultures, religions and nationalities – a great experiment, perhaps, for the fashioning of the polity of the globe – and, in the twentieth century at least, a catalytic participant in the construction of a just and noncoercive world order. When this part of the American identity is suppressed, when the country turns inward to become totally preoccupied with its own maladies, it loses an essential part of its purpose.

An American leadership that was concerned to raise the spirit of the American people and, once again, the hopes of mankind, could begin today to reshape U.S. foreign policy along the following lines:

(1) The United States, by its own example, would play down the use of force as a sanction behind diplomacy, and encourage the dismantling of permanent military coalitions premised on an international clash of arms between major ideological groupings. This would not preclude the maintenance of the minimal military forces necessary to assure the Soviets or any other potential adversary that it would be futile for them to resolve their disputes with the United States by force. And to dissuade the powerful nations from picking on the weak, it may be necessary occasionally to underline the fact that the United States reserves the right to help the victims of military attack. At a minimum, the marginal role military power should play in contemporary big-power diplomacy could be conveyed by demilitarizing the vocabulary of power that has been featured in U.S. foreign policy pronouncements since World War II.

(2) The United States would seek out special opportunities for practical cooperative projects with those with whom it has had general ideological

disagreements. This would involve resisting temptations to mobilize cold-war allies to speak in concert on new issues or for alliance structures to form the scaffolding of new institutions. It might require more work, and some sacrifice of efficiency, to put together new functionally specific coalitions that cut across the preexisting military alliances. Without such initiatives by the United States, an open world of interdependent and mutually respectful communities has little chance of evolving. A necessary corollary to such initiatives, however, is self-restraint against inflating particular conflicts of interest into ideological conflicts over ways of life.

(3) The United States would cooperate in funneling substantial capital and other resources from the rich to the poor countries through international institutions. If this mode of effecting "North-South" resource transfers is to be enhanced, the people of affluent industrialized countries, particularly the United States, will need to be roused to share part of their wealth with those less fortunate on grounds other than economic self-interest or military security. It will be necessary to develop new world community and world interest rationales as motivating appeals.

(4) As the world's leading center of technological innovation, the United States would make it attractive to others to share in the opportunities now arising to develop global systems for exploiting the earth's wealth for the benefit of mankind. If access is to be granted to U.S. scientists and technologists into coastal and seabed areas containing sources of new mineral wealth; if preferred frequencies and orbital slots for space satellite systems are to be granted willingly to U.S. systems; and if other nations are to cooperate with the United States and other advanced industrial nations in constructing global networks for monitoring and regulating the use of the globe's atmospheric, water and terrestrial resources to assure that essential ecosystems are not dangerously destabilized—then the United States will have to stimulate other countries, particularly the technological have-nots, to cooperate with U.S. nationals in these ventures. This probably means that equity criteria will have to be significantly injected not only in the setting of funding responsibilities for the new multilateral ventures, but also in the distribution of benefits.

(5) Finally, in promoting greater reliance on multilateral institutions, the United States would support principles of representation that would give voice, in so far as possible, to all communities affected by the multilateral activities. This implies that in international lending institutions, the recipient countries would be given more responsibility than at present for the allocations and setting the conditions of repayment. It also implies that the consumers of the various resources of the sea as well as their producers and marketers should have a say in how the

ocean "commons" is administered. The same would hold for other transnationally used environments and resources, some traditionally considered subject only to domestic jurisdiction. The shared participation would be on more than a token basis, and would include decision-making functions as well as technical tasks. In short, the people of the United States in the first instance would have to be more forthcoming than they have been in dispensing with some of the traditional trappings of national sovereignty.

A foreign policy responsive to these guidelines would be consistent with the basic international objectives of the United States since the end of the Second World War. Those objectives—a world environment conducive to the survival of the American society; and a system of international relations in which disputes are resolved without war, and in which opportunities to partake of the good life are extended to others—were pursued for a generation through policies that now need to be supplanted by a new set of policies. The fact that it is time for a new American posture, less reliant on military power and alliances, does not mean we must condemn this country's entire cold-war role. It does mean that we must free ourselves from the snares of inertia and false pride so as not to confuse the policies and commitments of the past with the fundamental objectives they were supposed to serve.

NOTES

1. Opinion data as of 1971 show less than a quarter of the American public willing to approve the use of U.S. troops to defend major allies such as West Germany or Japan in the event they were attacked by Communist-backed forces. Even fewer would fight on behalf of smaller allies, with surprisingly large portions of those polled unwilling to provide any support at all. See Albert H. Cantril and Charles W. Roll, Jr., "Hopes and Fears of the American People." (Washington, DC: Potomac Associates, 1971).

DONALD J. PUCHALA
STUART I. FAGAN

3
International Politics in the 1970s: The Search for a Perspective

Puchala and Fagan argue that changes in the structure, process, and substance of international politics make the realist Cold War "national security paradigm" an anachronism. The proliferation of international and transnational actors contributes to profound structural changes. Integration and bargaining replace more violent competition. Although Cold War questions remain important, the substance of international politics increasingly involves economic and welfare issues.

At a recent meeting of academic specialists in the field of international relations, a distinguished scholar reportedly called for a one-year moratorium on methodological innovations in the discipline. His reason was "so that actual research into world politics can be started." While offered in jest, this scholar's intervention cut to the core of a central problem in the discipline. For all of our methodological sophistication, we probably do not understand contemporary international politics as well as we should, since theoretical development in our discipline is presently lagging behind the evolving reality of day-to-day practice in international affairs.[1] Consequently, some of our most generally employed conceptualizations, our images of the world out there, produce fewer insights than they once did. Indeed, it is high time that actual research into world politics got started. But first it is necessary that we remodel

Reprinted by permission from *International Organization* 28:2 (Spring 1974). Copyright © 1974 by the Board of Regents of the University of Wisconsin System.

some of the conventional ways in which we have been taught to think about international relations. To this end, this comment pinpoints some of the central features of what we call "the international politics of the 1970s."

What we offer below is much more a reflective and interpretative essay than an empirical study. While many of our points find partial documentation in the literature of international relations as enriched during the last few years, the total image we project of evolving system, process, and substance in contemporary international politics remains to be tested for validity.[2] Part of our intention here is to encourage efforts at such testing.

SECURITY POLITICS: THE PREVAILING PARADIGM

For many years, the prevailing image of international politics has been that of *states and nation states competing, conflicting, and intermittently fighting over questions of national military security*. Let us call this image of interstate competition for military security and its concomitants, territorial domain, ideological ascendance, and high prestige, the *security politics* paradigm. It has informed a great deal of research in our discipline for several generations; a survey of the literature of international relations shows immediately that concerns with military force, interstate rivalry, and national security have been overriding, indeed preoccupying, concerns.

The security politics paradigm was probably more analytically productive than any alternative throughout our firsthand experience with world affairs during the first half of the twentieth century and in our historical experience before that as well. Certainly, the most recent era, 1945–60, is best abstracted as a period wherein world politics was states competing, conflicting, and intermittently fighting over questions and issues of national military security, strategically and ideologically defined. Whatever else was going on in world affairs during this era of superpower confrontation simply added complexity to the times. National pursuits after military security characterized the period, and our disciplinary paradigms founded in assumptions about prevalent conflict aptly guided research toward better understanding it.

Surely, to imagine world politics as a continuing contest for "power, glory and idea"[3] has always been to simplify a vast and complex realm of human behavior. Other varieties of events – less competitive, less security-focused, and nongovernmentally precipitated – have regularly occurred in international politics through the centuries. Still, most major theorists of international relations have deemed these varieties of events to be of secondary importance in describing and explaining main currents in world affairs.[4] And perhaps they were of secondary importance.

However, is this any longer the case? A number of us currently engaged in the study of international relations sense that international politics have changed structurally, procedurally, and substantively during the last ten years. This is not to say that there has been a revolution in international affairs, and that a new order has displaced an old one. Rather, the change we sense is more subtle. Conventional and traditional statecraft, competition, and power politics remain prominent in the inventory of recurrent world political styles and events in the 1970s. In fact, all that the security politics paradigm directed us to look for in international affairs remains easy to find today.[5] Yet it no longer seems wholly appropriate or wise to direct the major part of our analytical attention toward the conflicting pursuits of states after military security. Instead, it would seem that many of today's most pressing international issues have little to do with the relative military security of states, with their relative coercive power, with their territoriality, or even with the ideology of their regimes. Governments today appear increasingly absorbed in enhancing the economic, social, and intellectual well-being of their citizens via their foreign policies and international interactions. Similarly, international outcomes generated via coordination and cooperation appear today as conspicuous and, perhaps, as momentous as outcomes generated through competition. Theoretically speaking, it would seem that the security politics paradigm has become overly restrictive in that it no longer appropriately distinguishes between international actors, processes, and outcomes of central importance and those of secondary or peripheral importance. As a result, it no longer accounts for anywhere near the full variety of significant international events.

BEYOND SECURITY POLITICS

Exactly what it is we would miss by continuing to think about and analyze international politics as essentially security politics remains unclear, mainly because we have not yet tailored an analytical framework to guide us in asking appropriate questions about international politics in the 1970s. Nevertheless, we do have a checklist of phenomena, which we are currently monitoring, that seem not to be easily or satisfactorily explained within older conceptual frameworks. Some of these phenomena appear to be qualitatively new products, results of contemporary technology and institutional, economic, and societal developments. Many others are apparently only quantitatively new in that they seem to be occurring with more frequency and intensity now than in the past. In general, most of these phenomena have to do with noncompetitive interactions, or interactions between and among nonmajor powers or even nonstates, or over nonsecurity issues, or with outcomes not determined by military power, or some combination of these, or even all of these together. As a first step toward sorting out and cataloging these phenomena of significance in the international politics of the 1970s, let us separate them into phenomena having to do with international political structure, process, and substance.

COMPLEXITIES IN INTERNATIONAL STRUCTURE

A Diversity of International Actors

The structure of the contemporary international system is probably a good deal more complex than we have been accustomed to imagining. Whereas the study of international politics by analytical convention has been primarily concerned with a single level of interaction, the national or government-to-government level, it is now clear that the international system is actually organized on at least four levels: subnational, national, transnational, and supranational. That is, national governments are but some actors among many on the international scene.[6] Other prominent actors include international organizations and directorates, multinational corporations, functionally linked transnational groups such as regional political parties and international guerrilla organizations, and subnational groups such as departments of agriculture, ministries of finance or major labor unions, business firms or philanthropic foundations – all formulating and executing their own foreign policies in quasi-autonomous fashion.[7] To be sure, these actors are not *new* in the sense that they were unknown to international politics in the past. The fact is, however, that until recently nonnational actors (save for intergovernmental international organizations) received relatively little analytical consideration; and when they were studied, they were most frequently looked upon as instruments used by national governments pursuing national interests. In addition, and much more important, while nonnational actors are certainly not new to the world politics of the 1970s, there is reason to believe that they are new in their heightened impacts on world affairs.[8] There are surely many more nonnational actors now than ever before.[9] Nonnational actors today control more resources than ever before. Then, too, as is discussed below, new varieties of issues and outcomes in the international politics of the 1970s have opened new opportunities to nonnational actors to intervene in world affairs. Therefore, to argue, as some have, that nonnational actors participating in world politics are not really a phenomenon of the 1970s since these have always been on the scene is to miss the point. Because there are more and more powerful nonnational actors today, and because there are new opportunities and imperatives for them to act, the total matrix of international interaction is altered in our time and so, too, must be our explanations for international outcomes.

Looking now more closely at the inventory of contemporary international actors, first and most conventionally speaking, there exist today more than 130 formally sovereign states whose governments act and interact in pursuit of national interests. This government-to-government level of international activity is, of course, most familiar and, as a result of generations of research, best understood. Moreover, regardless of the relative space that we allot here to discussing various other international actors, we emphasize that government-to-government interaction in the 1970s remains the most prominent, conspicuous, and far-reaching in impact among the many different kinds of interaction in the world system. While international interdependence in our day tends to restrict the external autonomy of governments, and while new scarcities in resources coupled with new domestic needs and demands constrain their international activities, states certainly have not been eclipsed and the international system remains essentially an interstate system. Therefore, the image of the structure of world politics in the 1970s that we are trying to project is not an alternative to the traditional state system but an augmentation.

One factor accounting for this augmentation has been a remarkable proliferation of international organizations in recent years.[10] Since 1945 new charterings of international intergovernmental organizations have averaged several dozen per year. Moreover, when we add figures indexing the growth of nongovernmental international organizations during the same period, we discover, rather astoundingly, that virtually hundreds of new international organizations are created each year. Most important, many of these international organizations function effectively to influence the policies of governments and affect the lives and welfare of people in almost every country of the world. Furthermore, what scant quantitative evidence we have suggests that countries today are channeling increasing proportions of their total diplomatic transactions through international organizations.[11] Therefore, international interaction via international organizations is rapidly becoming an ever more important feature of world politics today.

In addition, what is interesting and what may be new about international organizations in our time is that their existence and functioning have introduced a certain amount of bureaucratization, routinization, continuity, and predictability into international politics, so that we may be presently taking at least small steps away from the anarchy of the traditional state system. Most obviously, international organization has given us a set of procedures for international conflict control applicable (and proven effective) in a variety of conflict situations.[12] Peacekeeping via the United Nations and collective security under regional organizational auspices are certainly not the last words in international conflict control. Nonetheless, what is important, but often ignored, is that responses to crisis situations where peacekeeping and collective security are practicable need no longer be ad hoc. Statesmen need no longer start *de novo* in devising procedures for meeting a crisis each time one occurs. The procedures exist; they are available to those who choose to use them; they need no longer be improvised. When we survey other issue areas in international affairs, we find again that international organization has, to an extent, bureaucratized international relations. Such is certainly the case with regard to the international economic relations of Western Europe, Central America, and East Africa. Such may well also be the case increasingly in transatlantic financial relations, in North-South aid transactions, in international dealings in peacetime atomic energy, and in the esoteric domains of ecology, space, weather, and the oceans. Procedures, rules, and routines are being explored and instituted in all of these areas so that international communication is facilitated and international conflict is avoided or resolved. To be sure, we are nowhere near world government; and, what is more, it remains as unlikely as ever that the state system will ever be subordinated to a world regime. Nevertheless, the either/or choice between international organization as a facade for power politics or international organization as incipient world government, frequently posed by analysts and critics of international organizations, is unrealistic in our day. Contemporary international organization is clearly neither a facade for power politics nor an incipient world government. The really fascinating question now is whether, when, and to what extent has the existence and functioning of international organizations become compatible with, and indeed functional to, the existence and functioning of the international state system? Do we in the 1970s *need* to cooperate internationally via international institutions and international bureaucracies? Do we in the 1970s need to channel increasing proportions of our international interactions through international organizations? If our present international organizations did not exist, would we have to create them?[13]

Somewhat less conventionally speaking, the analysis of contemporary international relations seems just now to be awakening to the existence and impacts of nongovernmental and extragovernmental international organizations and interactions, the realm of international behavior labelled "transnational relations" by Joseph Nye and Robert Keohane. Certainly, nongovernmental groups and forces, as well as subgovernmental agencies, units, and factions and extragovernmental movements, have always been active in world affairs. But how poorly we understand their activities, and how little we know of their impacts. In fact, we have become so accustomed to working with input-output, group theory, and pluralism models, which picture subnational groups pressuring governments and governments in turn interacting with one another, that we find it rather difficult to conceptualize governments reacting not directly to pressures exerted by pressure groups but to situations created by nongovernmental groups acting upon one another in the international arena. Some indication of these conceptual difficulties is found, for example, in the current absence of an analytical vocabulary that takes inventory of outcomes in transnational relations. That is, we have not yet developed helpful terms, labels, or concepts to identify and categorize outcomes and relationships that occur in transnational affairs.[14]

Nevertheless, even with the conceptual fuzziness that surrounds the area of transnational relations, the meaningfulness of this area and our need to understand it – if we are going to better understand contemporary international politics – become apparent from episodes that seem to be occurring with increasing frequency. Witness, for example, the petroleum price negotiations in Teheran, Iran, in 1970, that produced agreements directly affecting the national economies of several dozen states. Who were the international actors? National governments? Yes, but only in part. Participating also were: (1) a group of major international oil companies, acting individually and as members of a nongovernmental international organization; (2) the Arab League, an international intergovernmental organization; (3) the Organization of Petroleum Exporting Countries (OPEC), another international organization; and (4) a roving ambassador from the United States, acting not as an interested diplomat but as a disinterested mediator. The outcome of this petroleum price dispute was the result, then, of a matrix of multilevelled interaction between a variety of actors, only some of which were national governments acting as national governments. Similar matrices best describe interaction patterns characterizing the world currency crisis of 1971, the Chilean nationalizations that same year, preparations for the UN Conference on the Human Environment in Stockholm, UNCTAD III, and a great many other important events in world politics in our time. Certainly, too, the activities of the European Communities, with their networks of interest groups and political factions linked across national frontiers, have in effect transnationalized important aspects of intra–Western European international relations. In addition, the oil swapping situation in the eastern Mediterranean, where Western oil companies and the Soviet government exchange Middle Eastern for Black Sea oil, is a rather peculiar variety of transnational relations. Such swaps enable the Soviet Union to maintain trading relations with customers along the East African coast, in spite of the closing of the Suez Canal, while the Black Sea oil gained by Western companies in exchange is shipped to Western Europe. Finally, and more seriously, would our early analyses of the Vietnam War have been different, for example, if we had conceptualized the Viet Cong as a transnational actor rather than as a military instrument of North Vietnam?

In sum, world politics in the 1970s involve interaction among diverse actors whose nature and behavior cannot be accounted for by conventional government-to-government analytical paradigms. If we, as students of international relations, believe that understanding events such as those noted in this section is important, then we must revise our images of the international system by replacing single level "billiard ball" models with multilevel actor and interaction matrices.

A Politics of Subsystems

Still structurally speaking, contemporary international politics are global. But *global* today means something more than and something different from what it meant in the 1950s and 1960s, when we first conceptualized a new international system that included all of the new states emerged from former colonial empires. By and large, the older image of the global system was one that pictured a many-theatered cold war with the superpowers pursuing their competitive interests worldwide.[15] *Global*, therefore, was most descriptive of the range of superpower interests and actions. Certainly this image was largely accurate and useful for international political analysis during the last two decades, and it remains useful today as long as the many-theatered cold war continues. But it is too simple. When we talk about global international politics today, we mean that events of far-reaching significance are taking place all over the world, not only in superpower relations as formerly, or even in large state relations, but in countless interaction channels. Symbolically speaking, whereas we formerly could do rather well by focusing upon East-West relations almost exclusively, we now must cope with and understand, not only East-West, but also North-South, North-North, South-South, East-East, and West-West relations as well. This being the case, it seems most analytically promising to conceive of the present day international system as several different subsystems of activity—one encompassing the superpowers and their peculiar concerns, one containing the advanced industrial societies with their special international problems, one made up of the advanced industrial nations plus the less developed nations with the issues that join them, one comprised of the less developed countries alone with their particular international problems, and one containing the Communist states.

Certainly the subsystems are interrelated and overlapping, but each nonetheless has its own rather distinct structures, processes, and problems. Therefore, conceptualizing and understanding international politics in the 1970s may better begin by breaking the global complex down into subsystems of activity.

Again, the point here is not that the cold-war system has disappeared. Rather, it has been augmented as important aspects and issues of international relations in our day are no longer related to the East-West contest. What is unfortunate at the present state of our scholarship is that we really do not know very much about non-cold-war international politics. How much do we really know, for example, about North-South relations? What emerges, for instance, when we take a dispassionate look at the politics of the dominance-dependency relationships between northern economic giants and southern dwarfs? Do the weaker states really come off as poorly as the power disparities would lead one to expect?[16] Who really influences whom, and how much, to do what, when, and why? Moreover, how far do we get here analytically by limiting our investigations to the government-to-government level? And, if we will admit that we do not really know very much about North-South relations, what can we say about South-South relations? A major new aspect of the international system of the 1970s is that underdeveloped countries are interacting with one another with increasing frequency and intensity. What is this South-South dimension of international politics really all about? What do the governments of the underdeveloped countries want from one another? How are they going about getting what they want?[17] And again, how far do we get in our analyses by remaining at the government-to-government level? Similarly, what of North-North relations and the peculiarities of international relations among modern industrial democracies? How, for example, do aspects of postindustrial society get reflected in foreign policy?[18]

Overall, the new image of the international system that we suggest is complex, but not unfathomable. The system consists of several (at least five) subsystems of activity defined by clusters of issues (about which we will say more in a moment) relating clusters of actors. These actors, moreover, are of several different varieties, ranging from supranational to subnational and including multinational and nonnational. International politics today consists of interaction between and among actors within and between subsystems.

INTEGRATIVE INTERNATIONAL PROCESSES

Complexity in the international politics of the 1970s is reflected, not only in systemic structure, but also in systemic processes. Aspects of this procedural complexity, too, become rather difficult to cope with within the framework of conventional disciplinary paradigms which tend to focus most attention upon international competitiveness and outcomes determined by military power. Undeniably, much of contemporary international politics is competitive, and violence is almost constant. Though national armies have been crossing international borders with somewhat less frequency in our era than in times past, almost every other index of frequency and intensity in international conflict in our time signals constant, profound bloodletting. This, of course, is to say nothing of international jealousies, animosities, revanches, sensitivities, incidents, and crises that continue to crowd the "newspaper" world of the 1970s. Still, what living uncritically in this newspaper world fails to call to our attention is that, in the 1970s, international integration in bilateral relations significantly, in regional relations especially, and at the universal level sparingly also may be displacing competitiveness as the modal world political process.

To avoid conceptual confusion, by *integration* we mean *peaceful transnational problem solving*. Moreover, by *integrative processes* we mean *the fashioning and use of instruments for such transnational problem solving*. These instruments may be supranational institutions; they may be international legal norms; they could be tacitly accepted behavioral patterns; they even may be such things as international telephone linkages in the form of "hot lines." What is important is that they symbolize as well as facilitate movement toward positive-sum international outcomes. Typically, the integrative process – bilateral, multilateral, governmental, or nongovernmental – is manifested in several phases, beginning with the recognition of a common or convergent international problem or problems, following to discussion and negotiation concerning appropriate measures for solving the problem, moving to the fashioning of instruments for solving the problem (in the form of agreements, programs, or institutions), and continuing in the actual use of the instrument thus fashioned.

In this vein, most obviously, regionalism is certainly alive and well in the 1970s, in Western Europe where the Six recently became the Nine, in Central America where a common market agreement seems to have withstood an international war, in South America where the Andean Group is grasping the development dilemma by the horns via international cooperation, and in Africa where the "try, try again" ethic prevails despite any number of false starts.[19] What is most fascinating about contemporary regionalism is that this integration phenomenon, upon close analysis, appears to be a genuinely new kind of happening in international affairs. That is, regional integration, economic, political, or more narrowly functional, circa 1970 is not simply a rerun or revised version of more familiar traditional phenomena such as federalism or nation building. Nor is it imperialism.[20] For example, contemporary regional integration creates no new superstates with supergovernments, and it apparently builds no new nations from older nationalities. Neither, certainly, does it appear to be a process whereby stronger states expand in traditional fashion by gobbling up weaker neighbors. Regionalism today is rather a collection of procedures and techniques, set in particular attitudinal environments, by which governments and peoples maximize mutual positive payoffs by exploiting their interdependence. Furthermore, regionalism may be no longer, as it was during the 1950s, the cooperative exception that proves the rule of pervasive competitiveness in the international system. Today, rather, it seems to reflect forces, feelings, and processes that are central to world politics – increasing economic and technological interdependence, increasing reliance upon international organization for problem solving and for conflict control and conflict resolution, and increasing legitimacy accorded to international organization operations and outputs.

Still, despite impressive accomplishments under the heading *regionalism* (and some impressive failures too), when we say that the international politics of the 1970s are in notable measure a politics of integration, we are not really saying that we see, or even foresee, a world of multinational federations, common markets, huge conglomerate corporations, or any of the kinds of entities that the popular concept *international integration* tends to evoke in peoples' imaginations. As noted, some such experiments in far-reaching international cooperation via elaborate institutionalization are occurring, and others may well be forthcoming. But, more than this, what we actually envisage, and indeed already perceive, is a proliferation of institutionally less complex and certainly less conspicuous integrative ventures prompted by actors' attempts to solve a growing number and variety of transnational problems. SALT, the Soviet-American Hot Line, the Franco-German institutionalization of periodic summit-level consultation, the building of the Concorde, the World Weather Watch, INTELSAT, OPEC, the Group of Ten, and the Club of Rome are all examples.

As alluded to already, it seems that heightened international integration in our time – as reflected in an increased frequency of intergovernmental treaties and agreements over a widening range of concerns, a growing inventory of international organizational programs and projects, as well as in a vastly increased number of nongovernmental international contracts, joint ventures, exchanges, and programs over a broad functional field – is related to several conditions novel and peculiar to our time. Most of these have to do with the fact that today a great many national problems may be resolved only by securing assistance and cooperation from abroad. Most obviously, for example, world economic interdependence erases distinctions between internal and external economic policies.[21] While many of the less developed countries are truly wards of the international economic system, it is also true that even the economic giants cannot insulate their domestic economies from world forces. Then, too, full exploitation of the beneficial results of modern technology in transportation and communication, in production and marketing, and in fostering health, welfare, and enlightenment raises imperatives for international cooperation, regulation, and often institutionalization. By the same token, controlling the environmentally damaging impacts of modern technology also requires international coordination. Finally, it almost goes without saying that, for every country, enhancing national defense has come to mean fostering international cooperation with allies and suppliers and fashioning international instruments to this end. Hence, international integration in our time is largely the result of the fact that the traditional nation state is obsolete for most functional intents and purposes. Yet it remains a vibrant symbol of human identification and is, therefore, not about to disappear. In the 1970s, then, we have the appearance and the public rhetoric of national autonomy cloaking a reality of profound interdependence.

Of course, integrative processes are not necessarily conflict free. In fact, there is often a good deal of conflict involved in transnational problem solving. But, interestingly, we may be witnessing today the emergence of a kind of international conflict distinctly different from that which prevailed during past eras. In contrast to the past, when continuing conflict could be observed as arising from incompatibilities in men's values and goals, a goodly proportion of present-day conflict between international actors seems to stem from differences in preferences for means rather than from differences over ends. Most simply put, many international actors today seem to be disagreeing about appropriate ways to cooperate. Conflict, therefore, occurs within the larger framework of understandings that mutual rewards will follow from international cooperation if only procedures can be worked out so that these rewards can be gained and equitably distributed while specific interests are protected.[22] In this context, then, conflict concerns procedures and not ends. Compare, for instance, the Arab-Israeli conflict, a traditional clashing of incompatible ends, with Franco-British differences over British entry into the EEC, much more a clash over means than ends, at least since de Gaulle. Or compare the People's Republic of China–Formosa conflict, another traditional clash over ends, with Japanese-American differences over textile trade, another contest over appropriate means for realizing mutual benefits. Our distinct impression is that while traditional incompatibilities will remain with us as long as the international system remains state centered and as long as states pursue traditional ends, the more frequent variety of international conflict for the 1970s is likely to be conflict about cooperation, or short-run disagreement fought through so that long-run cooperation may proceed in the direction of mutual benefits. In other words, international politics may be becoming much less a constant-sum and much more a positive, variable-sum game.

For the sake of proper perspective, we are not suggesting here that transnational problem solving, cooperation, coordination, and institutionalization are novel phenomena in the 1970s. To say this would be silly. Nonetheless, what we do suggest is that the frequency of integrative undertakings has so increased in recent years as to alter the ratio of cooperative to competitive outcomes in international politics and, consequently, to alter the very nature of international relations. This is but a suggestion and it must be subjected to empirical testing. But if it is validated, then our basic conceptualization of international politics as essentially a constant-sum conflict game or even a mixed-motive conflict game must be refashioned. In any event, whether or not integration is to be the predominant mode of international politics in the 1970s, the student of contemporary international affairs, much more than his predecessor a research generation ago, must be able to account for and incorporate into his understanding an impressive array of day-to-day international outcomes generated in the course of integrative interaction.

COMPLEXITY AND NOVELTY IN THE SUBSTANCE OF INTERNATIONAL POLITICS IN THE 1970s

In the last analysis, the heart of the complexity as well as the novelty of contemporary international politics is in the range of issues that are today the substance of world affairs. Old issues remain with us. Cold-war questions about the expansion and containment of ideological empires are still validly asked. Twenty-year-old political and military stalemates over Berlin, central Europe, Korea, Formosa, and Indochina continue. Burden sharing, strategic decision making, and cohesion remain problems within the Western and Eastern alliances. The United States and the Soviet Union are still trying to entice each other into arms control and disarmament. But the two superpowers also continue their arms race at a feverish pace while nuclear proliferation to Nth countries remains likely despite the Non-Proliferation Treaty. Little has actually been settled in the Middle East, and, if anything, the tense situation in Asia is becoming more ominous. Lingering white minority rule in parts of sub-Saharan Africa continues as an incendiary problem. Certainly we cannot ignore such issues. They are parts of the substance of international politics today. But they may no longer be the overshadowing substance.

The older issues are almost all problems of military security – American, Russian, Chinese, German, or someone else's. They are mostly questions about how to cope with the other side's military capabilities. These issues became issues, and remain issues, because governments of the world clash in their respective pursuits of the traditional set of political goals, that is, territorial integrity, political autonomy, military preeminence, ideological universality, and universal deference. Most governments today continue to seek these traditional goals. But they seek other more mundane and more practical goals too, such as full employment and education for their populations, stability for their currencies, capital and technology for their industries, purification of their physical and natural environments, and nutritional adequacy. Of course, to some extent governments have always sought these more mundane and practical goals, but rarely have these been central foreign policy pursuits. Today, however, these may be pushing the traditional, more heroic drives away from the centers and toward the peripheries of governmental external concern.

Ernst Haas and others have drawn the distinction between "power" pursuits and "welfare" pursuits in international politics.[23] Whether *welfare* is the most descriptive term for the newly important cluster of international goals is incidental. What is most important is that governments in our era appear to be going to the international arena for purposes of procuring, allocating, channeling, and regulating flows of resources deemed essential for improving the material well-being of their countries' inhabitants.[24] Moreover, foreign policies toward welfare ends are as, if not more, characteristic of the modern industrial democracies of the northern quadrant as they are of poor, unstable countries of the southern quadrant, which we may expect to be interested in improved living conditions for their peoples. Governments attending to welfare goals tend to look upon other actors in the international system as possible partners or benefactors, or as possible threats to their attainment of domestic ends. But in contrast to traditional international politics, partnership, beneficence, and threat are more likely to be conceived, perceived, and evaluated *economically* than *militarily*. Therefore, a more salient, more vital politics of international economics seems a major dimension of the substance of international politics in the 1970s. The issues in this new politics of international economics are generated as actors collaborate and collide in pursuit of internal welfare ends – those of employment, stability, and food, rather than of territory, power, and glory.

Newly salient issues, then, include: (1) *issues of trade*, such as questions about preference, prices, and blocs, and problems of Asian textiles, Middle Eastern oil, French foodstuffs, Norwegian fish, and Brazilian coffee; (2) *issues of aid*, such as questions about volume, rate, and direction, about public versus private and bilateral versus multilateral, about economic sense and moral responsibility, and problems of foreign-owned subsidiaries and political sovereignty, of technological diffusion and brain drains; and (3) *issues of money*, such as questions about payments balances, exchange rates, currency blocs, currency reserves, and currency convertabilities, and problems of domestic monetary policies confronted by international capital flows, domestic inflation controls confronted by the "gnomes of Zurich," and domestic capital markets pitted against the Eurodollar market. Certainly, studying such issues may seem rather unexciting to scholars attuned to a heroic international politics of nuclear crisis and other grand enterprises of peace and war. However, if we fail to understand these issues and the political forces and pressures that make them issues in a world of strong and weak, capitalist and socialist welfare states, we may fail in a major way to understand the sources of world politics in the 1970s.

Exactly why international welfare issues have emerged as *high politics* questions in our time has not yet been fully explained. One immediate reason, of course, is that welfare issues have attracted more attention as it has become possible to pay somewhat less attention to security issues. East-West détente, in particular, has permitted some relaxation in military preparedness and consequently allowed governments greater freedom to attend to nonsecurity concerns.[25] It is also fair to say that attention to security issues and active participation in great questions of global politics became for some countries an expensive luxury that could not be afforded, especially in light of fleeting resources and demands for domestic allocations (as discussed below).[26]

But even more important, we believe, in heightening the significance of welfare questions in international politics have been secular trends toward welfare statism manifested in some degree in almost every country in the world. These, in turn, reflect the rise of mass society the world over with concomitant political populism which has affected even the totalitarian governments. Governmental responsibility for mass social and economic welfare is a political norm of our time. Citizens expect, indeed demand, economic planning, economic policy, employment, housing, education, and a host of welfare services from their governments. Consequently, governmental stability and tenure have come increasingly to depend upon the performance of these welfare functions. This is most true, certainly, in democracies where populism, pluralism, and electoral and parliamentary politics can combine to place governments under immense pressure. But authoritarian regimes are also not immune to populist pressures from below. Hence, governments today are prone to be more attentive than in times past to international developments that either pose challenges to or present opportunities for their administration of domestic economic programs. Again, since such factors and outcomes as inflation, recession, employment, capital supply, skill distribution, critical resources, and even food supply are presently internationally linked in sensitive networks of interdependence, external challenges to and opportunities for domestic welfarism are more likely to arise today than they were in the past.[27]

While the strongest case for new or newly important substance can properly be made about the pragmatic international politics of welfare ends, an equally intriguing discussion can be generated about an apparently newly emerging cluster of ideological issues. The great ideological clash of the 1950s and 1960s was, of course, the confrontation between the political-economic prescriptions of communism and those of liberal capitalist democracy. Let us bear in mind that this conflict is primarily over the legitimacy of different ways to politically and economically organize societies. It rests upon questions about right and wrong patterns of human relationships within societies. This contest continues today.

But since the early 1960s, we sense a new ideological cleavage in the international system. This is the contest between what we will call *nationalism* and *cosmopolitanism* as alternative philosophies of international relations. It rests, not upon questions of right and wrong human relationships within societies, but upon legitimate and illegitimate modes of relations between societies. Nationalism values the integrity, autonomy, continuity, and prosperity (in the broadest sense) of the nation state above all else. It sanctions a variety of international interactions all along the cooperation-competition spectrum. But, very fundamentally, it suspects foreigners, attributes malevolent goals to them, calls for external defensiveness, and demands exclusive attention to national interests narrowly defined. Most significantly, nationalism rejects the legitimacy of rule making, its processes, and its institutions above the national level. It further rejects the legitimacy of all transnational forces and organizations and all foreign penetration for whatever reason into national affairs. Cosmopolitanism, on the contrary, is a very different kind of ideology.[28] It values efficiency and accomplishment in social, economic, and political problem solving above all else; and it takes as a given that many problems today are transnational in nature and hence demand international efforts toward their solution. Cosmopolitanism does not reject the nation state or its institutions, though it does reject *nationalism* as defined here. While cosmopolitanism tends to value international cultural diversity and while it accepts that there are peculiar national interests and reserved domains for national problem solving, it nonetheless legitimizes rule making and rule-making institutions at the international and supranational level. Indeed, it views operations at these levels as essential to approaching and solving problems that are transnational and international in character.

Most generally speaking, the nationalism-cosmopolitanism cleavage divides the contemporary world along the Northwest-Southeast axis (though it also divides the populations of countries within the different quadrants). While many of the industrial democracies of the northern quadrant seem currently to be passing into a postnationalist era of social and economic interdependence, benevolent interpenetration, and international and supranational regimes in functional sectors, the majority of countries in the southern quadrant appear to be moving into an intensely nationalistic era, extolling, cherishing, and ideologically embellishing their newly gained independence. Ominously, nationalism in some new states recently has appeared as unabashed racism. Communist regimes, too, espouse nationalistic principles in their international relations, despite the rhetoric of proletarian internationalism, since they tend to fear political-ideological "contamination" from the non-Communist Northwest, imperialism from larger socialist confreres, and "beggar thy neighbor" policies from smaller ones.

Specific issues generated by the normative differences between nationalism and cosmopolitanism seem to be growing in number and importance. Some of these have to do with tensions created by multinational corporate operations in underdeveloped, newly independent countries. Fundamental to disputes over ownership, royalties, profit margins, nationalization, technological transfer, and other issues may be more deep-seated questions about the legitimacy of transnational business organizations as such. Other issues raised in the confrontation between nationalism and cosmopolitanism include tensions over perceived strings attached to North-South aid flows, perceived conspiracies of rich men, and perceived neo-colonialism. Then, too, fundamental differences over the legitimacy of international organization programs and rulings, legitimacy recognized by cosmopolitan proponents and emphatically denied by nationalists, have generated clashes over questions of human rights, international waterways, UN peacekeeping, UN budgeting, and UN leadership. Similar ideological cleavages have affected regional international organizations as well. While it is difficult at this time to be very conclusive about the magnitude and impact of new ideological cleavages in the international system, we speculate that much of the *newness* of our new system of the 1970s will be preserved or will perish depending upon the outcome of the contest between nationalism and cosmopolitanism.

Clearly, the substantive complexity of international politics in the 1970s arises from the fact that while older issues of national security and international military stability remain very much with us, other concerns that were once peripheral or, for some issues, nonexistent have become urgent. Urgency has followed partly from growing human welfare needs in a deteriorating world resource environment, partly from the entrance of the less developed countries into world politics and the persistence and ominousness of their demands, and partly from the twenty years' neglect from 1945 to 1965 when the world was preoccupied with the cold war and awed by the spectre of nuclear doom. Whether the urgent nonsecurity issues will again be second rated by national governments is something we must wait to observe. It seems clear to us, however, that they presently cannot be ignored by scholars.

NOTES

1. F. S. Hinsley identifies another such lag between perceptions of international politics and evolving day-to-day reality at the very beginning of the Western state system. Therefore, comparing Hinsley's case with ours is interesting and enlightening. See F. S. Hinsley, *Power and the Pursuit of Peace* (Cambridge: Cambridge University Press, 1967), pp. 153–85, especially 167–68.

2. Some of the most stimulating and insightful recent attempts at reconceptualization in international relations are displayed in Harold Sprout and Margaret Sprout, *Toward a Politics of the Planet Earth* (New York: Van Nostrand Reinhold, 1971), pp. 3–12, 348–460. See, also, Ernst B. Haas, *Tangle of Hopes* (Englewood Cliffs: Prentice-Hall, 1969), passim; Ernst B. Haas, *Beyond the Nation-State* (Stanford: Stanford University Press, 1964), passim; and Joseph S. Nye, Jr., *Peace in Parts* (Boston: Little, Brown & Co., 1970), especially the "Foreword" by Stanley Hoffmann and passim.

3. Raymond Aron, *Peace and War: A Theory of International Relations* (Garden City: Doubleday, 1966), p. 71.

4. While there has been, earlier, a good deal of discussion and debate among theorists about idealism versus realism and, more recently, about traditionalism versus scientism or behavioralism, one need only closely compare the works of the different theorists from the different schools to find rather sweeping agreement in the image of international politics as security politics described here. See, for example: Hans J. Morgenthau, *Politics Among Nations*, 4th ed. (New York: Alfred Knopf, 1967); Aron, *Peace and War;* Morton Kaplan, *System and Process in International Politics* (New York: John Wiley, 1957); Stanley Hoffmann, *The State of War* (New York: Praeger, 1965); Kenneth Boulding, *Conflict and Defense* (New York: Harper and Row, 1963); Harold Lasswell, *World Politics and Personal Insecurity* (New York: Free Press, 1965).

5. For a description of this contemporary world of security politics as perceived by one of the present authors, see Donald J. Puchala, *International Politics Today* (New York: Dodd, Mead & Co., 1971), pp. 243–355.

6. Joseph S. Nye, Jr., and Robert O. Keohane, eds., "Transnational Relations and World Politics," *International Organization* 25 (Summer 1971): entire issue.

7. Nye and Keohane; see also Karl Kaiser, "Transnational Politics: Toward a Theory of Multinational Politics," *International Organization* 25 (Autumn 1971): 790-818. Also illuminating in this regard is Roy Godson, "Non-Governmental Organizations in International Politics: The American Federation of Labor, the International Labor Movement and French Politics, 1945-1952" (Ph.D. dissertation, Columbia University, 1972).

8. Nye and Keohane, pp. 329-49.

9. David Singer and Michael D. Wallace, "International Organization in the Global System, 1815-1964: A Quantitative Description," *International Organization* 24 (Spring 1970): 239-87. See, also, Paul Smoker, "Nation-State Escalation and International Integration," *Journal of Peace Research* 9, no. 4 (1967): 61-73.

10. Singer and Wallace, pp. 272-73.

11. Donald J. Puchala, "International Transactions and Regional Integration," *International Organization* 24 (Autumn 1970): 759-62.

12. Ernst Haas, "Collective Security and the Future International System" in Richard A. Falk and Wolfram F. Hanrieder, eds., *International Law and Organization* (Philadelphia: Lippincott, 1968), pp. 299-344; Nye, *Peace in Parts,* pp. 3-19, 127-72.

13. This question was the topic of a lecture by Robert O. Keohane delivered before the Columbia University International Fellows in October 1971; Keohane's answer was affirmative.

14. Karl Kaiser makes some interesting thrusts in this direction: Kaiser, pp. 801-15.

15. See, for example, Andrew Scott, *The Revolution in Statecraft: Informal Penetration* (New York: Random House, 1965), passim.

16. I. William Zartman, *The Politics of Trade Negotiations Between Africa and the European Economic Community: The Weak Confront the Strong* (Princeton: Princeton University Press, 1971), pp. 200-230 and passim; Joan Edelman Spero, "Dominance-Dependence Relationships: The Case of France and Gabon" (Ph.D. dissertation, Columbia University, 1973), pp. 116-306 and passim.

17. I. William Zartman, *International Relations in the New Africa* (Englewood Cliffs: Prentice-Hall, 1966), passim; I. William Zartman, "Africa as a Subordinate State System in International Relations," *International Organization* 21 (Summer 1967): 545-64; I. William Zartman, "Intervention Among Developing States," *Journal of International Affairs* 22, no. 2 (1968); 188-97; Howard Wriggins, *South and Southeast Asia in the Asian State System* (New York: Columbia University Press for the Southern Asian Institute, 1971), pp. 28-61.

18. A great deal of writing is beginning to appear on this subject, for example: Louis Armand and Michel Drancourt, *The European Challenge* (New York: Atheneum, 1970); Robert Gilpin, *France in the Age of the Scientific State* (Princeton: Princeton University Press, 1967); Zbigniew K. Brzezinski, *Between Two Ages: America's Role in the Technetronic Age* (New York: Viking, 1970); Sprout and Sprout, *The Politics of the Planet Earth,* pp. 189-208, 348-77; Edward Morse, "The Transformation of Foreign Policies: Modernization, Interdependence and Externalization," *World Politics* 22 (April 1970): 371-92; Richard N. Cooper, "Trade Policy as Foreign Policy," *Foreign Policy* 9 (Winter 1972-73): 18-36.

19. Abdul Aziz Jalloh, "Regional Political Integration in Africa: The Lessons of the Last Decade," paper presented at the Conference on Regional Integration, Madison, Wisconsin, 24–26 April 1969.

20. Donald J. Puchala, "Of Blind Men, Elephants and International Integration," *Journal of Common Market Studies* 10 (March 1972): 267–84. Some authors, however, do claim that contemporary international integration schemes are ventures in imperialism; see, for example: Michel Teubal, "The Failure of Latin America's Economic Integration," in James Petras and Maurice Zeitlin, eds., *Latin America: Reform or Revolution* (New York: Fawcett, 1968), pp. 120–44; and Suzanne Jonas (Bodenheimer), "Masterminding the Mini-Market: U.S. Aid to the Central American Common Market," *Latin America and Empire Report* (publication of the North American Congress on Latin America) 7 (May-June 1973): 3–21.

21. Richard N. Cooper, *The Economics of Interdependence* (New York: McGraw-Hill, 1968), pp. 148–76 and passim; Richard N. Cooper, "Economic Interdependence and Foreign Policy in the Seventies," *World Politics* 24 (January 1972): 159–81.

22. Stuart Fagan, *Central American Economic Integration: The Politics of Unequal Benefits* (Berkeley: Institute of International Studies, University of California, 1970); Hugh W. Springer, *Reflections on the Failure of the First West Indian Federation*, Occasional Papers in International Affairs, no. 4 (Cambridge: Center for International Affairs, Harvard University, 1962); Puchala, "Of Blind Men, Elephants and International Integration," pp. 277–83.

23. Haas, *Beyond the Nation-State*, pp. 10–12.

24. Sprout and Sprout, *The Politics of the Planet Earth*, pp. 348–61; Harold Sprout and Margaret Sprout, "The Dilemma of Rising Demands and Insufficient Resources," *World Politics* 20 (July 1968): 660–93.

25. Brzezinski, *Between Two Ages*, pp. 274–93. See also Marshall Shulman, *Beyond the Cold War* (New Haven: Yale University Press, 1966), pp. 18–33, 86–111.

26. For an interesting case study of this phenomenon, see Lord Strang, *Britain in World Affairs: The Fluctuations in Power and Influence from Henry VIII to Elizabeth II* (New York: Praeger, 1961), passim.

27. Haas, *Tangle of Hopes*, pp. 119–64.

28. Our conceptualization of *cosmopolitanism* was influenced by Brzezinski's discussion of what he calls "rational humanism" (*Between Two Ages*, pp. 270–73), and by Daniel Lerner's and Morton Gorden's discussion of *pragmatism* in Lerner and Gorden, *Euratlantica: Changing Perspectives of the European Elites* (Cambridge: MIT Press, 1969), pp. 241–51.

ORAN R. YOUNG

4
Interdependencies in World Politics

Young notes that the degree of interdependence may vary among the component units of the international system and in such functional areas as economics and politics. In contrast to most idealists, who envision the emergence of a global community, the author addresses the issue of whether interdependence is rising or declining. He criticizes Karl Deutsch's contention that "national self-determination is becoming more intensive and extensive in the contemporary world." Young goes beyond Deutsch's trade and communications indexes to argue that managerial personnel and techniques; international monetary institutions; military, communication, and transportation technologies; cosmopolitan ways of looking at the world; and the rise of nonstate actors have increased levels of interdependence. Young then speculates on the implications of this increase for world politics.

This essay explores the phenomenon of interdependence in world systems[1] from three separate perspectives. To begin, it attempts to pin down and clarify the concept "interdependence." Secondly, it assesses the debate on the factual question of whether the level of interdependence is rising or falling in the contemporary world system. Finally, it offers a number of hypotheses dealing with the links between systemic interdependencies (as an independent variable) and various aspects of world politics.

I

The concept "interdependence" will be defined in this essay in terms of the extent to which events occurring in any given part or within any given component unit of a world system affect (either physically or

Reprinted by permission from *International Journal* 24 (Autum 1969), pp. 726–750.

perceptually) events taking place in each of the other parts or component units of the system. By definition, therefore, the greater the extensiveness and weight of the impact of events occurring in any given part of a system for each of the other parts, the higher the level of interdependence in the system. In these terms, it is possible to conceptualize the opposite of interdependence in two ways. When a system is described in terms of its component units, the level of effective autonomy of the units is the inverse of the systemic level of interdependence. That is, the more autonomous the units, the lower the level of the system's interdependence. When a system is described without reference to specific component units, on the other hand, the concept "isolation" seems more appropriate as the opposite of interdependence. In this sense, the level of isolation in a system increases as events taking place in any given part of the system have less impact on events occurring in each of the other parts of the system.

It also seems helpful to distinguish between the composite level of interdependence in a system and variations among different segments of the system. When the level of interdependence among all the component units of a system with respect to all relevant functions is high (low), the composite level of interdependence can be said to be high (low). In world systems, however, there are often substantial variations along these lines. The level of interdependence among some of the component units of any given system is commonly higher than the level of interdependence among others. In the contemporary system, for example, the level of interdependence among the industrialized states of the north Atlantic area is considerably higher than that among the states of the "third world."[2] Similarly, the level of interdependence in world systems is apt to vary from one functional area to another. In nineteenth-century Europe, for example, it appears that economic interdependencies were more constricting than more straightforward political interdependencies.

The conceptual implications of the prevailing state-centric world view often obscure discussions of interdependencies in world systems.[3] Above all, the *formal* independence and equality implied in the doctrine of sovereignty tend to become confused with effective autonomy.[4] And since it is difficult to square the constraints placed on states by the operation of systemic interdependencies with the imagery of state sovereignty, limitations on autonomy in interdependent world systems are often simply ignored in rhetorical affirmations of the formal prerogatives of sovereign states. In addition, the emphases of the state-centric world view on states or nation-states as the principal actors in world politics, the relative impermeability of states, and the watershed quality of the boundaries of states often tend to exaggerate the level of effective autonomy of the component units of world systems. It is easier to maintain effective autonomy in a system of hard-shelled states that are clearly and neatly demarcated in territorial terms, for example, than in a system characterized by crosscutting relationships and interpenetrations among a number of qualitatively different types of actor. Similarly, effective autonomy is easier to maintain in cases where the boundaries of states mark qualitative shifts in the nature of most human activities and domestic policies are largely impervious to external influences than in cases where effective boundaries vary from one functional area to another and extensive intrusion of external influences on the internal policies of actors is commonplace.

There is also a persistent "idealist" interpretation of the growth of interdependencies in world systems that has long been a source of confusion in the analysis of world politics.[5] This interpretation is characteristic of commentators who argue that a states system is dangerously obsolete given the development of modern technology and who concern themselves with the problem of moving as rapidly as possible from a states system to some more viable structural arrangements for world politics. In brief, the idealist interpretation looks upon indications that the level of interdependence in the world system is rising as signs of great hope. The principal argument here is that if the level of interdependence in the system continues to rise, this will eventually precipitate the emergence of a world "community" or a world "culture" which will in turn lead to the development of a world "state" capable of managing the rising level of interdependence.

This argument, however, is logically deficient in several respects. First, the rise of systemic interdependencies generally creates new opportunities for conflict as well as increased scope for co-operation in world politics. As has long been recognized in the analysis of economic relationships, the growth of interdependencies among actors is equally if not more often a source of conflict than an impetus toward co-operation.[6] Interdependencies may well be subject to effective management, therefore, but there is no *a priori* reason to suppose that a rising level of interdependence will precipitate the emergence of a world community. Secondly, the idealist interpretation tends to confuse prescriptive notions with descriptive statements. In fact, a good argument can be constructed to the effect that under conditions of rising interdependence, increases in the extent of organized regulation (or government) will be required to maintain the stability of any given sociopolitical system. (More on this below.) But this in no way indicates that the conditions of stability will actually be met in any given case. To suppose that this will happen is to fall into the fallacy of structural teleology. While the idealist interpretation is understandable, therefore, it has been more a source of confusion than enlightenment in the analysis of world politics.

II

There has for some time been a debate concerning the factual question of whether the level of interdependence is rising in the contemporary world system. There is little doubt that the notion of a rapid rise in the level of interdependence is part of the popular wisdom of the day. But a number of empirical studies have cast sufficient doubt on this conclusion to make the question worth re-examining.

Several preliminary points are in order in approaching this question. To begin with, it is true by definition that world systems are characterized by a relatively low ratio of systemwide interdependencies to interdependencies within their component units.[7] This of course does not imply, in empirical cases, that the ratio cannot shift or that the absolute level of systemic interdependence cannot rise. It does indicate, however, that studies documenting the low ratio of systemwide to subsystemic interdependencies do little more than confirm the empirical existence of a world system. In addition, it follows from the discussion in the preceding section that the compilation of a composite index of trends in the level of interdependence in any given system is apt to be a difficult task to accomplish satisfactorily. Shifts along these lines may well affect units or segments of the system differentially. And the problem of variation along functional lines is likely to be a particularly difficult one in the analysis of world systems. The question of whether the level of interdependence in the contemporary world system is rising, therefore, is a more complicated question than it seems at first. Nevertheless, it appears to be of sufficient importance to merit further consideration.

Perhaps the most persuasive and influential arguments against the notion that the level of interdependence in the world system is rising are contained in a series of writings by Karl Deutsch.[8] Deutsch's central argument is that "national self-preoccupation" is becoming more intensive and extensive in the contemporary world. This argument does not *necessarily* imply that there has been no increase in absolute terms in the level of interdependence in the world system. It does suggest, however, that a far more striking and important development is an increase in the ratio of interdependencies within component units to interdependencies characteristic of the world system as a whole. That is, nation-states are becoming more preoccupied with their own internal affairs relative to their involvement in activities cutting across national boundaries.

Deutsch has marshalled a considerable amount of empirical data to support this conclusion in recent years. His most central bit of evidence appears to be that "during the last sixty years, the foreign trade sectors have declined."[9] Taking an average of all the countries of the world, that is, the sum of exports and imports as a percentage of national income has declined. As a result, in the nineteenth century foreign trade potentially involved a larger proportion of the interest groups of a country than is the case at the present time.[10] In addition, Deutsch has mustered several other sets of empirical indicators to support the idea that national self-preoccupation is increasing. Human migration across national boundaries, for example, involved greater numbers of people in the nineteenth century than in the current era. The percentage of letters crossing national boundaries has declined in the contemporary period. The demands for resources to deal with essentially domestic problems such as social welfare, education, and environmental pollution are increasing rapidly.[11] And, according to Deutsch, "wage interdependence" between countries has declined markedly since the middle of the nineteenth century. That is, marked shifts in the wage structure of one country appear to affect the wage structures of other countries less than was the case in the past. Moreover, Deutsch is inclined to argue that popular and élite perceptions of interdependence across national boundaries are either unchanging or actually declining in the contemporary world.[12] Thus, there is a rather weak sense of common identity or "belongingness" throughout the world system, and people do not come to each other's aid quickly, massively, spontaneously, or effectively across national boundaries.[13]

There is no doubt that this is a provocative and important argument. Nevertheless, it appears to be subject to important criticisms along several separate lines. First, it is severely restricted by the tacit assumption that nation-states are the only important actors in world politics.[14] Thus, the argument that foreign trade sectors have declined in interstate relations is deceptive when used to draw conclusions about world politics more generally. Such an index fails to account for many of the important activities of "multinational" enterprises, the flow of scientific and technological ideas through transnational channels, and the role of a wide range of non-state actors dealing with political and social questions.[15] It also fails to indicate the impact on the level of interdependence in the world system of the rapid expansion of "international" organizations in the twentieth century.

Secondly, Deutsch's argument is based upon a rather narrow and selective range of indicators of interdependence in the world system. In most cases, his indicators deal with tangible and highly iterative transactions among nation-states such as the exchange of commodities or the flow of letters. Even in economic terms, this procedure de-emphasizes sharply a variety of factors leading to interdependence. It fails to account for the flow of managerial personnel and techniques, the workings of the international monetary system, the impact of what Richard Cooper has called the "increased sensitivity of foreign trade,"[16] and so forth. Moreover, it is an open question what the links are between these economic factors and the level of interdependence with respect to political activities in the world system. How much do the workings of the international monetary system constrain the political activities of the actors in world politics? Are the contemporary revolutions in military technology and the technologies of communications and transportation more important sources of political interdependence in the world system than the iterative economic factors that Deutsch focuses upon? It seems evident that, other things being equal, a rise in the level of economic interdependence in the world system is apt to lead to a rise in the level of political interdependence in the system.[17] But it is far from clear whether a rise in the level of economic interdependence is a necessary condition for a rise in the level of political interdependence or even an important contributing factor in many shifts affecting levels of political interdependence.

Thirdly, Deutsch frequently (though not always) focuses on indicators of interdependence that are primarily associated with the development of co-operative activities across national boundaries. The growth of foreign trade sectors, for example, is characteristic of situations in which there is substantial scope for co-operation based on economic complementarities.[18] An actor may be highly interdependent with another actor, however, and yet experience a decline in its foreign trade sector. Consider in this connection the case of two non-industrialized states with a single and similar product (such as coffee or tobacco) to market in the world economy.[19] And there is some evidence to suggest that interdependencies of this type in contrast to the type emphasized by Deutsch's analyses are increasing in the contemporary world. Similarly, a number of Deutsch's other indicators (such as mail flows) are essentially measures of co-operative (or positive) interdependencies in contrast to competitive (or negative) interdependencies. In this light, contrast the political links between the United States and numerous other states arising from the American involvement in Vietnam with the impact of the shifts in international mail flows reported by Deutsch. In so far as there is a real bias in Deutsch's work along these lines, therefore, it casts substantial doubt on the validity of his basic argument about the rise of national self-preoccupation.

Fourthly, there is a certain deceptiveness in Deutsch's general emphasis on percentages and ratios, especially when coupled with his focus on iterative transactions as indicators of interdependence. While shifts in the ratio of interdependencies between the world system and its subsystems are obviously of substantial importance, shifts in absolute levels of interdependence are important in other contexts. Thus, the development of military technologies based on intercontinental delivery systems has far-reaching implications regardless of shifts in the ratio of systemwide interdependencies to subsystemic interdependencies. And since these new technologies have precipitated the emergence of a variety of important though intangible political links in the system, this case also illustrates the problems of relying too heavily on tangible indicators of interdependence such as the exchange of commodities. Moreover, there is some reason to believe that a number of the most important developments leading to a rise in the level of interdependence in the world system do not manifest themselves in iterative transactions. This would appear to be the case, for example, with the revolution in military technology as analyzed by writers like Boulding[20] and with recent developments in the technologies of communication and transportation outside the military sphere. Furthermore, such factors as the intercontinental ballistic missile have no direct analogues in the context of intranational developments.[21] Here too, therefore, Deutsch's argument about the rise of national self-preoccupation appears to be of doubtful validity.

Fifthly, there are some tricky methodological issues that plague efforts to determine the level of interdependence in the world system in empirical terms. Many writers, for example, have recently commented on the phenomenal growth of international trade in the contemporary world.[22] Yet Deutsch emphasizes a decline in the foreign trade sector as a critical indicator of the rise of national self-preoccupation. The difference here is easily explained in terms of the time span analysed. Compared to the economic autarky of the 1930s, the growth of international trade and the reduction of artificial barriers to international trade in the current era are unquestionably remarkable. Nevertheless, by contrast with the middle of the nineteenth century international trade does presently constitute a smaller percentage of national income (though it is important to note that the roster of countries involved in the two time periods is substantially different), and Deutsch is quite justified in his reference to this shift. In specific terms, this example indicates the problems involved in relying on volatile factors subject to fully reversible change as indicators of trends in the level of interdependence in the world system. The volatility of such factors is such that they make dubious indicators of long-term secular trends at best. More generally, this example points to the importance of paying careful attention to the methodological issues involved in efforts to construct composite indices of shifts in the level of interdependence in the world system.

If the question is turned the other way, an impressive case can be constructed for the proposition that the level of interdependence in the world system has risen sharply in the contemporary period. Though many of the relevant factors do not show up clearly in an enumeration of iterative transactions, there can be little doubt that political decision-makers in any given part of the system are far more sensitive to events occurring in other parts of the world than was the case in the past. The determinants of this development are sufficiently well-known so as not to require elaborate discussion in this essay. Nevertheless, it may be helpful to place these factors in context to indicate the full weight of the evidence against the argument that national self-preoccupation is rising.

Above all, it is important to emphasize the revolutionary increases in the physical capacities of man as a source of expanding inter-dependencies in world politics. It seems clear that sheer physical limitations have been the single most important source of effective autonomy and isolation in world systems throughout recorded history. In ancient times, these limitations were such as to preclude definitively political interactions on a global scale.[23] And even in the nineteenth and early twentieth centuries, world politics were global in scope only if the level of interaction or interdependence required to meet this designation was very low indeed.[24] In the contemporary period, however, technological revolutions in three areas have virtually wiped out the effects of distance as a necessary source of autonomy and given events occurring in any part of the world system an instantaneous relevance to political activities in every other part of the system.

First, the development of modern communications has made possible the transmission of detailed verbal and graphic accounts of activities on a worldwide and instantaneous basis.[25] Moreover, modern technology makes this type of communication almost as accessible to the masses as to élites specializing in "foreign affairs." Thus, the war in Vietnam can be followed in minute detail in the United States on a day-to-day basis; the Apollo moon shots become worldwide subjects of popular discussion within hours after their launching; and detailed elements of the internal racial problems of a country like the United States become an important determinant of both mass and élite attitudes toward American policies in every part of the world.

Secondly, one of the traditional barriers to the development of interdependencies in the world system arose from absolute physical limitations on transportation or from the prohibitive costs (either in time or in dollars) of transportation over long distances. Under the circumstances, the accidents of geography were a critical determinant of the patterns of interaction among the actors in world politics.[26] A country like the United States, for example, was able to maintain an extraordinary level of effective autonomy throughout the nineteenth century because of its geographical location, even though it was a debtor nation in the world economy during most of the century. As Albert Wohlstetter has recently shown, however, the barriers to interaction and interdependence associated with the costs of transportation are now breaking down in a truly revolutionary fashion.[27] With modern means of transportation, transportation costs in either time or dollars are rapidly declining in influence as a determinant of both economic and political activities in the world system. And although there are considerable variations in the speed with which these developments are taking place between the industrialized and non-industrialized parts of the world, the process is a striking one throughout the world system.

Thirdly, the contemporary revolution in military technology – in part a derivative of developments in the areas of communications and transportation – has produced a qualitative shift in the patterns of interdependence among the component units of the world system. Since weapons systems such as intercontinental missiles are not employed regularly in physical terms, it is difficult to pin down in any quantitative (or even precise) fashion the dimensions of the impact of the revolution in military technology on the world system. Nevertheless, it is clear that recent developments in this area have produced a qualitative increase in the level of interdependence in the world system in the sense that it is now impossible for any actor in the system to operate on the assumption that its survival is guaranteed regardless of the actions of other actors.[28] Thus, in Boulding's terms, the world system has evolved decisively toward relations of conditional viability in the interactions among its component units.[29] This development does not necessarily indicate, as Boulding suggests, that the probability of system transformation has increased drastically in the contemporary period. It does make it necessary, however, for decision-makers in any given actor to become more sensitive to events taking place in the internal arenas of other actors in developing policies designed to maximize the security of their own unit.

Along with the expansion of interdependencies arising from increases in the physical capacities of man, the contemporary period has witnessed growing shifts in the patterns of human attention, information, and expectations which have had the effect of increasing the impact of events occurring all over the world on internal activities within the individual units of the system. Fashions both in patterns of consumption and in political attitudes, for example, now spread rapidly across national boundaries on a popular as well as élite basis. And the details of an American election campaign become a preoccupation for large groups of people in every part of the world.

The influence of these developments on the expansion of interdependencies in the world system can be separated into at least two categories. In the first instance there has been a movement away from parochialism in the perceptual horizons of broad segments of the world's population. It is of course evident that "local" concerns are still dominant in the world view of most men and that human attention and concern still slope downward as a function of distance. Nevertheless, the effective boundaries of human perception appear to be expanding in the contemporary world so that the downward slope of attention as a function of distance is less precipitous than it once was. Thus, human expectations are significantly influenced by events taking place in larger and larger segments of the world system. And the level of interdependence within the system goes up as these perceptions and expectations are translated into political actions. Beyond this, shifts in the patterns of human attention have led to a growing exchange of ideas and skills on a worldwide basis. Exchanges of this kind are frequently difficult to document because they are not apt to occur in the form of physical transactions as in the case of an exchange of commodities. Instead, they occur in such forms as the transmission of intellectual movements (e.g., the present student movement), the exchange of technical skills and know-how, the communication of management techniques, the contagion of fashions and patterns of consumption, and the impact of tourism on human perceptions and expectations.

Next, the level of interdependence in the world system has risen in recent years as a function of the tightening of the links between the external policies and actions of states and the constraints imposed by the demands of internal policy. In the economic realm, this development is closely related to what Richard Cooper has called the "increased sensitivity of foreign trade."[30] This increased sensitivity arises from a number of factors such as the decline in transportation costs, the accumulation of capital, and the transmission of technical knowledge rather than from quantitative increases in the size of the foreign trade sector. Under the circumstances, the impact of the phenomenon of comparative advantages has declined in the world economy, and states have become more sensitive to disturbances in their international economic relations quite apart from shifts in the total volume of their trade. Moreover, these developments are reinforced by the fact that in many countries domestic objectives involving social welfare (such as full employment) have achieved such high priority that they cannot easily be sacrificed in order to maintain a position of equilibrium in the world economy. In the nineteenth century statesmen were often able to engage repeatedly in policies requiring domestic deflation in the interests of maintaining their international freedom of action without suffering unacceptable political losses at home. In the contemporary world, however, the margin of freedom of action in the international arena is sharply curtailed by the rigidities of numerous domestic commitments.

Similar things can be said about the tightening links between internal and external activities in the political realm. On the one hand, the sensitivity of popular opinion to external events has increased in a striking fashion in the contemporary world. World politics are no longer the province of small élite groups whose effective autonomy in dealing with each other was radically enhanced by their autonomy from their own publics and their consequent ability to ignore many potential constraints on their international activities. In the contemporary world, interdependencies are rising continuously as a function of the growing pressures on statesmen to include in their calculations the consequences of the interactions *among* states for all segments of the population *within* states rather than restricting their calculations to the concerns of small élite groups. At the same time, the opportunity costs associated with many external options are rising as a function of the elevation of various domestic objectives in terms of priorities. Here too the margin of freedom of action in external affairs is becoming narrower and the links between internal and external activities are becoming tighter. As a result, the level of interdependence among the component units in the world system has risen markedly not so much as a function of any increase in the volume of transactions among the units as because the units are becoming increasingly sensitive to the activities of each other as their internal freedom of action becomes more and more circumscribed.

Finally, the level of interdependence in the world system has risen in the contemporary period as a result of the expanding role of various non-state actors and the development of those patterns of interpenetration among actors which are characteristic of systems that are heterogeneous with respect to basic types of actor.[31] In general, interdependencies tend to rise when the actors in a system interpenetrate each other since such conditions make it virtually impossible to isolate the effects of the actions of any given actor from the concerns and interests of other actors. In the contemporary world system, this process manifests itself with particular sharpness in two distinguishable areas. First, we are witnessing a rapid expansion of the activities of multinational enterprises whose domains do not coincide with the jurisdictional boundaries of states.[32] As a result, the autonomy (though not the formal authority) of all the actors is reduced by the necessity of paying careful attention to the requirements of regulating activities that overlap formal jurisdictions. Secondly, the rise of non-state actors has precipitated the growth of discontinuities in the patterns of organization characteristic of the different functional segments of the world system. In systems where national political boundaries mark a qualitative shift in the status of most human activities, it is not so difficult to maintain the image of independent states providing all the important bases of their own subsistence unassisted. When the organizational patterns for different functional activities begin to diverge significantly, however, it is impossible for any actor to survive without paying increasing attention to the impact of the activities of other actors on its interests.

The preceding discussion has made it clear that the task of constructing a composite index of the level of interdependence in the world system is an extremely complex one. And there appears to be little doubt that a number of the most influential interdependencies in the contemporary world are of such a nature that they are difficult to pin down through an analysis of iterative transactions such as the exchange of economic commodities. On balance, however, the evidence from a wide range of disparate indicators seems to warrant the provisional conclusion that the level of interdependence in the world system is rising in the current era.

III

If the level of interdependence among the component units of the world system is in fact rising, what consequences can this development be expected to have? This section explores several changes in world politics which are likely to flow from a rising level of interdependence.

At the outset it is necessary to make explicit the several assumptions underlying this analysis:

1. The actors in the world system will be treated as collective entities. This means that any given actor can be thought of as a single unit with respect to its participation in world politics.

2. The actors will be assumed to be rational. This means that they evaluate alternatives in their environment in terms of their preferences; their preferences constitute a transitive ordering, and they always choose the preferred alternative.

3. Each actor in the world system makes choices on the basis of self-interest. That is, no actor values the utility of other actors as an end in itself.

4. Actors calculate their choices on an expected-value basis. This allows them to take into account risky situations as well as certain options.

5. The information available to each actor is imperfect. While additional information can always be acquired, it can only be acquired for a price.

These assumptions are all highly restrictive in nature, and many analysts would be inclined to reject them out of hand as patently unrealistic. Some assumptions along these lines, however, are essential if we are to construct formal analyses of any kind in the field of international relations. Moreover, the value of any given assumptions lies in the conclusions to which they lead rather than in any *a priori* judgment of their descriptive accuracy. As a result, it is of little use to reject any given set of assumptions out of hand. What conclusions about the links between world politics and a rising level of interdependence in the world system, then, can be reached on the basis of the assumptions set forth here?

1. The higher the ratio of interdependencies among the component units of a world system to interdependencies within the component units, the greater the proportion of any given unit's resources that will be devoted to external affairs. That is, *relative* levels of interdependence are a major determinant of the allocation of resources in world systems. Other things being equal, it takes more resources to accomplish any given objective under highly interdependent conditions than under conditions of effective autonomy. In the first place, interdependencies generate problems requiring the allocation of resources (e.g., defense or the international monetary system) that do not exist in fully autarkic situations. In addition, under conditions of interdependence there are the costs of dealing with other actors affected by efforts to achieve any given objective which must be added to the basic costs of achieving the objective even under conditions of effective autonomy. If interdependence is strongly oriented toward competition, these costs of interdependence arise from the sanctions or obstructive actions of other actors. Even if interdependence is weighted toward co-operation, however, there are the costs of regulating the overlapping interests of a number of actors.[33]

If this hypothesis is correct and the level of interdependence is in fact rising in the contemporary world system, Deutsch's thesis concerning the growth of national self-preoccupation would appear highly questionable. Under these conditions, the only escape would be to rely on the argument that subsystemic interdependencies are rising more rapidly than systemwide interdependencies. Although the evidence is far from conclusive on this point, the arguments presented in the preceding section certainly cast doubt on this position. In addition, this hypothesis may shed some light on the problem identified by the Sprouts as the dilemma of rising demands.[34] If systemwide interdependencies were rising while subsystemic interdependencies were falling or remaining the same, the result would be a straightforward shift in the allocation of resources toward external affairs. If the level of interdependence is in fact rising at both levels, however, a real dilemma arises with respect to resource allocation. The only apparent escape from this dilemma would involve a rapid increase in the total volume of resources available in the system, an escape that has frequently worked in the past in sociopolitical systems but that may well be impossible in the contemporary world system.

2. The higher the level of interdependence among the component units of a world system, the greater the probability of system transformation. This hypothesis asserts that the probability of a change of state affecting one or more of the defining variables of any given system will increase as a function of the level of interdependence in the system.[35] It does not imply, however, that this will necessarily lead to an increase in the probability of transformation through violent or highly destructive processes. The basic idea underlying this hypothesis is that changes of all kinds become more difficult to contain or keep isolated as the level of interdependence in a world system rises. Where effective autonomy prevails, far-reaching changes affecting numerous functional activities can take place within the individual component units of a system without any substantial impact on the nature of the system as a whole. Where the component units are tightly linked through a network of interpenetrating relationships and, therefore, highly sensitive to changes occurring within any given unit, however, changes originating within any unit are apt to generate spread (or contagion) effects between units. And the more the impact of all changes occurring in a world system is magnified by the nature of the system's structure, the greater the probability that these changes will ultimately lead to a transformation of the system.

A factor that may mitigate the force of this relationship arises from incentives to contribute to regulatory mechanisms for the maintenance of a world system. If, other things being equal, a rising level of interdependence increases the probability of transformation in an existing system, the rational response for those actors that are major beneficiaries of the system would be to contribute to the development of mechanisms designed to manage the rise in interdependencies. Should the regulatory mechanisms resulting from these contributions prove adequate to handle the problems produced by the rise in the level of interdependencies, the probability of system transformation would not increase. But there are two significant limitations on this argument. First, the size of the contributions made to set up new regulatory mechanisms would be a function of elasticities in the calculations of the relevant actors, and the contributions needed to offset the growing probability of transformation might not be forthcoming. And the fact that information would be imperfect reinforces this conclusion. Secondly, the establishment of the new regulatory mechanisms themselves might have the effect of transforming the system. Under the circumstances, the factor under discussion here may mitigate the force of the original hypothesis, but it does not vitiate this hypothesis.

3. The higher the level of interdependence among the component units

of a world system, the greater will be the ratio of activities involving collective goods to those involving only private goods in the transactions among the units. A collective good is any "good such that nonpurchasers cannot feasibly be excluded from its consumption" whereas private goods are "goods such as nonpurchasers *can* be kept from consuming them."[36] The units in a world system characterized by a very low level of interdependence are much like families in a subsistence economy. They interact very little with each other because they provide mostly goods for themselves and, as a result, there are few collective goods from the perspective of the system as a whole. Moreover, the few exchanges that do take place among the component units occur on an *ad hoc* basis with little need for regulatory procedures or security arrangements, which would involve the production of collective goods. As a rising level of interdependence in a world system increases the scope and frequency of interactions among the system's units, however, the requirements for regulatory mechanisms, arrangements for the maintenance of order, and procedures to handle conflicts expand. And each of these problems involves the provisions of collective goods.

This hypothesis is not of critical importance as an end in itself. If it is correct, however, it has far-reaching implications for world systems, including the present one. It can be shown that the supply of collective goods in any sociopolitical system will generally require some form of organization to collect sources and provide the collective goods.[37] Such an organization can sometimes be set up on the basis of voluntary donations. Another classic solution to this problem is the creation of a government, some formal and centralized mechanisms of authority which can employ coercion to acquire the resources necessary for the production of collective goods. In many sociopolitical systems operating below the level of world systems, the rise of governmental institutions can be explained in large part along these lines.

In world systems, the problems of supplying collective goods are apt to be particularly acute. There are several barriers to the supply of collective goods through voluntary actions on the part of a large number of the actors in such systems. The number of units is generally large enough to make it impossible to organize the system along the lines of a small club. The actors tend to be highly diverse and often engaged in competitive interactions that overshadow the problems of collective goods.[38] And many of the actors may not regard themselves, for the most part, as beneficiaries of the existing system in any case. As a result, voluntary contributions to the provision of collective goods are apt to be quite inadequate. Witness, for example, the size of the United Nations budget by contrast with the budgets of the individual states in the contemporary world system.

At the same time, there are severe difficulties in world systems associated with the idea of supplying collective goods through the creation of formal institutions of government. Given the horizontal authority structures and low level of community that characterize systems of this type, it would be difficult for formal institutions to emerge in any given world system which were both broadly based and able to employ coercion successfully. In addition, the emergence of viable institutions of government in a world system would in itself lead to a transformation of the system.

If the level of interdependence is actually rising in the contemporary system, therefore, the world may soon face a severe dilemma concerning the supply of collective goods on a worldwide scale. It should be noted here, however, that there are several potential processes through which these needs may be met without precipitating a transformation in which some other form of sociopolitical system would supersede the world system. First, it may be possible for one (or a consortium of several) of the prime beneficiaries of the existing system to provide the minimum collective goods necessary to prevent transformation through a combination of contributions on its own part and coercive pressures directed against various lesser actors. Note, however, that this arrangement can only work where the pattern of power relationships is highly asymmetrical, a condition which may not hold in the contemporary system. Secondly, it is possible that some collective goods may be supplied without the establishment of formal governmental machinery through the evolution of informal procedures or tacit rules of the game that provide guidelines for the contribution of resources for collective goods.

4. The higher the level of interdependence in a world system, the more important functional specialization among the units becomes for the maintenance of the system. This hypothesis emerges from the same underlying problem as the preceding hypothesis. As the level of interdependence in a system rises, it becomes less possible for any actor to operate on the autonomous basis characteristic of subsistence (or autarkic) arrangements, and the scope and frequency of the interactions among the system's units increase. As mentioned above, extensive interactions produce the problems of supplying important collective goods. At the same time, however, a growth in the scope and frequency of interactions in a system increases the importance of functional specialization among the units of the system. The basic relationship is the same whether economic or political activities are in question. The more extensive the interactions among the units, the greater the probability that unspecialized actors will duplicate each other's efforts, thereby producing conflicts rather than complementarities and increasing the pressures for coercive or even violent change. A rising level of interde-

pendence without a concomitant increase in specialization, therefore, will tend to destabilize a system both because of the conflicts arising from redundancy and because of the added barrier to the supply of important collective goods such as regulatory mechanisms produced by these conflicts.

If the level of interdependence is in fact rising in the world system, this hypothesis has extensive implications for the future. It should not of course be assumed that growing specialization among the actors of the world system will automatically occur in the foreseeable future since the hypothesis in question is prescriptive rather than descriptive on this point. Nevertheless, it seems likely that the problem of rational specialization among actors will become a focus of conscious and extensive analysis in the near fuure. In the realm of economic relations, developments along these lines are already becoming evident.[39] This is the case, for example, in the development of worldwide financial arrangements, the growth of multinational enterprises, and the rise of efforts to allocate specific industries among the developed states of the world. In the realm of world politics, however, the problems of achieving a viable pattern of specialization in an interdependent system have only just begun to attract attention. The analysis of these problems is impeded both by the commitment to political autarky enshrined in the doctrine of sovereignty and by the difficulties in developing operational concepts in terms of which to analyse political specialization.

5. As the level of interdependence among the component units of a world system rises, the opportunities for any given actor to exercise power over others increases but the costs of exercising power rise at the same time.[40] The power of any given actor refers to the changes its actions cause in the actions of others when these changes are sought on a conscious basis. And the power of an actor can be said to increase as the cost (in terms of its own values) of changing the actions of others goes down. By definition, rising interdependencies increase the sensitivity of the individual units in a system to events occurring in other parts of the system and, therefore, to the actions taken by other actors. It follows that a rising level of interdependence will expand the capacity, though not necessarily the desire, of each actor in the system to exercise power over the others. Note that this does not indicate anything about the patterns of power relationships in highly interdependent systems. Moreover, the cost to any given actor associated with the exercise of power over others in interdependent situations is apt to be high because the actor in question will, in turn, be highly sensitive to the reactions of both the target actor and the other actors in the system.

That the opportunities to exercise power in such situations are mutual is of critical importance. Most conceptions of power in world politics are predicated on some notion of dependence rather than *inter*dependence. Thus, an independent actor can cause changes in the actions of a dependent actor at a relatively low cost to itself. And it is this inexpensive exercise of power that is generally at issue in efforts to specify the sources of national power or to identify the "great powers" in world politics. As the level of interdependence in a world system rises, however, it becomes more difficult for any actor in the system to exercise power over others at a low cost to itself. As a result, it is doubtful whether the concept of a "great power" has any real meaning in highly interdependent systems except in cases where the pattern of interdependence is asymmetrical in the extreme. This may well account in considerable part for the often noted paradox that those actors controlling the greatest quantities of resources in the contemporary world system (i.e., the United States and the Soviet Union) more often than not experience great difficulty in accomplishing their objectives even in relations with small actors.[41] Given the mutual sensitivity arising from high levels of interdependence, small actors are often able to make the costs greater than the benefits for large actors who attempt to effect specified changes in the actions of the small actors.

6. It follows from the preceding hypothesis that the higher the level of interdependence in a world system, the harder it becomes to maintain qualitatively unequal (i.e., superordinate-subordinate) relations among the units of the system. Fundamentally, the maintenance of such relationships (as in the case of colonialism) is a function of the combination of a high degree of dependence on the part of the subordinate actors and a high degree of independence on the part of the superordinate actors. The rise of *inter*dependencies, however, increases the costs that the subordinate actor can impose on the superordinate actor for the exercise of power even though it does not reduce the capacity of the latter to exercise power over the former. While the rise of interdependencies does not necessarily increase the effective autonomy of subordinate actors, therefore, it does militate against qualitatively unequal relations by increasing the retaliatory capacity of subordinate actors in their relations with superordinate actors.

If the level of interdependence has in fact been increasing in the contemporary period, this hypothesis goes far toward explaining recent difficulties in maintaining imperial relationships in the world system. The great empires in history have typically been based upon arrangements in which the colonies were highly dependent upon the imperial power but the imperial power was relatively independent of the activities of any individual colony. This is why the far-reaching impact of the Boer War on the internal politics of Britain, for example, was so portentous for the future of the British empire.[42] Similarly, one major reason why contemporary conflicts in southeast Asia and Algeria precipitated the end of the French empire was their far-reaching impact on the internal politics of the imperial actor. With all due respect to the force of nationalism and the "spirit of the age," therefore, the rising level of interdependence in the world system may well have been the crucial determinant of the "end of empire" in the contemporary world.[43] Moreover, this development also casts considerable doubt on the realism of many of the fears underlying the idea of neo-colonialism at the present time.[44]

7. The higher the level of interdependence among the component units of a world system, the greater the frequency of intervention on the part of individual units in the affairs of others. Intervention refers here to organized activities across recognized boundaries aimed at affecting the authority structures of the target.[45] Intervention is therefore a specific type of power relationship. In highly interdependent systems, interference by any given actor in the affairs of others is more nearly a matter of necessity than a matter of conscious design or political machination. That is, it is impossible to avoid interference along numerous lines in such situations no matter what the intentions of decision-makers within the various actors may be. Under the circumstances, it is rational for any given actor to give intentional direction to its interference in the affairs of others since its actions will have a substantial impact on others in any case. Thus, it makes good sense for other actors – whether friendly or hostile – to attempt to influence presidential elections in the United States as much as possible. And it is hardly surprising that the United States deliberately attempts to influence the power structures of various other actors in the system. Inescapable interference, therefore, will tend to become intervention in highly interdependent systems.

If this argument is correct, analyses of the possibilities of regulating intervention are apt to be far more relevant than efforts to reduce the extent of intervention in the foreseeable future. Note, however, that this conclusion is not necessarily incompatible with Deutsch's recent argument to the effect that "world politics is now entering upon a stage of rising costs of foreign intervention."[46] As argued above, the costs to any individual actor of exercising power may generally increase as a function of rising levels of interdependence. What does *not* follow from this, however, is the implication in Deutsch's argument that the volume of intervention among the actors in the system will accordingly decline if only because "politicians who fail to see this [i.e., the rising costs of intervention] will eventually fail to win reelection."[47] On the contrary, intervention may well increase in volume even as it becomes more costly.

IV

The phenomenon of interdependence in sociopolitical systems is considerably more complex than it is often thought to be. Interdependence involves numerous dimensions that may vary asymmetrically, and it is frequently difficult to find operational indicators in terms of which the level of interdependence in a specific system can be measured accurately. Nevertheless, the level of interdependence appears to be a powerful explanatory variable in the analysis of sociopolitical systems. In the analysis of world systems, this conclusion has at least two specific consequences. First, analyses formulated at this level of generality may well lead to considerably more interesting theoretical propositions than the analyses at lower levels of generality that have always been prominent in the study of world politics. Secondly, the importance of the level of interdependence among actors in analysing world politics suggests the need to develop far better empirical techniques for the measurement of trends in the level of interdependence in world systems than those available at the present time.

NOTES

1. World systems are defined in this essay as a subset of the broader class of all sociopolitical systems characterized by the following attributes: (1) they are the most inclusive sociopolitical systems with empirical attributes; (2) they have a relatively low *ratio* of systemwide interdependencies to interdependencies within their component units; and (3) they are oriented strongly toward horizontal rather than hierarchical patterns with respect to authority structures.

2. For an interesting discussion of the level of interdependence among the industrialized states in the contemporary world see Edward L. Morse, "The Politics of Interdependence," *International Organization* 33 (spring 1969).

3. For a systematic formulation of the principal features of the state-centric world view see Oran R. Young, "The Actors in World Politics," in James N. Rosenau, Vincent Davis, and Maurice A. East, eds., *The Analysis of International Politics* (New York: Free Press, 1970).

4. For a discussion of the distinction between sovereignty and autonomy in this context see Richard N. Cooper, *The Economics of Interdependence* (New York: Columbia University Press, 1968), pp. 4–6.

5. For a relatively sophisticated version of this interpretation consult Amitai Etzioni, *The Active Society* (New York: Free Press, 1968), esp. chap. 19.

6. For a discussion of problems of this kind focusing on the industrialized world consult Cooper, chap. 6.

7. This is no doubt the source of Karl Deutsch's comment to the effect that "international relations is that area of human action where interdependence

meets with inadequate control." Karl W. Deutsch, *The Analysis of International Relations* (Englewood Cliffs: Prentice-Hall, 1968), p. v.

8. See Deutsch, *ibid.*; Karl Deutsch and Alexander Eckstein, "National Industrialization and the Declining Share of the International Economic Sector, 1890-1959," *World Politics* 13 (January 1961); Karl Deutsch, Lewis Edinger, Roy C. Macridis, and Richard L. Merritt, *France, Germany, and the Western Alliance* (New York: Scribner, 1967); Karl Deutsch, "The Impact of Communications upon Theory of International Relations," in Abdul Said, ed., *Theory of International Relations* (Englewood Cliffs: Prentice-Hall, 1968); and Karl Deutsch, "Transaction Flows as Indicators of Political Cohesion," in Philip E. Jacob and James V. Toscano, eds., *The Integration of Political Communities* (Philadelphia: Lippincott, 1964).

9. Deutsch, "Impact of Communications," p. 84.

10. *Ibid.*

11. On this question see Harold and Margaret Sprout, "The Dilemma of Rising Demands and Insufficient Resources," *World Politics* 20 (July 1968).

12. See, for example, Deutsch et al., *France, Germany, and the Western Alliance.*

13. Deutsch, "Impact of Communications," pp. 88-9.

14. For further discussion of the problems posed by this assumption for the analysis of the contemporary world system see Young.

15. For further information on these factors consult Cooper, chap. 4. See also Raymond Vernon, "Economic Sovereignty at Bay," *Foreign Affairs* 67 (October 1968).

16. Cooper, chap. 3.

17. As a working hypothesis, it seems reasonable to suppose that the higher the level of economic development of the actors involved, the greater will be the impact of a rise in the level of economic interdependence among the actors on the level of political interdependence among them. This point follows from the general argument that the difficulties in making clear distinctions between political and economic phenomena increase as a function of the degree of modernization of sociopolitical systems.

18. For a discussion of the notion of complementarities in this connection see Mancur Olson, Jr., "Economics, Sociology, and the Best of All Possible Worlds," *The Public Interest* (summer 1968), esp. pp. 108-14.

19. The only way out of this problem is to increase the total size of the world market. Otherwise, the interdependence of the two states will lead to a decline in the foreign trade sector of one of them whenever there is a shift in their relative competitiveness in the world economy.

20. Kenneth Boulding, *Conflict and Defense* (New York: Harper, 1962), chaps. 12 and 13.

21. This is not only a consequence of the geographical scope of ballistic missiles, but also a result of the fact that at the level of the world system technologies of destruction are coupled with a low level of effective community.

22. See, for example, Cooper, *Economics of Interdependence*, pp. 59-68.

23. For a wealth of substantive information dealing with this question consult Adda B. Bozeman, *Politics and Culture in International History* (Princeton: Princeton University Press, 1960).

24. On the relationship of specific levels of interdependence to the basic concept of a world system see Oran R. Young, *A Systemic Approach to International Politics* (Princeton: Princeton University Center of International Studies, 1968).

25. There is some evidence that the availability of graphic accounts on a mass basis through the medium of television is presently producing a substantial impact on public attitudes toward the problems of world politics. It is too early to tell, however, what the substantive thrust of this impact will be.

26. For a classic effort to employ geographic factors as independent variables in the explanation of world politics see Halford J. Mackinder, *Democratic Ideals and Reality* (New York: Holt, 1942). And for a discussion of the ways in which increases in the physical capacities of man (mostly in the form of technological developments) have undermined many of these geopolitical hypotheses consult Harold Sprout, "Geopolitical Hypotheses in Technological Perspective," *World Politics* 15 (January 1963).

27. See Albert Wohlstetter, "Illusions of Distance," *Foreign Affairs* 67 (January 1968); Albert Wohlstetter, "Theory and Opposed System Design," in Morton Kaplan, ed., *New Approaches to International Relations* (New York: St. Martin's, 1968); and Albert Wohlstetter, "Strength, Interest and New Technologies," in *The Implications of Military Technology in the 1970's*, Adelphi Paper No. 46 (London: Institute for Strategic Studies, 1968).

28. For a discussion of some of the effects of this shift on planning for security from the perspective of the individual actor see Glenn Snyder, *Deterrence and Defense* (Princeton: Princeton University Press, 1960), chap. 1.

29. Boulding, chap. 4.

30. Cooper, chap. 3.

31. For a more extended discussion of world politics in systems that are heterogeneous with respect to basic types of actor see Young, "Actors in World Politics."

32. On the concepts "domain" and "jurisdiction" as employed in this discussion see Cooper, pp. 91-4.

33. Consider, for example, the costs of infrastructure and related arrangements associated with the maintenance of an alliance such as NATO.

34. Sprout and Sprout.

35. For a fuller discussion of the concept of system transformation see Young, *A Systemic Approach to International Politics.*

36. Olson, "Economics, Sociology, and the Best of All Possible Worlds," p. 108.

37. For a thorough discussion of the theoretical arguments underlying this conclusion see Norman Frohlich, Joe A. Oppenheimer, and Oran R. Young, *A Theory of Leadership: The Supply of Collective Goods*, mimeographed (Princeton: Princeton University Center of International Studies, 1969).

38. The importance of factors such as the diversity of the units in world systems is especially striking when non-state actors as well as states are taken into account.

39. For some indications of developments along these lines see Raymond Vernon, "The Role of U.S. Enterprise Abroad," *Daedalus* 98 (winter 1969).

40. The discussion of power in this essay draws on several concepts developed by Robert Dahl and John Harsanyi.

41. For one discussion of this paradox see Oran R. Young, *The Intermediaries* (Princeton: Princeton University Press, 1967), chap. 9.

42. On this case consult A. P. Thornton, *The Imperial Idea and Its Enemies* (Garden City: Macmillan, 1968), chap. 3.

43. It might be argued, however, that the growth of nationalism in the twentieth century has itself been an important determinant of the rising level of interdependence in the world system. Although this is a plausible argument, the discussion of the earlier sections of this essay does not lend much weight to it.

44. The feasibility of "neo-colonialism" would appear to be a function of the importance of independent-dependent relationships as opposed to *inter*dependent relationships in a world system. For a brief account of some of the principal factors involved in arguments about "neocolonialism" see Raymond F. Betts, *Europe Overseas* (New York: Basic Books, 1968), chap. 6.

45. For a discussion of this definition as well as a more extended analysis of intervention in world politics see Oran R. Young, "Intervention and International Systems," *Journal of International Affairs* 22 (summer 1968).

46. Deutsch, "Impact of Communications," p. 92.

47. *Ibid.*

5
The Myth of National Interdependence

Contrary to the globalist contention that interdependence is on the increase, Waltz argues that "interdependence is low and, if anything, is on the decrease." Drawing on the history of trade and investment since the end of the nineteenth century, he asserts that interdependence characterized much of the European state system before World War I. By contrast, the world today displays more independence and dependence. Furthermore, even the limited degree of interdependence that now exists is not necessary for peace.

"Peace is indivisible," a slogan of the 1930s, suggests that a small war anywhere means war everywhere unless the small war can somehow be stopped. The domino theory is an old one. Its economic equivalent is found in statements, frequently made, that America cannot exist as an island of affluence in a sea of impoverished nations. From such statements the mistaken conclusion is often drawn that a growing closeness of interdependence would improve the chances of peace.

But close interdependence means closeness of contact and raises the prospect of at least occasional conflict. The fiercest civil wars and the bloodiest international ones have been fought within arenas populated by highly similar people whose affairs had become quite closely knit together. It is hard to get a war going unless the potential participants are somehow closely linked. Interdependent states whose relations remain unregulated must experience conflict and will occasionally fall into violence. If regulation is hard to come by, as it is in the relations of states, then it would seem to follow that a lessening of interdependence is desirable.

Reprinted by permission from Charles P. Kindleberger, ed., *The International Corporation* (Cambridge, MA: MIT Press, 1970), pp. 205–223.

Focusing on the international corporation, however, has led many economists to believe that international interdependence is high and is rapidly becoming higher. The thought is forcefully put by the various people who claim that the national state has become an obsolete economic unit. If the interdependence of nations is high and becoming higher, we must expect international difficulties to multiply. I am inclined to be sanguine because I believe that interdependence is low and, if anything, is on the decrease. Those who come to the opposite conclusion apparently do so for two reasons. What interdependence entails is often incorrectly understood. Because this is so, economic developments are looked at aside from their proper context.

THE MEANING OF INTERDEPENDENCE

A comparison of the conditions of internal and external interdependence will make it clear that in international relations interdependence is always a marginal affair. The political elements of a state are formally differentiated according to the degrees of their authority, and their distinct functions are specified. Specification of roles and differentiation of functions characterize any state, the more fully so as the state is more highly developed. The parts of a highly developed polity are closely interdependent. Some parts depend on others for services and supplies that they cannot easily, if at all, provide for themselves. Thus Washington depends on Kansas for its beef and its wheat, and Kansas depends on Washington for protection and regulation. In saying that in such situations interdependence is close, one need not maintain that the one part could not learn to live without the other. One need only say that the cost of breaking the interdependent relation would be high. Where the political and economic division of labor is elaborately developed, high inequality may be found; and yet a mutuality of interest among unequals may be said to prevail.[1]

The domestic order is composed of heterogeneous elements; the international order is composed of homogeneous units. Each state regulates its own affairs and supplies largely out of its own resources the food, clothing, housing, transportation, and amenities consumed and used by its citizens. The international order is characterized by the coaction of like units. Since the functions of all states are highly similar, differentiation among them is principally according to their varied capabilities.

Because the units that populate the international arena are the same in type, interdependence among them is low even if those units are of approximately equal size. Interdependence is further reduced by the immense disparity in the capabilities of states. This last point can be stated as an iron law: high inequality among like units *is* low interdependence.

How interdependent are these not very interdependent states, and what difference does the answer to this question make? In the European-centered great-power politics of the three centuries that ended with World War II, five or more great powers sought to coexist peacefully and at times contended for mastery. Since World War II, only two states have perched at the pinnacle of power. It follows from the law just stated that the interdependence of states is less now than it was earlier. But this deduction will not be accepted unless the force and meaning of the law are made clear. The validity of the proposition can be established by looking at international trade and investment, not simply at a moment in time and as absolute amounts, but by viewing them in relation to the volume of internal business and in comparison with the patterns of previous periods.[2]

TRADE: CHANGES IN NATIONAL INVOLVEMENT

Even if the interdependence of nations is in general low, we nevertheless want to know whether it is lower or higher now than in earlier times. In the late nineteenth and early twentieth centuries, the external sector loomed large. Not only was the level of external transactions high in comparison with internal production, but also the internal order was characterized by a low level of governmental activity. Even if the interdependence of nations has increased in the meantime, the progress of internal integration and the increased intervention of governments in their domestic economies means that for most states the internal sector now looms larger than it once did. But it is not even clear that the interdependence of states has increased overall.

Prior to World War I, most of the great powers of the world were also great traders; economically they were closely tied together. In the years preceding World War I, for example, Germany was Britain's second-best customer, both as a source of imports and as a market for exports. Measured in terms of their own economies, the two greatest powers in the world today trade little with each other or with the rest of the world.[3] Most of this change can be accounted for by the fact that the present great powers of the world are geographically much larger than the old ones.[4] Britain, France, Italy, and Japan, it should be noticed, also trade a smaller proportion of their national product now than they once did.[5]

From the recent growth of world trade, however, one might be tempted to conclude that the relative decreases in trade are only temporary and that the interdependence of nations is now tending toward the old level. In the years from 1953 to 1965, both trade in manufactured goods and trade in primary products grew more rapidly than world output in each of the two categories.[6] In the economic data for the first half of this century, however, there is a strong component of war and depression. To a considerable extent we are dealing, in the past two decades, with recovery rates; and the recovery is rooted in the economic resurgence of Western Europe and Japan. In the years from 1926 to 1930 world manufactures grew more rapidly than trade in manufactured goods–about 40% as compared to less than 15%. This was in part because of the faster economic growth of the United States, a relatively self-sufficient country, as compared to the economic growth of West European countries, which are more dependent on imports. Beginning in the 1950s, the rapid growth of Japan and of West European countries has given a corresponding boost to world trade.[7]

As well as considering the decline of trade in relation to GNP and the recent growth of world trade overall, we should ask whether changes in the composition and direction of trade have affected the extent of interdependence. In advanced industrial countries a larger proportion of the national product is now composed of products whose raw-material content is low. This is true not only because the service sector has grown but also because more value is added to raw materials as they are transformed into technologically more complicated goods. The GNP's of advanced countries have thus grown faster than their demand for primary products.[8] In 1953, trade among developed countries accounted for 37.2% of world trade; 12 years later the amount had increased to 46.5%. In 1953, the trade of less-developed with developed countries accounted for 19.3% of world trade; 12 years later the amount had decreased to 14%.[9] The exchange of finished goods for primary products has grown less rapidly than trade in finished goods among industrial countries. A lesser portion of trade now is done out of near necessity, and more of it is merely for profit. The present relation of less-developed to developed countries is less close than was the old imperial tie.

Shifts in the composition of trade, with primary products in decline relative to manufactured goods, change the political as well as the economic significance of trade. Before World War I, as Richard Cooper points out, large differences in comparative costs meant that "trade was socially very profitable" but "less sensitive to small changes in costs, prices, and quality."[10] I would add that trade then, as well as being socially very profitable, was politically very significant. States are mutually dependent if they rely on each other for goods and services that cannot easily be produced at home. That kind of interdependence is difficult (costly) to break. The other kind of interdependence – sensitivity of response to variations in factor prices – may be economically more interesting; it is also politically less important.

Even though trade in relation to production and the proportionate amount of raw materials imported have declined, one might nevertheless imagine a country being heavily dependent on a small quantity of imports. But is this really the case? In the decades during which congressional renewal of the Reciprocal Trade Act was recurrently at issue, it was customary for the friends of free trade to emphasize the extent of American dependence on imported minerals and ores. The Report of the Commission headed by Clarence B. Randall, for example, stated that: "we depend on foreign sources today for over 30 percent of our requirements of copper, lead, and zinc; over 50 percent of our requirements of tungsten, bauxite, and antimony; over 75 percent of our requirements of chrome and manganese; practically all of our nickel requirements; and all our requirements of tin, natural rubber, and jute."[11] Bad economics may make good political strategy; we should, however, notice that the economic case was distorted.

The quantity of imports is not just a function of scarcity; it is also a matter of price. Reliance on imports at a particular time does not necessarily represent dependence, as the following points make clear.

1. The nearness of a country's approach to autarky cannot be measured simply by amounts imported. It is not possession but rather reliability of access that counts. Whether Lorraine was part of France or of Germany, those countries were less sure of the availability of its iron than the United States is of bauxite and nickel from Latin America and Canada.[12]

2. Not only the location of suppliers but also their numbers are important. Wayward political movements or revolutions or wars elsewhere in the world may well shut off some of a country's supplies. The larger a country's trade, in absolute terms, the larger the number of its suppliers is likely to be. The United States, as the world's largest trader, enjoys a multiplicity of sources of supply. Here as in other matters, there is safety in numbers. Worries are further reduced by remembering that the market for primary products is one that favors the buyer. Manganese, for example, is often cited as an instance of America's dependence on imports; but those imports come from a large number of eager suppliers, Brazil and India among them.[13]

3. Suppose, however, that war engulfed much of the globe and disrupted many or most of the channels of trade. This possibility was a more active worry in the late 1940s and early 1950s than it has been in the 1960s, and the response to it was more than sufficiently effective. In the considerable efforts made to stockpile strategic materials, the problem was not to acquire and store enough of them but rather to prevent domestic producers from unloading unduly large quantities upon the American government. Glenn Snyder, for example, has pointed out that as of June 1964, "about 60 per cent of the stockpile was surplus and

subject to disposal . . . more than 80 per cent of the total excess was concentrated in 12 materials – aluminum, chromite, cobalt, copper, lead, manganese, molybdenum, nickel, rubber, tin, tungsten, and zinc."[14] Often domestic interests resisted the government's efforts to dispose of the surplus for fear of reducing prices.

4. The resiliency of the economy is increased, and dependence on imports is lessened, by improved methods for the use and recovery of materials. The electroplating process in tin-plating, introduced in 1949, resulted in a steady drop in imports. In recent years, the secondary recovery of antimony has yielded a larger supply than imports of the metal itself.[15] The ability to make do in the face of adversity is one of the most impressive qualities of large and advanced economies. The synthetic production of rubber provides the most impressive example. The need was not recognized until the fall of Singapore in 1942. The United States was able to develop an entirely new large-scale industry while fighting a global war on two fronts. The worry of primary producers that synthetics will further shrink their markets is more sensible than American worries about access to raw materials.

Large and economically well-developed countries, the very ones that are crucial in world politics, can more quickly move toward an autarkic condition. I am not suggesting that we should forgo imports and rely on our own resources, but merely that we can move in that direction at relatively low cost if we have to. The low cost of disentanglement is a measure of low dependence.

If not dependent on particular items of import, may the economy nevertheless be sensitive to adverse economic movements that originate outside of the national arena? Here also big countries are at an immense advantage. I shall give only a few illustrations of this. If a country exports a large portion of its manufactured output, as advanced countries smaller than the United States and the Soviet Union tend to do, then changes in trade will have major effects on that country's economic growth.[16] Of more relevance to the less-developed countries is the tendency for foreign trade to be most important where incomes are lowest and for the fluctuations in the trade of those countries to be unusually large.[17] Countries of large GNP are doubly protected from such effects. The circle of their customers and suppliers is wider, thus increasing the chances that some external fluctuations will balance off others. And since their trade is relatively small, even sharply adverse foreign developments do not greatly affect the domestic economy. From 1950 to 1956, for example, the year-to-year fluctuation in national income derived from changes in the terms of trade was 2.8% for less-developed countries and 1.5% for developed countries. For the United States, it was only 0.2%.[18]

A small portion of America's trade is a big portion of the trade of many another country. In 1966, for example, 42.5% of Peru's total exports and 18.2% of India's were sent to the United States; but the exports of each of those countries amounted to only 1.2% of total United States imports. The asymmetrical relation also holds for industrial countries. Japan, the United Kingdom, and France sent 30.7, 12.3, and 6.0%, respectively, of their total exports to the United States. The respective shares of U.S. imports that these totals represent were 11.8, 6,8, and 2.5%.[19] Smaller countries are strongly constrained to make domestic economic decisions with an eye on their external accounts. The United States is much less constrained to do so, and yet our domestic economic decisions will affect other states more than theirs will affect us. The political importance of this condition arises from the asymmetry of the relation.[20] Decisions by the United States, whether or not intended to harm or to bring pressure against another state, can have grave effects.

What looks to some like a thickening web of economic interdependence obscures relations that are best described as a compound of independence and dependence, and that is quite a different thing. But this point can be developed better if we add consideration of foreign investment to the discussion of international trade.

INVESTMENT: NATIONAL AND CORPORATE STAKES

Statements about whether interdependence is higher or lower now than it used to be easily obscure the fact that recent economic changes within and among nations and the political consequences attendant upon them are changes of kind rather than merely of degree. When the great powers of the world were small in geographic compass, they naturally did a higher proportion of their business abroad. The narrow concentration of power in the present and the fact that the United States and the Soviet Union are little dependent on the rest of the world produce a very different international situation. Since at the same time the size of America's foreign business in terms of world totals is large, its impact on others is considerable.

It may be, however, that the enterprise of international corporations and the recent increase of foreign investments modify these trends and move the world back toward a closer integration. But is this really happening?

When Britain was the world's leading state economically, the portion of her wealth invested abroad far exceeded the portion that now represents America's stake in the world. In 1910, the value of total British investment abroad was 1½ times larger than her national income. In 1966, total American foreign investments, both official and private, were only 18% as large as its national income. In 1910, Britain's return on investment abroad amounted to 8% of national income; in 1966, the comparable figure for the United States was only 1%.[21]

Although, in comparison, the stock of American investment is not high, the rate of its recent growth is impressive. Britain's foreign investment had tripled in the 30 years prior to 1910. From 1958 to 1966, American investment abroad grew at an average rate of 8% yearly, which in 18 years would increase the total fourfold. One should, however, be wary of assuming that such a high rate will continue long enough to raise American investments to the point where they become a much higher percentage of GNP. One may expect continued growth although I rather doubt that it will be as rapid. Not just American technology but also skills in management and marketing enabled American subsidiaries operating in the less-advanced and less-well-organized European environment to earn a higher return on capital invested in Europe than on capital invested at home. As with the opening of mines in Latin America or the drilling of oil wells in the Middle East, businessmen properly and usefully responded to the possibility of increased profits. As we have known since Adam Smith and Ricardo, the effect of everyone's seeking to increase his profits is to drive the profit rate downward. Something of the same sort is happening here. American capital in Europe earned 18% yearly in 1959 as compared to 13% at home. In 1965 return abroad and at home stood at 13% and 15%, respectively.[22] On economic grounds, one would expect a leveling off.

On political grounds, one might entertain the same expectation. Precisely because the operations of American corporations abroad have concentrated in those sectors of the economy that are thought by the host countries to be most significant for economic growth and for their military establishments, political resistance to the encroachment of American firms has occurred and will continue to do so.

But such resistance has been of limited effect. Just as political fragmentation invites imperial control, so low economic capability easily leads to dependence upon another state of higher economic capability. The higher the costs of disentanglement, the higher the degree of dependence; the lagging state will only get weaker if foreign capital and technology are excluded.

The American computer industry can get along without the assistance of French companies, but Machines Bull felt it could not survive without American capital and technology. In 1962, the French government resisted the purchase by General Electric of 20% of Bull's shares. Unable to find another French or European partner, the French government was constrained in 1964 to accept a 50-50 arrangement with General Electric. By the middle 1960s General Electric's share in the company had grown to approximately two-thirds.[23] General Electric, Control Data, and other American firms may require foreign affiliations in order to compete with IBM. There may be genuine interdependence at the level of the firm. It is a mistake, however, to identify interdependence at that level with the interdependence of states. The attempts of European firms to band together are impeded by the greater attraction of establishing connections with American firms, for they are the ones with the most advanced technology, the most plentiful capital, and the most impressive managerial abilities. When German aviation companies sought ties with firms in other countries, they did not go to Britain or France. Larger benefits were to be gained by association with American companies.

Nor is it easy for foreign firms to catch up. The size of the home market enables American firms to operate on a large scale and to generate resources that can be used abroad to compete with or even to overwhelm native industries. General Motors could have given away every Opel it produced in 1965 and still have made $1 billion in profit.[24] As long as IBM spends yearly on research and development an amount equal to the gross sales of Britain's largest computer company, the American industry is likely to retain its lead. Two-thirds of the world's and two-thirds of Europe's markets in computers have been captured by IBM.[25] The size of its operations enables the company to spend money on a governmental scale. The $5 billion that IBM committed to the development of its model 360 computer was equal to the amount that France planned to spend on her nuclear force in the years from 1965 to 1970.[26]

The disadvantages of foreign firms are paralleled by the difficulties their governments face. In 1962, America's gross expenditure on research and development amounted to $17.5 billion; Britain, France, Belgium, Holland, and Germany together spent $4.3 billion. American expenditure amounted to about 3% of GNP or about $100 per capita, and for the European states named, to about 1½% of their GNP's or about $25 per capita.[27]

Under these conditions, national governments are constrained to permit domestic firms to make arrangements with American companies. The smaller states' opportunities to maneuver are further limited by competition among them. If, say, France follows an effective policy of exclusion, American capital and firms, and the technology these firms carry with them, will locate in neighboring countries. Even one who believes that the economies of those countries would become beholden to America cannot help but notice that they would also be enriched and be enabled to compete more effectively in European markets, including the markets of countries that had excluded American firms.

In 1967, the output of American firms operating abroad amounted to some $120 billion. This product represented, in effect, the world's third largest economy, surpassed only by the United States and the Soviet Union.[28] In 1965, residents of the United States owned 44% of the capital invested in Canadian manufacturing firms and those firms accounted for 48% of Canada's exports of manufactured goods. In the United Kingdom, American subsidiaries accounted for 7½% of the capital, 10% of the sales, and 17% of the export of manufactured goods.[29] In France, American firms "control" only 5 to 7% of the economy, according to Robert Gilpin, but America's influence is wider than the figures suggest because the companies that Americans do control are strategic ones.[30]

Who is able to regulate these vast undertakings? Most Americans who have considered the question conclude that the American government is not able to do so with very much success. Foreigners more often incline to the opposite view. On the basis of their study, the authors of the Canadian report previously cited draw "the general picture . . . of a tight legal and administrative network capable of being turned to any objective in foreign policy or to meet any future stringency, such as a further deterioration of the American balance of payments position."[31] Rules made under the authority of the Export Control Act of 1949 control not only American exports but also those exports of other countries that contain American components and embody American technical data. Under the Trading with the Enemy Act of 1917, the Office of Foreign Assets Control regulates the exports of American subsidiaries abroad whether or not the commodities they produce incorporate American components or technology. Enforcement can be secured by holding the American parent criminally liable for its subsidiaries' activity.[32]

By an executive order issued in January of 1968, President Johnson made previously voluntary guidelines mandatory. The American government can now control the payments of foreign subsidiaries to their American parents and can regulate companies that are incorporated abroad, that operate under foreign law, and that may in part be foreign owned. Further, by requiring the approval of the Secretary of Commerce for private investments abroad, the American government may, if it chooses, control both the amount and the direction of capital flow.[33]

Whatever the extent of American control over various operations, one may nonetheless believe that with well over $100 billion of assets abroad the vulnerability of American interests to punitive regulation by foreign governments, or even to confiscation, must be proportionate to the size of the stake. Just as the sudden severance of its trade would be a hard blow for the United States to absorb, so would the nearly complete loss of its investments abroad. Surely, if all or much of this capital were suddenly wrenched from us, the American economy itself would be seriously damaged. I would not care to deny that. We do have plenty to lose, and we can emphasize the "plenty" or we can emphasize the possibility of its loss. But if we imagine a situation in which American assets in Canada, Latin America, Europe, and the Middle and Far East are simultaneously confiscated, we are imagining a situation comparable in its impact to a global war. Indeed, short of such a catastrophe, it is hard to see why or how all or most foreign governments would suddenly set upon American capital and enterprises.

Partly, as suggested earlier, the question becomes one of who needs whom more. Confiscation would result in the loss of assets and profits of American firms, and for those few of them whose foreign operations are a major part of their business, that could be fatal. It is widely agreed, however, that physical plant and capital investment have not been as important as the managerial and organizational abilities of American firms and their capacity for technological innovation. Foreign economies would lose capabilities that could not easily be reproduced. Partly, also, the diversity of American investment, both in terms of types of enterprise and of their geographic location, itself provides insurance against sudden and sharp reversals. Nations do not easily bring their policies into concert, and that is a comfort for the nation whose operations are global.

RHETORIC AND REALITY

The American rhetoric of interdependence has taken on some of the qualities of an ideology. The word "interdependence" subtly obscures the inequalities of national capability, pleasingly points to a reciprocal dependence, and strongly suggests that all states are playing the same game.

If interdependence is really close, each state is constrained to treat other states' acts as though they were events within its own borders. A mutuality of dependence leads each state to watch others with wariness and suspicion. Near self-sufficiency and the possession of great capabilities, however, insulate a nation from the world by muting the effects of adverse movements that originate outside of the national arena. One who looks only at the activities of American firms and at their considerable stake in foreign countries, may then in one misdirected leap reach the conclusion that the size of this stake renders America vulnerable. At the level of the firm, it may be all right to dwell upon the extent of integration. At the level of international politics, it is grossly misleading to do so. It often seems that the approach of international economists would, if applied to domestic economics, cause it all to be written in terms of the firm and not at all in terms of the market. It is necessary to look at the matrix of action rather than simply at the discrete activities that fill it. One who does so reaches a different conclusion.

Someone who has a lot to lose can afford to lose quite a bit of it. This maxim is, of course, a common proposition of oligopolistic economics. That a large and well-placed firm can afford to run at a loss for some years is taken not as a sign of weakness and vulnerability but as being a considerable advantage. Where disparities are great, whether among firms or among states, the largest of them need worry least about the bothersome activities of others. Since in such situations interdependence does not reduce to zero, we can rightly say that all of the parties are vulnerable, but we should hasten to add that some are much less so. Some states, of course, are closely interdependent economically, but neither the United States nor the Soviet Union is among them. In economic terms and from their points of view, the world is loosely coupled.

Finally, as well as the insulation that permits lassitude, the highly skewed distribution of resources gives rise to the possibility of those with the largest share exercising some control. When the point is made that multinational corporations make their decisions on a global basis, one gets the impression that nations no longer matter. But that is grossly misleading. We should not lightly conclude that decentralization of operations means that centers of control are lacking.

From about the middle of the nineteenth century, the quicker transmission of ideas resulted, in the words of R. D. McKenzie, in "centralization of control and decentralization of operation." As he put it, "the modern world is integrated through information collected and distributed from fixed centers of dominance."[34] The complaints of some Europeans strikingly echo these words. One has to ask where most of the threads come together, and the answer is not in London, or Brussels, or Paris, but rather in New York City and Washington.

Decisions are made in terms of whole corporations and not just according to the condition and interest of certain subsidiaries. The picture usually drawn is one of a world in which economic activity has become transnational, with national borders highly permeable and businessmen making their decisions without even bearing them in mind. But most of the largest international corporations are based in America; most of their research and development is done there; most of their top personnel is American. Under these conditions, it is reasonable to suppose that in making corporate decisions the American perspective will be the most prominent one. Similarly, though both American and foreign governments try to regulate the activities of these corporations, the fact that most of them are American based gives a big advantage to the latter government. The advantage is made much stronger by the ability of the American government to grant or withhold a variety of favors, for example, in matters of trade, aid, loans, financial arrangements, and the supply of atomic energy for peaceful purposes. If means for bringing other countries into compliance with preferred American policies are desired, the American government does not have to look far to find them. The customary response of American commentators when the regulatory instruments available to their government are mentioned is to dwell on the ease of evasion. There is something to that response, though it underplays the fact that control – domestically as well as internationally – is often difficult to achieve.

What is really important, however, is to notice that we do not need much control. The size of American operations abroad does give the United States influence in the affairs of other nations, a situation that prevails whether or not we wish it. But the fact that, in relation to our resources, the stake is small means that the exercise of influence and control is less needed. These points can be clearly seen if both the similarity and the difference between America's present and Britain's past positions in the world are kept in mind.

Britain in its heyday had a huge stake in the world, and that stake also loomed large in relation to her own national product. From her immense and far-flung activities, she gained a considerable leverage. Because of the extent to which she depended on the rest of the world, wise and skillful use of that leverage was called for. When the great powers of the day depended on foodstuffs and raw materials imported from abroad much more heavily than the United States and the Soviet Union do now, that very dependence pressed them to make efforts to control the sources of their vital supplies.

Today, the myth of interdependence both obscures the realities of international politics and asserts a false belief about the conditions that may promote peace. The size of the two greatest powers gives them some capacity for control and at the same time insulates them to a considerable extent from the effects of other states' behavior. The inequality of nations produces a condition of equilibrium at a low level of interdependence. In the absence of a system of international regulation, loose coupling and a certain amount of control exerted by large states help to promote the desired stability.

NOTES

I am grateful to the National Science Foundation for supporting my research on this subject, to Harvard's Center for International Affairs at which the research and writing were done, and to Ellyn Hessler, who assisted me on every aspect of this paper.

1. Cf. R. E. Park, *Human Communities: The City and Human Ecology* (Glencoe, Ill.: Free Press, 1952), p. 80: "People live together on the whole, not because they

are alike, but because they are useful to one another." Cf. also J. G. March and H. A. Simon, *Organizations* (New York: John Wiley & Sons, 1958), p. 159: "The greater the *specialization by subprograms* (process specialization), the greater the *interdependence among organizational subunits.*"

2. I have, of course, had to leave some things out of this paper. To draw a fuller picture would require consideration of monetary and balance of payments problems, short-term capital movements, etc. The conclusions reached would, I believe, be similar to those arrived at by examining international trade and investment.

3. The situation of low economic interdependence along with high political-military interdependence suggests the limits of drawing conclusions from economic conditions alone. I have, however, confined myself to worrying about the international political implications of economic developments.

4. Cf. K. W. Deutsch, C. I. Bliss, and A. Eckstein, "Population, Sovereignty, and the Share of Foreign Trade," *Economic Development and Cultural Change* 10 (July 1962), pp. 353–366; S. Kuznets, "Economic Growth of Small Nations," in E.A.G. Robinson, ed., *Economic Consequences of the Size of Nations* (London: Macmillan, 1960), pp. 14–32; H. B. Chenery, "Patterns of Industrial Growth," *American Economic Review* 50 (September 1960), pp. 624–654; C. P. Kindleberger, *Foreign Trade and the National Economy* (New Haven: Yale University Press, 1962), pp. 32–37.

5. K. W. Deutsch and A. Eckstein, "National Industrialization and the Declining Share of the International Economic Sector, 1890–1959," *World Politics* 13 (January 1961), p. 275. Cf. S. Kuznets, *Modern Economic Growth* (New Haven: Yale University Press, 1966), pp. 312–314. Decline is marked for all of the great powers except Germany. The comparison made, however, is between all of Germany earlier and Western Germany now. The change in the size of the state, of course, affects the level of its foreign trade.

6. M. Z. Cutajar and A. Franks, *The Less Developed Countries in World Trade: A Reference Handbook* (London: Overseas Development Institute, 1967), Table 1, p. 21.

7. A. Maizels, *Industrial Growth and World Trade* (Cambridge: Cambridge University Press, 1963), pp. 79–81.

8. The point is often made. See, e.g., R. Nurkse, Wicksell Lectures for 1959, published as *Patterns of Trade and Development* (Stockholm: Almquist & Wiksell, 1959), p. 23.

9. Data taken from Cutajar and Franks, Table 2, p. 22.

10. R. N. Cooper, *The Economics of Interdependence: Economic Policy in the Atlantic Community* (New York: McGraw-Hill, 1968), p. 152. On p. 68, Cooper identifies a "gradual convergence of cost structures among the industrial countries – an evolution which results in narrowing the economic basis on which foreign trade rests."

11. Commission on Foreign Economic Policy, *Report to the President and to the Congress* (Washington, D.C.: U.S. Government Printing Office, 1954), p. 39.

12. (a) Department of the Interior, Bureau of Mines, *Minerals Yearbook, 1967,* Vol. I (Washington, D.C.: U.S. Government Printing Office, 1968), p. 36; (b) W. S.

Woytinsky and E. S. Woytinsky, *World Population and Production* (New York: Twentieth Century Fund, 1953), Table 335, p. 791.

13. Department of the Interior, p. 711. See also P. W. Bidwell, *Raw Materials: A Study of American Policy* (New York: Harper, 1958), p. 192.

14. G. H. Snyder, *Stockpiling Strategic Materials* (San Francisco: Chandler, 1966), p. 247.

15. Woytinsky and Woytinsky, pp. 804, 820; cf. Department of the Interior, pp. 187, 1119.

16. Maizels, pp. 222–224.

17. H. W. Singer, "U.S. Foreign Investment in Underdeveloped Areas: The Distribution of Gains between Investing and Borrowing Countries," *American Economic Review* 40 (May 1950), p. 473.

18. M. Michaely, *Concentration in International Trade* (Amsterdam: North-Holland, 1962), Table 18, p. 113.

19. Figures computed from data in United Nations Statistical Office, *Yearbook of International Trade Statistics, 1966* (New York: United Nations, 1968). West Germany is the only country for which the difference in proportions is small.

20. The 4% of its 1966 GNP that the United States exported amounted to 14.7% of the world's total exports. The corresponding figures for the United Kingdom were 15.3 and 6.8%. Calculated from (a) U.S. Bureau of the Census, *Statistical Abstract of the United States: 1968,* 89th ed. (Washington, D.C.: U.S. Government Printing Office, 1968); (b) Central Statistical Office, *Annual Abstract of Statistics, No. 105, 1968* (London: Her Majesty's Stationery Office, 1968); (c) United Nations Statistical Office.

21. Computed on the basis of figures on British foreign investment: A. H. Imlah, *Economic Elements in the Pax Britannica* (Cambridge, Mass.: Harvard University Press, 1958), pp. 70–75; on British national income, Woytinsky and Woytinsky, p. 385; on U.S. national income and foreign investment, U.S. Bureau of the Census.

22. W. Guzzardi, Jr., "Why the Climate is Changing for U.S. Investment," *Fortune* 75 (September 1967), p. 117.

23. R. Gilpin, *France in the Age of the Scientific State* (Princeton: Princeton University Press, 1968), p. 50; Guzzardi, p. 116.

24. C. Layton, *Trans-Atlantic Investments* (Boulogne-sur-Seine: Atlantic Institute, 1968), p. 47.

25. *Ibid.,* p. 98.

26. T. A. Wise, "I.B.M.'s $5,000,000,000 Gamble," *Fortune* 74 (September 1966), p. 118; Gilpin, p. 65.

27. Gilpin, p. 27.

28. E. Littlejohn, "The Influence of Multinational Corporations on International Affairs," paper given at the Ninth Annual Convention of the International Studies Association, March 28–30, 1968 (unpublished), p. 1.

29. M. Watkins et al., Report of the Task Force on the Structure of Canadian Industry, *Foreign Ownership and the Structure of Canadian Industry* (Ottawa: Queen's Printer, 1968), pp. 199–200.

30. Gilpin, p. 51.

31. Watkins, p. 339.

32. *Ibid.*, pp. 313–314, 317–318.

33. Cf. Watkins, p. 336; Littlejohn, pp. 3–4; A. de Riencourt, *The American Empire* (New York: Dial Press, 1968), pp. 228–290.

34. R. D. McKenzie, "The Concept of Dominance and World-Organization," *American Journal of Sociology* 33 (July 1927), pp. 34–35.

RICHARD ROSECRANCE
ARTHUR STEIN

6
Interdependence: Myth and Reality

Taking issue with Waltz's contention that interdependence is in decline, Rosecrance and Stein suggest that the world is more complex than Waltz recognizes. After developing a working definition of interdependence, they measure its development in four areas: trade, investment, finance, and politics. Although Rosecrance and Stein note substantial increases in transnational interaction, they also find that nationalism is on the increase and that it not only contributes to transnationalism but also poses a significant challenge. They conclude that "the earth today is poised between a world of nationalism and a world of transnationalism."

One of the uncertainties of modern international relations is the degree of interdependence among states. Some theorists have asserted that interdependence is high and/or growing, and others have maintained that it is low and/or declining. Essentially, the debate about interdependence has proceeded in three separate phases. (1) In the aftermath of World War II, technology was heralded as the stimulus to an interrelationship among states: the world was shrinking; technological, military, and economic factors would produce interdependence even among erstwhile enemies.[1] (2) Later this conventional wisdom was challenged by Karl Deutsch and his associates, who purported to show that various economic indicators of external reference were declining.[2] International transactions were lessening relative to intranational transactions. More and more, citizens were turning to the nation-state for the satisfaction of their needs, and national economies were taking precedence over the

Reprinted by permission from *World Politics* 26:1 (October 1973), pp. 1–27. Copyright © 1973 by Princeton University Press.

previous international economy of the nineteenth century. This theme
has recently been powerfully reinforced by Kenneth Waltz.[3] (3) In
reaction to the claims of the Deutsch group, which initially predicted
stalemate in European unification efforts and a greater autarchy for
industrial states, new presentations of the argument in favor of
interdependence have been made.[4] According to this view, interdependence among states is certainly increasing. A symposium on the
international corporation partly reinforces Deutsch's view, while one on
transnational processes argues against it.[5] The result of these theoretical
vectors remains uncertain. In this essay we hope to offer new data and to
provide a modest reconciliation of the contending claims, drawing a trial
balance between them.

One of the problems in unravelling disagreements about interdependence is the absence of an agreed definition of the term. At least three
different notions have been employed. In its most general sense,
interdependence suggests a relationship of interests such that if one
nation's position changes, other states will be affected by that change.[6]
A second meaning, derived from economics, suggests that interdependence is present when there is an increased national "sensitivity" to external economic developments.[7] This "sensitivity" presumably can be either perceived or unperceived.[8] The most stringent
definition comes from Kenneth Waltz, who argues that interdependence
entails a relationship that would be costly to break.[9] This definition is
different from the others in two senses: (1) it presumes a positive relationship between the interdependent units, such that each will suffer if
the relationship is harmed; (2) relationships in which one party is
affected by what another does would not necessarily be interdependent
by Waltz's definition, because the effect might not be "costly." Since ob-
servers use such different definitions of the central term, it is easy to understand why they draw different conclusions about the presence or absence of interdependence in the contemporary world.

At the same time, Waltz's conclusion that interdependence is low or
declining can be disputed even on the basis of the stringent definition he
employs. The Waltz contentions run approximately as follows: interdependence exists where there is a division of labor or a specialization of
functions. Unlike units perform different functions or offer specialized
services; they become interdependent when they perform these services
for each other and when units come to rely on such specialization. On
the other hand, if units are alike, they cannot offer different commodities
or services; interdependence declines. Waltz also asserts that interdependence is lowest where like units have unequal capacities: then,
powers either cannot or do not have to take each other into account. As
juridically like units, therefore, states can have little interdependence at

any time and place. Since differences in *de facto* capacities among states have grown since World War II, interdependence is now at a nadir. This is not dismaying, however, for it is contended to be a "mistaken conclusion" that "a growing closeness of interdependence would improve the chances of peace."[10] To summarize this argument, interdependence is high (1) where there are unlike units; and (2) where the units are relatively equal in capacity.

A number of comments can be offered in rejoinder. First, if interdependence is taken entirely in the positive sense (where interests of states vary directly, not inversely), it is difficult to understand how a high degree of interdependence could be a cause for conflict. If relationships really were costly to break on all sides, this would be a factor for general international cooperation. Second, while it is true that interdependence may be high where there are unlike units involved in the relationship, it is by no means clear that such differentiation is the *necessary condition* of high interdependence. A most important form of interdependence, that of military alliance, arises when states offer the same defense resources to each other. By pooling their resources, they gain a joint security that each could not attain in isolation, and yet there is no necessary division of labor. Clearly such defense ties might be very costly to break.[11]

If military allies have relationships that are positively interdependent, enemies or adversaries manifest a high degree of negative interdependence in their relationships. Their interests are crucially linked in that it is assumed that if one improves his position, the other suffers. Yet, where such a high degree of interdependence (albeit negative) exists, there is no necessary differentiation of functions or division of labor. Rather, the interdependence of antagonists arises in part because rivals are alike: they compete for the same goals, utilize similar techniques, and seek to win over the same allies or to acquire the same real estate. The very continuance of competition over time, moreover, is likely to make them even more alike. Eventually, rivals may even develop certain positively interdependent goals. If they reside at the top of a hierarchy of nations, it may be a common interest to prevent any inroads on their joint position by other states. If war is likely to result in widespread mutual devastation, they may have a common interest in mutual accommodation and coexistence.

It may also be argued that the greatest interdependency in contemporary world politics subsists among the most highly developed powers, powers whose economic systems bear the greatest similarity to each other. In military terms, these powers could hurt each other grievously; in economic terms, they have the capacity to help or harm each other. At this juncture, the error of following the comparative-advantage, product-specialization argument too far is clearly portrayed. The basis for international trade today is not only marked product differentiation, but also the capacity of the domestic market. Europeans, Americans, and Japanese sell the bulk of their goods in each other's markets, even though typical approaches to comparative advantage would have them import raw materials from and sell industrial goods to the less developed countries.[12] The products which major industrial countries offer are not highly differentiated in the Ricardian sense; they all offer automobiles, consumer electronics, and industrial equipment. Differences exist, however, in marketing, pricing, quality, and sophistication. As we shall see later, the exchange of manufactured goods for manufactured goods is becoming *more* typical in international trade, not less so. It therefore does not follow that interdependence is low today, even if Waltz's strict definition of the term is employed.

At the same time, Waltz correctly points to the fact that nationalism and national interests are not secondary or obsolete phenomena in the contemporary world. Indeed, nationalism is a far more prominent factor in economic and political arrangements today than it was in the halcyon days of the nineteenth century. Prior to 1914, economic internationalism was the order of the day. Passports were unnecessary. Tariffs had only been recently reintroduced. National secrecy in military plans and the demand for patriotic loyalty on the part of citizens were surely less stringent than they are now. Nationalism was in fact strengthened by the reformist orientation of modern politics: Franklin Roosevelt, a domestic reformer who tried to put the United States on the road to economic recovery after the Depression, did so at the expense of the international economic and, to some extent, political system. When governments are expected to regulate the economy to obtain maximum welfare for their citizens, they must often slight the interests of economic and political partners. Citizens may also reflect such attitudes. They do not look to the international system for economic and political benefits, but to their national government. Socialism, nationalization, and domestic economic planning interpose national criteria on international economic forces. By almost any definition of the terms, economic and political nationalism have grown since the last decades of the nineteenth century. What effect has this development had upon interdependence?

By all three definitions, nationalism might have been expected to reduce interdependence. It might be argued that, if nations seek only to achieve their own goals without any reference to the rest of the system, the linkage between units must decline. If nationalistic goals depend on supportive actions by other members of the international community, however, nationalism cannot be achieved in isolation. Not only does interdependence not decline in such circumstances, aggressive nationalism may lead to higher negative interdependence. The greater nationalism of the twentieth century therefore need not entail a reduction of interdependence. We still do not know whether interdependence will rise or fall, whether it will be positive or negative. The rest of this paper will be devoted to an answer to these questions in economic and political terms, considering data and developments of the past century.[13]

THE TRADE SECTOR

If we are to gain a greater understanding of present-day interdependence, the trade sector is critical. One of the long-standing contentions of those who assert that interdependence is low or declining is that national industrialization, at least in its later stages, involves a decreasing reliance upon foreign trade. As manufacturing economies develop, states rely more upon themselves for necessary goods and less upon imports from other countries. Karl Deutsch and Alexander Eckstein, in a pioneering study, tried to measure this phenomenon by the ratio of foreign trade to GNP over time.[14] They concluded that the ratio of foreign trade to GNP increased during the early stages of economic development, but decreased in the later stages of national industrialization.

It is not certain, however, that Deutsch's and Eckstein's data support their conclusions. Ratios for the 1950's, as given by the two investigators, are sometimes quite close to the highest of the series for several countries.[15] Moreover, the Deutsch-Eckstein study is based on current dollar figures.[16] Over the last century, domestic rates of inflation have tended to inflate GNP figures while, due to revolutionary advances in transportation, export and import prices have not risen as sharply.[17] Robert E. Lipsey, therefore, recalculated the ratio of American exports to GNP in constant 1913 dollars. As Table 1 shows, there is no secular trend of a decline in foreign-trade ratios.

Calculations on other bases support the same conclusion. Table 2 shows that data to 1970 may even portray a slight increase in the ratio of American exports to GNP.

The conclusion that ratios have not fallen and may even recently have increased is strengthened by the knowledge that the ratio for the nineteenth century is inflated because of the downward bias in GNP calculations. Deutsch and Eckstein admit that their national-product estimates "tend to understate the subsistence sector of the economy."[20] They accurately point out that much of the growth in GNP in industrialized states is due to the growth of the service sector, and that that very sector was substantially underestimated in GNP calculations for the previous century. It is therefore very difficult to square the available

TABLE 1

RATIO OF EXPORTS TO GNP AVERAGED BY DECADES,
IN CONSTANT 1913 DOLLARS[18]

	Ratio of Exports to GNP
1880-89	6.25
1890-99	7.24
1900-09	6.64
1910-19	7.69
1920-29	6.35
1930-39	5.06
1940-49	7.93
1950-59	6.65

TABLE 2

RATIO OF EXPORTS TO GNP AVERAGED BY DECADES,
IN CONSTANT 1958 DOLLARS[19]

	Ratio of Exports to GNP
1930-39	4.91
1940-49	4.34
1950-59	4.93
1960-69	6.06

data with the conclusion that foreign trade as a share of GNP has declined as a consequence of higher industrialization.

Changes in the structure of trade, however, may lead to lower interdependence even though the foreign stake of many developed countries is high or increasing. If interdependence existed only when the relationship would be costly to break, it might be contended that trade at the turn of the century was more truly interdependent than it is today. Before World War I, a typical trade transaction probably involved an exchange of manufactured goods for raw materials; today, much of world trade consists of the exchange of manufactured goods among developed countries. Since these countries could theoretically adopt programs of import replacement, it is contended that interdependence has decreased.[21]

It is indeed true that trade in manufactured goods has greatly increased with time. Table 3 shows the trend in world exports of primary products, petroleum, and manufactured goods since 1950. While primary exports have almost doubled and petroleum exports nearly trebled,

TABLE 3

TREND IN WORLD EXPORTS OF MANUFACTURES, PETROLEUM, AND
PRIMARY COMMODITIES, 1950-1969
(IN BILLIONS OF DOLLARS)[22]

	Primary Commodities	Petroleum	Manufactures
1950	30.28	-----	22.97
1955	31.13	8.59	33.77
1960	36.71	10.63	57.74
1965	46.02	15.05	92.45
1969	56.02	21.54	149.73

manufacturing exports have grown by a factor of seven. These trends are
reinforced by Table 4, which shows that raw materials have dropped and
manufactured goods have risen as a percentage of imports and exports
among developed countries since 1954. The increasing trade in
manufactured goods, not surprisingly, is linked with an increase in the
trade among developed countries. Table 5 shows that trade among
industrial states has increased most dramatically in the last three
decades.

These trends are consistent with the conclusion that interdependence
has not increased, however; industrial countries, with flexible economies, should be able to reduce their dependence upon each other
without great cost. But this argument must take account of yet another
point. Not only do developed countries trade with one another mainly in
manufactured goods: there is also, in trade among developed nations, an
increasing dependence upon particular countries and particular
commodities. Albert Hirschman has used an index running from 100
(when a country's exports go solely to one trading partner) to very low
numbers (when a country's trade is evenly divided among a large
number of countries).[25] This measure is known as the Gini coefficient,
which is the square root of the sum of the squares of the fractions of
trade with each country, multiplied by 100. Its upper limit is 100; the
lower limit, assuming trade is evenly divided among 100 countries,
would be 10. In 1945 Hirschman used it to calculate the dependence of
one nation upon the trade of another. Thirteen years later, Michael
Michaely furnished an estimate of the dependence of countries on trade
in particular commodities.[26] We have updated these estimates with
figures for 1961 and 1968. The evidence is incontrovertible: the recent
growth of trade in manufactures among developed societies has not
freed economies from the thrall of a few suppliers, nor has it reduced

TABLE 4

RAW MATERIAL AND MANUFACTURED IMPORTS AND EXPORTS AS A PERCENTAGE
OF TOTAL TRADE FOR SELECTED INDUSTRIAL COUNTRIES[23]

		Imports		Exports	
		Raw/ Total	Manufactured/ Total	Raw/ Total	Manufactured/ Total
Germany	1954	71	27	15	84
	1968	43	53	9	90
Japan	1954	86	14	14	85
	1968	72	27	5	94
France	1954	70	24	28	65
	1968	39	60	22	74
Italy	1954	65	34	40	58
	1968	54	45	16	82
United Kingdom	1954	76	20	13	81
	1968	48	48	8	85
United States	1954	63	32	28	68
	1968	32	62	26	70

TABLE 5

VALUE INDEX OF DIRECTION OF EXPORTS,
DEVELOPING COUNTRIES AND DEVELOPED COUNTRIES
(1950 = 100)[24]

	From Developed to Developed	From Developed to Developing	From Developing to Developed	From Developing to Developing
1938	42.1	31.0	31.3	28.3
1948	95.5	100.0	85.8	108.7
1950	100.0	100.0	100.0	100.0
1954	143.7	134.5	119.4	117.4
1959	213.8	176.1	140.3	126.1
1964	352.2	223.9	185.8	158.7
1969	598.7	331.6	271.7	223.3

their dependence on imports of particular commodities. Perhaps surprisingly, industrial countries have become more dependent on particular countries for their trade, and are generally more dependent on the supply of particular commodities. Less developed countries may have increased their independence within the system. Table 6 shows the change in Gini coefficients for selected industrial and developing countries in dependence upon trade with particular states. Separate indices are given for imports and exports, indicating the degree to which trade has become geographically dependent.

It is noteworthy that among developed countries (with the exception of imports to Japan) the changes are all in a positive direction, indicating that trade has become more geographically concentrated among suppliers and markets with time. For the developing countries shown, with the exception of Turkey, trade has become less concentrated geographically, and therefore it reflects a smaller degree of dependence. Table 7 gives similar evidence of the dependence on trade in particular commodities. With the exception of changes in imports for France and the United Kingdom, commodity concentration for the major developed countries has increased in the past decade. Developed countries are now more dependent upon the import and export of particular commodities than they were previously. Developing countries show no such pattern, and Mexico's reduction of dependence on particular commodity imports and exports is striking. These findings modify conclusions about a reduction in interdependence among industrial countries. The concentration in trade among developed countries is growing. Diversification of suppliers and markets is harder to accomplish. To this degree, dependence and mutual interdependence of all industrial countries increased.[29]

There is a further point. The most satisfactory measure of interdependence is not the cost of breaking the relationship, but the degree to which economic interests are direct functions of one another. If the economic position of state *A* changes, will state *B* be affected? In the nineteenth century, there was a *de facto* interdependence of economic units, but political governors did not act in such a way as to maximize the economic interests of their unit. They therefore neglected external economic changes that had a great effect upon the domestic economic system. During the past half-century, political changes within society have made it impossible for political leaders to ignore the domestic impact of external economic forces. Today, therefore, they respond vigorously to external economic changes. Economic effects are now fully comprehended within the political realm. Thus, politically significant interdependence is much higher today than it was during the nineteenth century.

TABLE 6

CHANGE IN GINI COEFFICIENTS IN THE GEOGRAPHIC CONCENTRATION
OF TRADE FOR SELECTED DEVELOPED AND DEVELOPING COUNTRIES
(CHANGE FROM 1954 TO 1968)[27]

	Exports	Imports
Germany	3.5	4.2
Japan	9.9	- 7.3
France	4.4	8.8
Italy	6.2	2.2
United Kingdom	1.9	1.0
United States	.5	4.9
Brazil	- 4.7	- 1.2
Mexico	-15.1	-17.1
Ghana	-10.8	-19.4
Turkey	- 1.6	+ 3.2

TABLE 7

CHANGE IN GINI COEFFICIENTS IN THE COMMODITY CONCENTRATION
OF TRADE FOR SELECTED DEVELOPED AND DEVELOPING COUNTRIES
(CHANGE FROM 1961 TO 1968)[28]

	Exports	Imports
Germany	1.21	.53
Japan	2.98	.93
France	1.18	- .95
Italy	.03	3.27
United Kingdom	.04	.81
United States	2.86	3.86
Brazil	- .19	-1.49
Mexico	-21.14	-2.92
Ghana	- 1.38	-3.68
Turkey	+ 8.98	-6.77

THE INVESTMENT SECTOR

The investment sector reveals similar patterns. Those who argue that interdependence is decreasing can point to the change in the pattern of overseas investment over the past century.[30] Those who assert that it is rising can center their attention on the tremendous recent growth in foreign investment and on changing patterns of investment.[31] Much of the growth in foreign investment since World War II has been in direct investment (investment which results in an important share of ownership or control of a foreign corporation). By contrast, the leading authority on capital flows in the late nineteenth century observes that "portfolio investment was a far more important component of long-term capital movements before 1914 than direct investment; and it consisted much more of transactions in bonds and other debt instruments than in equities."[32] What direct investment there was in the nineteenth century tended to proceed from capital-abundant to capital-deficient areas.[33] While one-third of British long-term investments were in Europe, much of this was in capital-deficient areas such as Russia. Even when direct investment in other developed countries increased after World War I, investment in capital-deficient areas remained a large fraction of the total. In this period, American direct investment abroad typically flowed to Latin America.

The recent growth in overseas long-term investment has not only taken the form of direct investment, it has also increasingly gone to other developed countries. Tables B and C of the Appendix demonstrate this change. In 1936 and 1950, American investments were evenly divided between developed and less developed countries; in 1968, two-thirds of the book value of direct American investments were in developed countries. American direct investments in manufacturing have risen from 25.6 per cent of the total in 1936 to 40.6 per cent in 1968. These changes are revealed even more dramatically by an analysis of capital flows. In 1957, 55.5 per cent of the net capital flows from the United States went to less developed countries, with 46.9 per cent going to Latin America. In 1968, 58.4 per cent of American capital flowed to developed countries, with 31.2 per cent going to Europe – an increase of 11.6 per cent since 1957.[34]

With these changes, American investments have become more concentrated geographically and in terms of specific industries. Table 8 indicates this concentration.

The conclusion to be drawn from these trends is that the stake of the developed countries, and particularly of the United States, in the international economic system has risen as it has become more concentrated.[36] Direct investments imply a higher stake in a foreign

TABLE 8

GEOGRAPHIC CONCENTRATION OF U.S. INVESTMENT, 1929-1959[35]

	1929	1936	1943	1950	1959
Gini Coefficient	33.02	34.41	34.20	34.68	37.60

country than portfolio investments. Investments in manufacturing enterprises and in other developed countries have narrowed the focus of American investor activity and concern. More is at stake in specific markets, and in specific kinds of enterprises; there is more to lose than there was formerly.

The absolute increase in American direct foreign investment is matched by its relative growth as compared to other GNP indicators. Measured against domestic GNP, in current or constant dollars, the foreign-investment sector has grown rapidly. Table 9 makes this clear.

These comparative growth rates are even more remarkable if 1950 is taken as the base year. (See Table 10.)

This tremendous growth in the book value of American direct investment has been paralleled by a growth in the volume of operations of foreign affiliates compared with U.S. domestic concerns.[39] Domestic sales did not double between 1957 and 1968; however, the sales of foreign manufacturing affiliates rose by more than a factor of three. In 1968, the volume of sales abroad in manufacturing amounted to 10 per cent of domestic sales in manufacturing.

Foreign earnings on direct investments of American corporations have also increased more rapidly than domestic earnings. Since 1950, domestic profits of corporations have risen by about 50 per cent. But earnings on direct foreign investments have increased by more than 450 per cent.[40] By 1969, foreign earnings on direct investments had risen to 28 per cent of domestic earnings.[41]

This increased preoccupation with the foreign economic sector, moreover, was not confined to the United States. The growth of the multinational corporation has been so spectacular that today, "of the 50 largest economic entities (in the world), 37 are countries and 13 are corporations. Of the top 100, 51 are corporations."[42] It has been estimated that about one-quarter of the gross national product of the non-Communist world is earned by the business of such enterprises outside their home countries.[43]

It is of course true that foreign investment as a percentage of national income has decreased since 1913, but the type of investment which has

TABLE 9

INDEX OF GROWTH OF FOREIGN DIRECT INVESTMENT AND U.S. GNP, 1968[37]

(1959 = 100)

GNP in current dollars	179
GNP in constant dollars	148
GNP in foreign investment	219

TABLE 10

INDEX OF GROWTH OF FOREIGN DIRECT INVESTMENT AND U.S. GNP, 1968[38]

(1950 = 100)

GNP in current dollars	303
GNP in constant dollars	199
Direct foreign investment	551

occurred is such as to give its owner a substantial stake in the foreign sector. In contrast to the experience of the nineteenth century, current foreign investment is not simply credit, it is partial ownership. Control of productive facilities is involved. Today, transfers of technology are an exceedingly important part of direct investment. Since they are so important, it would be foolhardy for host countries to threaten them. But if the cost of breaking the relationship is so high, interdependence must also be high.

The political significance of interdependence is low when its salience is low. In 1913, economic interdependence had very low political salience; governments were not supposed to be responsive to or control external economic influences. Thus, the absolute high value of investment in 1913 had little political significance. Today the rate of increase of the foreign-investment sector and the increasing political responsiveness of governments have given high salience and significance to foreign investment.

THE FINANCIAL SECTOR

The financial operation of the international economic system has changed greatly since World War I. Under the gold standard of 1880-1913, short-term capital movements were neither as extensive nor as disruptive as they have been in recent years.[44] The amount of funds available for "hot money" flows has now reached an all-time high. Table H of the Appendix shows that $71 billion is available in various currencies (mainly dollars) for short-term transactions. This huge pool of assets, sloshing from country to country, can easily undermine domestic monetary policy and strength. In 1968, an inflow of foreign funds into West Germany amounted to as much as 8.9 per cent of the domestic money supply, greatly circumscribing attempts at an anti-inflationary policy. In the same year, France suffered an outflow of 22 per cent of her international reserves, forcing her central bank to put a brake on expansionist policies.[45] In July 1972, speculation against the dollar was so intense that in just one day European central banks bought $1.5 billion to prevent the dollar from going beneath the level fixed by the Smithsonian Agreement of December 18, 1971.[46] Less than 14 months later, speculation forced a further 10 per cent devaluation of the dollar, and in one day Germany took in $2.7 billion in exchange for marks. The Smithsonian Agreement, which once appeared to be a long-term solution, has now been abandoned.

If the sudden speculative movements of this vast pool of currencies are not to undermine domestic monetary stability and economic progress, and perhaps to cause a collapse of the whole Western trading system, governments will have to concert their countermeasures. Increasing recognition of the problem in the past fifteen years has led to the General Agreement to Borrow (GAB), various currency-swap arrangements, an enlargement of IMF quotas, and the creation of Special Drawing Rights (SDR's). Yet it is by no means certain that these and various pending arrangements will fully control the short-term flow of funds among Western and developed nations. The interdependence of the financial structure of trade is growing, but still higher cooperation among governments is necessary to ensure that it will not become a negative interdependence.[47]

Other changes have transformed the system since World War I. The old gold standard was based (not surprisingly) on gold as a medium of exchange. Minimum use was made of foreign currencies as reserves. At the end of 1913, the nations of the world held only $963 million in foreign-exchange reserves, and over half of these were possessed by Russia, India, and Japan.[48] Official gold holdings, in contrast, were more than five times as much.[49] With the move to a gold-exchange standard, the percentage of national reserves accounted for by foreign-exchange holdings has gone up dramatically. Table I of the Appendix makes it clear that in 1945 gold accounted for 70 per cent of international reserves, while foreign exchange totaled 30 per cent. By the end of 1971, on the other hand, gold amounted to only 30 per cent of world reserves, while foreign exchange represented 60 per cent, and a new category of international reserves (SDR's and gold *tranche*) represented 10 per cent.

These figures are even more instructive when analyzed in conjunction with the growth of world trade in the same years. In 1945, world exports in the non-Communist world totaled $34.2 billion. By the end of 1971, world exports were estimated at $334 billion, 977 per cent of the previous figure. This means that since 1945, the value of world exports has more than doubled every eight years. This growth is more than double the growth rate of foreign-exchange holdings, more than four times that of total international reserves, and almost eight times the growth rate of gold holdings. In 1945, total international reserves were 39 per cent greater than the value of world exports; by the end of 1971, total international reserves were only 40 per cent of the total value of exports in one year. Thus, while the holdings of international reserves have not kept pace with the growth in trade, the degree to which they have kept up is due to vast increases in the holdings of foreign exchange.

This change also represents an increase in international interdependence. Gold was an undifferentiated asset; it could be earned from any sector, and spent in any sector. A nation had to discipline its trade overall, but not with specific countries. Today, bilateral trading relationships are far more important, and among those trading countries interdependence has increased. What is more important, while the countries whose currencies are media of exchange have some responsibility for disciplining their own financial policies, other countries also have a direct financial stake in their solvency. These other countries have an interest in not allowing reserve currencies to sink too low on international exchanges. Hence the rescue operations for the British pound and the U.S. dollar. Now that Swiss francs, German marks, and Japanese yen are being held as reserves, other nations also have a stake in maintaining the value of such reserves. These currencies may be able to benefit from rescue operations at a later stage. Gold holdings in the nineteenth century did not produce this same stake, this same interdependence. Governments, recognizing this dependence upon currencies, have now gone so far as to create a new reserve unit, the SDR, the use and further extension of which will be entirely dependent upon international agreement. The interdependence of the financial system has now become formal.

THE POLITICAL SECTOR

The development of political relations among states since 1913 has witnessed two major trends. Between 1919 and 1939, an essentially autarchic trend held sway, with nations striving to reduce their dependence upon others, first in political and later in economic terms.

Because of the role of prewar alliances, World War I strengthened the tendency for nations to rely on themselves. The peacetime alignments which emerged in the 1930's had little significance in time of crisis or war. Indeed, the only major powers which stood by their alliance commitments were Germany and Japan. The Soviet Union, France, Britain, and Italy all vacillated, and the United States remained out of the bargaining.

After World War II, however, nations came to believe that they could not ensure their own defense without help. National self-sufficiency would no longer provide security. In the wake of Hiroshima, many nations also concluded that major wars would be so horrendous that they could not be tolerated at all. Henceforth, minimal cooperation would be necessary even among adversaries. Arrangements were made for crisis communication and management.

In recent years, however, intergovernmental cooperation and interdependence have grown apart from military stimuli. It can even be argued that the alienation of publics from their governors has strengthened such trends. Contemporary government depends upon such a wealth of information and specialized expertise that the man in the street cannot keep up with what is happening, to say nothing of being able to make informed judgments. Under these circumstances, elections have come to be symbolic processes, largely devoid of intellectual content. Since people do not fully understand their governments, they tend to distrust them and to become resentful toward those in authority. But distrust of those in power nationally does not lead to any new foci of international loyalty and support. If national bureaucracies are immobile, international or supranational institutions are either weak or unresponsive to popular demands. Even in Europe there has been no marked substitution of international for national loyalties.

The difficulties of domestic governance have, paradoxically, forced governmental elites together. Although the masses cannot fully communicate with elites, and elites cannot talk to the masses except in the simplest terms, elites *can* talk to each other. National leaders are coming to recognize that, with individual variations, they are all in the same boat. Among developed societies at least, they face similar problems: the problem of remaining in power as the electorate becomes sullen and resentful; the problems of economic progress and of making their way in international politics while avoiding major war. Leader-to-leader diplomacy has been a way of learning from each other.

The failure of ideology to cope with real governmental problems has also brought leaders together. The barrage of information and the communications revolution have today either destroyed or rendered irrelevant most ideological systems of belief.[50] Rigid doctrinal approaches are discredited by new information. Rulership requires so much expertise and detailed adjustment that ideological systems offer few guidelines. Elites learn from each other, perhaps more than they do from their own publics; in one sense they help each other solve the problem of domestic governance.

• • •

Increased communication among leaders has not, however, put an end to nationalism. It is true, as Kenneth Waltz argues, that "the progress of internal integration and the increased intervention of governments in their domestic economies means that for most states the internal sector now looms larger than it once did."[51] While elites are looking outward, publics are turning to their national governments for the solution of social and economic problems. What Karl Kaiser calls "vertical interaction" (between government and society) has grown greatly in recent decades. Kaiser argues that "a high degree of horizontal interaction [between units of world politics] . . . does not lead to transnational politics unless there is vertical interaction." He goes on: "The higher the degree of interventionism on the part of national governments, the more vulnerable governmental policies become to processes on the level of transnational society which might thwart these policies. A democratic structure intensifies this relationship since it forces governments to be more responsive to disturbances."[52] He then concludes that a nation-state's participation in transnational politics is a function of the product of horizontal and vertical interaction:

$$tp = hi \times vi^{53}$$

This equation suggests that, if vertical interaction increased and horizontal interaction remained the same, transnational politics would increase. But if transnational politics is any measure of the amount of interdependence among states, this conclusion can scarcely be accepted. If vertical integration and interaction were to increase greatly, as for example with the establishment of a totalitarian state, transnational politics would almost certainly decline rather than increase. Such an increase in vertical interaction would probably stimulate a decline in horizontal interaction with other states and societies, again preventing any increase in transnationalism. It is also not an accident that states convulsed by revolutionary impulses have been the least amenable to horizontal interaction with other states and societies. The domestic preoccupation of the vertical revolutionary process tends to cut links with other units. It is also not surprising that the Communist countries, with the highest degree of vertical integration, where "the permanent intervention of governmental institutions in the social and economic life of society" has gone farthest, evince the fewest horizontal ties with other states and societies. There can be no conclusion, therefore, that vertical interaction *always* increases transnational politics and interdependence.

CONCLUSION

The earth is today poised between a world of nationalism and a world of transnationalism. The vertical interaction of nationalist processes has moved to a new peak. The horizontal interaction of transnational processes is higher than at any point since World War I. Moreover, it is growing rapidly. As both Kaiser and Morse have pointed out,[54] vertical interaction has made horizontal interaction relevant for political and governmental purposes. If vertical interaction were not so great, the world would be witnessing a return to the *apolitical* interdependence of 1913. However, a rapid further increase in domestic social change and vertical interaction, far from increasing transnational politics, could put an end to them.

Domestic governments lie at the nexus of vertical and horizontal interaction. They are impelled in one direction by the desire to satisfy the electorate and to build domestic support. They are impelled in another by the high degree of horizontal integration of the system. If they are to cope with the great transnational phenomena of the current age – the multinational corporation, the unrivaled impact of private financial transfers, and continuing trade problems – they must cooperate with one another. In some measure the two influences are complementary: if governments are to satisfy the demands of the electorate in economic and financial policies, they may have to cooperate more fully with other nations. Under the stimulus of economic nationalism, however, nations may also occasionally act *against* the multilateral cooperative framework.

Intergovernmental cooperation has slowly increased since World War II to provide for a steadily increasing level of international trade and financial stability. The gold pool, GAB, and swap arrangements were the achievements of the early 1960's. SDR's and last-minute rescue operations for the dollar or the pound are the remedies of today. Yet, given the huge pool of Eurodollars and other currencies which can spill in or out of the domestic economic reservoirs of Western states, it is by no means assured that intergovernmental cooperation will be great enough to meet the need. Devaluation has often been the practical recourse, even though it represents national action against an agreed set of currency values.

American economic nationalism stimulated the U.S. moves of August 15, 1971 and February 12, 1973. The first eventually led to the

Smithsonian Agreement of December 1971, but that agreement could not be maintained under the continued pressure of monetary speculation. A further 10 per cent devaluation of the dollar, on February 12, 1973, led to the float of European and Japanese currencies. Even after the second American devaluation, however, the dollar and a number of other currencies remained vulnerable to speculative assault. After each autarchic move, the damage to the Western trading mechanism has been patched or repaired. But it is not certain that intergovernmental cooperation will be great enough to meet all crises in the future. It is, for example, uncertain that the Common Market countries will be able to keep their currencies in fixed alignment under current pressures. Neither is it certain that the Europeans will be able to avoid import surcharges if their currencies float too high for domestic political acceptability. In this sense, the American precedent of August 1971 may now be employed by European states. The problem of speculative flows of hot money has by no means been solved.[55]

Today, therefore, whether interdependence will emerge as positive or negative will depend largely on old-fashioned cooperation among governments. Governments can heed nationalistic, autarchic, or reformist demands of the citizenry. Even if they do not do so, however, the onrush of economic transnationalism is so rapid that it is not certain that governments can keep abreast of it. When antiquated forms of cooperation fail, nationalistic alternatives may be substituted.

In the international system today there is a phenomenon akin to Ernst Haas's "spill-over" in the Common Market. Nations that strive to carry out existing functions required by the exigencies of transnational flows and domestic demands must move to a higher level of cooperation. Horizontal interaction is increasing so rapidly, however, that the past apparatus of intergovernmental institutions and policy is no longer adequate. Haas presumed that, within an already partially integrated structure, this would lead to further integration of policies and institutions. Whatever the mandates of functional cooperation within customs unions, however, the international system as a whole does not prescribe such results. The failure to meet the challenge of higher necessary cooperation could mean a higher possibility of conflict. The objectives at stake are much greater than heretofore, but it is not certain that the current structure of interdependence will permit them to be achieved.

NOTES

The authors would like to acknowledge their indebtedness to Professors Richard N. Cooper, Simon Kuznets, Robert Lipsey, Thomas Willett, and Raymond Vernon, and to Mr. Brian Healy, for advice or data used in preparation of this paper. They absolve them entirely, however, from any responsibility for errors of fact or argument in what follows.

1. See, *inter alia*, Emery Reves, *The Anatomy of Peace* (New York: Harper and Brothers, 1946), p. 268.

2. See, particularly, Karl W. Deutsch, Lewis J. Edinger, Roy C. Macridis, and Richard L. Merritt, *France, Germany and the Western Alliance* (New York: Scribner, 1967), chap. 13.

3. Kenneth N. Waltz, "The Myth of Interdependence," in Charles P. Kindleberger, ed., *The International Corporation* (Cambridge: MIT Press, 1970).

4. See Edward L. Morse, "Transnational Economic Processes," in Robert O. Keohane and Joseph S. Nye, Jr., eds., *Transnational Relations and World Politics* (Cambridge: Harvard University Press, 1972); Morse, "The Politics of Interdependence," *International Organization* 23 (Spring 1969); Oran R. Young, "Interdependencies in World Politics," *International Journal* 24 (Autumn 1969); and Richard N. Cooper, *The Economics of Interdependence* (New York: Columbia University Press, 1968).

5. See Keohane and Nye; Kindleberger.

6. This meaning is close to that suggested by Morse and Young. Morse writes: "Interdependent behavior may be understood in terms of the outcome of specified actions of two or more parties (individuals, governments, corporations, etc.) when such actions are mutually contingent." Morse, "Transnational Economic Processes," p. 29. See also Young, p. 726.

7. See Cooper, p. 59.

8. See also Robert D. Tollison and Thomas D. Willett, "International Integration and the Interdependence of Economic Variables," *International Organization* 27 (Spring 1973), pp. 255–71.

9. See Waltz, pp. 205–07.

10. *Ibid.*, p. 205.

11. Mancur Olson, Jr., and Richard Zeckhauser, "An Economic Theory of Alliances," in Bruce M. Russett, ed., *Economic Theories of International Politics* (Chicago: Markham Publishing Co., 1968).

12. This approach is that of the Heckscher-Ohlin theorem emphasizing factor proportions.

13. Interdependence may also increase due to scientific and technological developments. See Eugene B. Skolnikoff, *The International Imperatives of Technology* (Berkeley: Institute of International Studies, No. 16, 1972); see also his "The International Functional Implications of Future Technology," prepared for delivery at the 66th Annual Meeting, American Political Science Association, Los Angeles, September 8–12, 1979; John Gerard Ruggie, "Collective Goods and Future International Collaboration," *American Political Science Review* 66 (September 1972), pp. 874–93; John H. Dunning, "Technology, United States Investment, and European Economic Growth," in Kindleberger.

14. Karl W. Deutsch and Alexander Eckstein, "National Industrialization and the Declining Share of the International Economic Sector, 1890–1959," *World Politics* 13 (January 1961), pp. 267–99.

15. See also Robert E. Lipsey, *Price and Quantity Trends in the Foreign Trade of the United States* (Princeton: Princeton University Press, 1963), pp. 39–44.

16. There are no criteria by which to decide which ratio of foreign trade to GNP is more valid, the one based on current dollars or the one based on constant dollars. In its limiting case, the ratio based on current dollars would go to zero, and it would be irrelevant to point out that in constant dollars there was still some foreign trade of consequence. (We are indebted to Richard N. Cooper for this point.) However, in the Deutsch-Eckstein case, where even in current dollars the ratio for the 1950's was relatively high, it is more illuminating to look at ratios based on constant dollars.

17. The following table gives an indication of this phenomenon for the last decade:

EXPORT, IMPORT, AND CONSUMER PRICES FOR SELECTED COUNTRIES, 1970

(Expressed in U.S. Dollars; 1963 = 100)

	Export	Import	Consumer
Japan	110	106	149.5
West Germany	114	110	120.4
France	112	107	130.9
United Kingdom	112	110	139.3
United States	121	120	128.9

Source: International Financial Statistics 24 (December 1971), pp. 32, 33, 35.

18. See Lipsey, pp. 430–31. This table is constructed using Kuznets' estimate of the U.S. Gross National Product. Because the Kuznets estimates deflate GNP, official statistics cannot be used to extend the Kuznets series.

19. Source: United States Government, *Economic Report of the President* (1972). The lower ratios in this table are due to the use of official (undeflated) GNP indices.

20. Deutsch and Eckstein, p. 271.

21. See Waltz, p. 210.

22. Source: International Bank for Reconstruction and Development, *Trends in Developing Countries* (Washington, D.C.: International Bank for Reconstruction and Development, 1971). Beginning in 1955, petroleum is included as Section 3 of the Standard International Trade Categories. Data exclude trade among Communist countries. It is interesting to compare these results with those offered by Albert O. Hirschman, *National Power and the Structure of Foreign Trade* (Berkeley: University of California Press, 1945), pp. 141–45. He found either no percentage increase in manufacturing trade as a proportion of the total, or a slight decline for major powers from 1913 to 1937. Longer term figures, however, point to secular increases since 1954.

23. United Nations, *Yearbook of International Trade Statistics* 1954 and 1968

(New York: United Nations, 1955 and 1970).

24. Source: *Trends in Developing Countries.*

25. See Hirschman, pp. 98–100.

26. Michael Michaely, "Concentration of Exports and Imports," *Economic Journal* 68 (December 1958), pp. 722–36.

27. 1954 data based on Michaely, *ibid.*; 1968 data computed using D.o.T. totals from International Monetary Fund and International Bank for Reconstruction and Development, *The Direction of Trade Annual 1966–70* (Washington, D.C.: Government Printing Office, 1971).

28. Source: *Yearbook of International Trade Statistics* 1961 and 1968.

29. On balance, the foreign-trade sector does not appear to be quite as useful for the measurement of relative interdependence as previous analysts have maintained. Although foreign trade is increasing relatively and absolutely among developed countries, that trade represents an exchange of manufactured goods. As a number of economists have pointed out, if governments can find substitutes for import or export markets among a few industrial countries, the growing effects of concentration do not necessarily increase interdependence. But even if substitutability exists economically, the problems of the political costs of switching from one market to the other and of the circumscription of political latitude involved in the process remain. For the latest review of the literature on trade as a measure of integration, and an excellent bibliography, see Cal Clark and Susan Welch, "Western European Trade as a Measure of Integration: Untangling the Interpretations," *Journal of Conflict Resolution* 16 (September 1972), pp. 363–82. Integration theorists might find it useful to examine other transnational economic sectors as well as trade, including those discussed below. One such attempt is outlined in Tollison and Willett.

30. Kenneth Waltz notes, for example, that "in 1910, the value of total British investment abroad was 1½ times larger than her national income"; for the United States today, however, it is a meager 18%. Waltz, p. 215.

31. See Cooper, chaps. 3, 4, and 5; Morse, "Transnational Economic Processes," pp. 36–37.

32. Arthur Bloomfield, *Patterns of Fluctuation in International Investment before 1914* (Princeton Studies in International Finance, No. 21, 1968), pp. 3–4.

33. *Ibid.*, pp. 2–3.

34. See Tables D and E of the Appendix.

35. Source: U.S. Department of Commerce, *U.S. Business Investments in Foreign Countries* (Washington, D.C.: Government Printing Office, 1960), p. 92. Figures since 1959 would probably indicate an even higher degree of concentration, but Department of Commerce statistics no longer give country-by-country breakdowns of investment figures.

36. It could of course be argued that a reduction in the number of suppliers or buyers does not necessarily raise the costs of such transactions to the United States. A few sources may be cheaper than many sources. But the circumscription does diminish U.S. political initiative; it narrows America's political latitude and thus links her interests more closely with the remaining sources of supply or markets.

37. Sources: *U.S. Business Investments in Foreign Countries*, p. 92; *Survey of*

Current Business 50 (October 1970), p. 28; *Economic Report of the President,* 1972, pp. 195–96.

38. *Ibid.*

39. See Table F of the Appendix.

40. See Table G of the Appendix.

41. This figure of 28% would be even higher if income from other (non-direct) foreign private assets had been included.

42. Lester R. Brown, "The Nation State, the Multi-National Corporation and the Changing World Order," mimeo (U.S. Department of Agriculture, 1968), quoted in John McHale, *The Transnational World* (Austin: Bureau of Business Research, University of Texas, 1969), p. 8.

43. Raymond Vernon, *Sovereignty at Bay* (New York: Basic Books, 1971), p. 383.

44. See Bloomfield, p. 87.

45. See Lawrence Krause, "Private International Finance," in Keohane and Nye, pp. 181–83.

46. *New York Times,* July 19, 1972.

47. See Susan Strange, "The Dollar Crisis: 1971," *International Affairs* 47 (April 1972), p. 194.

48. See Bloomfield, p. 7.

49. *Ibid.*, p. 7. Peter Lindert disputes the traditional wisdom (and Arthur Bloomfield) by claiming that foreign currencies were used fairly extensively. However, even Lindert's data for 1913 show that only $1132 million were held in foreign-exchange reserves, which is 15.9% of the total world reserves. He also concurs that more than half of these official foreign balances were held in Russia, India, and Japan. See Peter H. Lindert, *Key Currencies and Gold, 1900–1913* (Princeton Studies in International Finance, No. 24, 1969), pp. 12, 13, 76, 77.

50. See Zbigniew Brzezinski, *Between Two Ages* (New York: Viking Press, 1971), Parts II–III.

51. Waltz, p. 208.

52. Karl Kaiser, "Transnational Politics: Toward a Theory of Multinational Politics," *International Organization* 25 (Autumn 1971), p. 812.

53. *Ibid.*

54. *Ibid.*, pp. 811–12; Morse, "Transnational Economic Processes," pp. 44–45.

55. See Strange, p. 215; Edward L. Morse, "Crisis Diplomacy, Interdependence, and the Politics of International Economic Relations," *World Politics* 24 (Spring 1972 Supplement), pp. 123–50. As many have noted, one response to the failure of agreed currency values could be to move to freely floating exchange rates. So far, however, there is little evidence that nations would not try to extract the maximum national leverage from such a situation. After August 15, 1971 and after the failure of the Smithsonian Agreement, many nations engaged in "dirty floating," supporting the dollar and preventing their own currencies from rising to market level.

APPENDIX TO CHAPTER 6

TABLE A*

PERCENTAGE DISTRIBUTION OF TRADE FOR SELECTED DEVELOPED
AND LESS DEVELOPED COUNTRIES IN ACCORDANCE WITH THE
VARIOUS TYPES OF INTERCHANGE: 1954 AND 1968

		Raw-Raw	Man-Man	Inv	Raw-Man	Total
West Germany	1954	16	25	8	51	100
	1968	9	47	14	30	100
Japan	1954	12	16	20	53	100
	1968	5	27	1	67	100
France	1954	28	24	7	41	100
	1968	21	63	7	9	100
Italy	1954	32	41	20	7	100
	1968	16	45	2	37	100
United Kingdom	1954	11	22	16	50	100
	1968	7	54	17	22	100
United States	1954	34	26	23	17	100
	1968	26	61	7	6	100
Brazil	1954	37	1	13	49	100
	1968	37	8	7	48	100
Mexico	1954	2	28	27	44	100
	1968	16	22	22	40	100
Nigeria	1954	15	1	15	70	100
	1968	17	8	6	69	100
Panama	1954	38	1	65	-3	100
	1968	45	1	48	6	100

Raw-Raw: Exchange of foodstuffs and raw materials against foodstuffs and raw
          materials.
Man-Man: Exchange of manufactures against manufactures.
Inv: Exchange of commodities against "invisible items."
Raw-Man: Exchange of manufactures against foodstuffs and raw materials.

*Computed using Albert O. Hirschman's method, National Power and the Strucuture of
Foreign Trade (Berkeley: University of California Press, 1945), chap. 7. Data
from Yearbook of International Trade Statistics, 1954 and 1968.

TABLE B*

PERCENTAGE OF U.S. BOOK VALUE OF DIRECT INVESTMENT
BY GEOGRAPHIC AREA: 1936, 1950, 1959, and 1968

	1936	1950	1959	1968
Developed Countries	51.2	48.3	56.5	66.9
Canada	29.2	30.4	34.2	30.1
Western Europe	18.8	14.7	17.8	29.9
Less Developed Countries	48.4	48.6	39.1	28.8
Latin America	41.9	37.7	27.6	20.2

*The percentage not accounted for is due to a category called international, unallocated.

TABLE C*

PERCENTAGE OF U.S. BOOK VALUE OF DIRECT INVESTMENT
BY CATEGORY: 1936, 1950, 1959, AND 1968

	1936	1950	1959	1968
Mining and Smelting	15.4	9.6	9.6	8.4
Petroleum	16.1	28.8	35.1	29.1
Manufacturing	25.6	32.5	32.6	40.6
Public Utilities	24.5	12.1	8.1	4.1
Trade	5.8	6.5	6.9	8.1
Agriculture	7.2	5.0	2.2	---*
Other	5.4	5.6	5.5	9.7

*No separate category.

Sources for Tables B and C: Survey of Current Business (Washington, D.C.: U.S. Government Printing Office, October 1970), 28; U.S. Department of Commerce, U.S. Business Investments in Foreign Countries (Washington, D.C.: Government Printing Office, 1960), 92-93.

TABLE D

PERCENTAGE OF U.S. NET CAPITAL FLOWS
BY AREA: 1957 AND 1968

	1957	1968
Developed Countries	40.1	58.4
Less Developed Countries	55.5	35.7
Canada	28.9	19.5
Western Europe	11.6	31.2
Latin America	46.9	21.1

TABLE E

PERCENTAGE OF U.S. NET CAPITAL FLOWS

BY CATEGORY: 1957 AND 1968

	1957	1968 (preliminary)
Mining and Smelting	8.0	1.7
Petroleum	56.7	33.3
Manufacturing	17.4	36.5
Public Utilities	7.7	*
Trade	1.7	*
Finance and Insurance	7.8	*
Miscellaneous	.6	28.4

*No separate category.

Sources for Tables D and E: Survey of Current Business (October 1970), 29; U.S. Department of Commerce, U.S. Business Investments in Foreign Countries (Washington, D.C. 1960), 137.

TABLE F

INDEX OF U.S. FOREIGN AND DOMESTIC SECTOR

IN MANUFACTURING IN 1968

(1957 = 100)

Manufacturing Exports	189	
Sales by Direct Manuf. Affiliates	325	
Total Foreign Sales		262
U.S. Value Added by Manuf.	193	
U.S. Manuf. Sales	175	

Sources:

Domestic Sales: United States Government, Economic Report of the President (Washington, D.C.: Government Printing Office, 1972), p. 244.

Valued Added: 1957: U.S. Bureau of the Census, Annual Survey of Manufactures (Washington, D.C.: Government Printing Office, 1969), II; 1968: Annual Survey of Manufactures 1968 (Washington, D.C.: Government Printing Office, 1971), Press Release #M68 (AS-6), pp. 1 & 2.

Manuf. Exports: U.S. Statistical Abstract (1970), 480; U.S. Statistical Abstract (1963), p. 875.

Sales by Affiliates: Survey of Current Business (October 1970); U.S. Department of Commerce, U.S. Business Investments in Foreign Countries (Washington, D.C., 1960), p. 110.

TABLE G

EARNINGS ON DISTRICT FOREIGN INVESTMENTS AND FOREIGN EARNINGS
AS PERCENTAGE OF DOMESTIC CORPORATE PROFITS

	Earnings on Direct Foreign Investments*		Foreign Earnings as Percentage of Domestic Profits
	Million $	Index (1950 = 100)	
1950	1,892	100	9
1951	2,365	125	13
1952	2,457	130	15
1953	2,386	126	15
1954	2,534	134	16
1955	3,036	160	14
1956	3,527	186	16
1957	3,799	201	18
1958	3,260	172	19
1959	3,589	190	16
1960	3,969	210	19
1961	4,278	226	21
1962	4,815	254	20
1963	5,247	277	20
1964	5,827	308	19
1965	6,384	337	17
1966	6,732	356	16
1967	7,170	379	19
1968	8,268	437	22
1969	9,497	502	28

*Earnings category was obtained by adding (1) earnings of U.S. direct investment abroad, and (2) direct investment receipts of royalties and fees. Income from other (nondirect) private assets has not been included.

Sources:

Profits: 1950-1962: Survey of Current Business, September 1965, p. 53; 1962-1963: ibid., July 1966, p. 5; 1964: ibid., July 1968, p. 24; 1965-1966: ibid., July 1969, p. 22; 1967-1970: ibid., July 1971, p. 18.

Royalties and fees: ibid., June 1970, pp. 34-35.

Earnings of U.S. direct investments abroad: 1950-1959: Balance of Payments Statistical Supplement, rev. ed. (Washington, D.C.: U.S. Department of Commerce, Office of Business Economics, 1963), p. 184; 1960: Survey of Current Business, August 1962, pp. 22-23; 1961: ibid., August 1963, pp. 18-19; 1962: ibid., August 1964, pp. 10-11; 1963-1970: ibid., October 1971, pp. 28-29.

TABLE H

NET[*] ESTIMATED SIZE OF EUROCURRENCY MARKET

(IN BILLIONS OF DOLLARS)

	Eurodollar Market	All Eurocurrencies
1964	9.0	**
1965	11.5	**
1966	14.5	**
1967	17.5	**
1968	25.0	**
1969	37.5	44.0
1970	46.0	57.0
1971	54.0	71.0

[*]Net of interbank deposits within Europe. However, net includes banks' assets and liabilities vis-a-vis their own countries (foreign currency position vis-a-vis residents).

[**]Not estimated by B.I.S.

SOURCE: Bank for International Settlements

   1964-68 Eurodollar: Thirty-Ninth Annual Report (Basle 1969), p. 149;
   1969-70 Eurodollar: Forty-First Annual Report (Basle 1971), p. 164;
   1969-71 Eurocurrency: Forty-Second Annual Report (Basle 1972), p. 155;
   1971 Eurodollar: Forty-Second Annual Report (Basle 1972), p. 148.

TABLE I

INTERNATIONAL RESERVES

(BILLIONS OF DOLLARS, END OF YEAR)

	1945	1955	1965	1971
Gold	33.3	35.8	41.4	39.2
of which: U.S.[*]	(20.1)	(21.8)	(14.1)	(11.1)
Foreign Exchange	14.3	17.0	23.0	79.5
of which: U.S. $	(4.2)	(8.3)	(15.9)	(51.1)
Sterling	(10.1)	(7.6)	(6.7)	(7.8)
Gold Tranche position at the IMF	---	1.9	5.4	6.9
SDR's	---	---	---	6.4
Total	47.6	54.7	69.8	132.0
Addendum: World Exports	34.2	84.0	165.4	334.0[*]

[*]Estimated quarterly data expressed as annual rate.
Sources: For 1945, 1955, and 1965, Richard N. Cooper, The Economics of Interdependence (New York: Columbia University Press), 1968, p. 51; for 1971, International Financial Statistics (September 1972).

RICHARD ROSECRANCE, ALAN ALEXANDROFF,
WALLACE KOEHLER, JOHN KROLL,
SHLOMIT LACQUEUR, JOHN STOCKER

7
Whither
Interdependence?

This chapter deals with the concept of interdependence, which Rosecrance and his colleagues define as "the direct and positive linkage of the interests of states such that when the position of one state changes, the position of others is affected, and in the same direction." *After reviewing the conflicting literature, the authors apply this definition to six industrial countries for the period 1890–1975. Rosecrance and his coauthors find a significant degree of interdependence before World War I, followed by a marked decline during the interwar period. Although interdependence did increase after 1945, the record has been mixed since 1959. This cyclical history casts doubt on the contention that the post–World War II period has seen linear increases in interdependence.*

It is a commonplace that the structure of world economic interdependence has changed in the past decade. One can no longer argue that sovereignty is universally at bay, or that the nation-state is just about through as an economic unit.[1] Those who, in the late 1960s, prophesied that economic power, trade, and influence would become more important than military power and its surrogates are now baffled by events. Those who believed that world interdependence was accelerating have to admit that nation-states have gone to considerable lengths to reshape the economic, technological, and ecological forces acting upon them, seeking to reduce interdependence. It is no longer clear what kind of international economic order obtains, and where it is moving. The essay which follows is an attempt to narrow the range of these uncertainties

Reprinted by permission from *International Organization* 31:3 (Summer 1977), pp. 425–445. Copyright © 1977 by the Board of Regents of the University of Wisconsin System.

(though not finally to resolve them) by offering a new and more properly economic concept of interdependence and new data on interdependent relations among six industrial countries, 1890–1975.

INTRODUCTION

The term "interdependence" has so many and varied meanings that it is no longer fully clear what investigators intend to signify when they use the term. In a very loose and general sense, one can say that interdependence is a state of affairs where what one nation does impinges directly upon other nations.[2] In this most general use, higher foreign trade, the ability to threaten atomic war, the development of worldwide inflation or recession all mean higher interdependence among states. The more one nation has to take into account what other states might do in charting its own international and domestic policy, the higher the interdependence. This use of the term, however, is quite unsatisfactory for analytic purposes. On this definition, knowing that there is high interdependence tells one very little about the actual state of relations between nations. The highest interdependence, one surmises, would actually be attained by opponents in war. Then any improvement in one state's position would directly and adversely affect the other. Their fates would be completely joined. Fully conflictual, as well as fully cooperative, relations among states would be characterized by high interdependence.

Most students, of course, have wished to use interdependence in a positive sense to see higher interdependence as a fundamental force for better relations among nations.[3] If interdependent relations are to be interpreted in this positive way, the loose and general notion of interdependence must yield to more precisely and narrowly defined concepts. In this paper, by "interdependence" we mean the direct and positive linkage of the interests of states such that when the position of one state changes, the position of others is affected, *and in the same direction.*[4] Interdependence, then, suggests a system in which states tend to go up or down the ladder of international position (economic strength, power, welfare, access to information and/or technology) together. Of course, some relationships which would be deemed "interdependent" on previous notions, would no longer be "interdependent" on the revised definition. But this more specific, narrower definition is more useful in understanding world politics for it means that wherever interdependence is high, there should be high cooperation.

The measures of interdependence have made definitions even less clear by blurring such distinctions. Up to now economic interdependence among industrial countries has largely been gauged by horizontal flows: transactions, trade, and other financial movements.[5] The greater the magnitude of trade, investment, or other transactions (absolutely or in comparison to the domestic sector) the greater the presumed interdependence. But, as we have seen above, a greater "connectedness" in international politics does not necessarily mean higher interdependence.[6] Whether it does or not depends upon how nations react to the increasing international sector. Some states may develop common policies while others fashion opposed policies. Some nations may try to reduce the domestic impact of international economic forces; others may shape policies to conform with their impact.[7] Such horizontal transactions, even if very large, tell us little about the responses of particular nations. It is possible, fortunately, to follow this pattern of action and reaction by examining factor prices of the two economies. In formal economic terms two economies can be considered integrated (very highly interdependent) when there is an equalization of factor prices between them.[8] Under such conditions any increase of consumer price, interest rate, or factor cost would be expected to stimulate flows of the more highly valued commodity, capital, or labor from one market to the other, producing a re-equalization of factor prices. An increase of such prices in Country A would bring a new supply of goods, capital, and labor from Country B, having the effect of raising prices in B and lowering them in A. Just as an increase in A will lead to an increase in B, a decrease in A will lead to a decrease in B and vice versa. Even within a single economy, of course, factor prices are not always equalized across all regions. There are limits to the mobility of factors of production, and wage labor is particularly immobile. Between two separate national economies, then, one should not expect a complete equalization of factor prices. It should be anticipated, however, that between highly interdependent economies factor prices would move in the same direction. The greater the simultaneity and similarity in their movements, the more the economies are identically responding to the movement of factors between them, and the higher the interdependence. At least two measures of such "vertical" (as opposed to horizontal) interdependence are obvious: (1) a correlation of the movement of factor price indices between the two societies; and (2) a correlation of the changes in such movements. The first gives the central tendency or trend, the second the fluctuation around it.[9]

These measures, charting the actual economic responses of one society to another, are considerably more sensitive indicators of interdependence than the size of the international sector. If governments allow international economic forces to impinge on their economies without compensatory action, these policies will be clear in factor price trends. If, on the other hand, governments seek to influence or reshape these forces, through high interest rates, contractionist fiscal policies, and other measures, different national policies will show up in different price trends. These responses reveal interdependence much more directly than notions of "vulnerability" or "invulnerability."[10] If governments are relatively invulnerable to interdependent effects but take no action to insulate themselves from foreign price movements, they are behaving as if they were vulnerable and interdependent. If governments are relatively vulnerable, but make major efforts in political and economic policy to reduce their vulnerability and to reshape the impact of external forces, they are to that degree less interdependent and less vulnerable. What is important in international politics is what nations perceive and what they do; not what they might do if they perceived things differently.

TWO CONCEPTS OF INTERDEPENDENCE

There are thus two different concepts and two sets of measures of interdependence. The size of the transactions between two societies is *horizontal* interdependence. It charts the flow of money, men, goods, and so on. (But even here, of course, horizontal interdependence is only interdependence in the *first* sense, defined above; it implies only "connectedness.") *Vertical* interdependence, in contrast, shows the economic response of one economy to another, in terms of changes in factor prices. It is possible to imagine conditions where there might be high horizontal interdependence (a large international sector, growing amounts of trade either absolutely or in relation to GNP) and yet low vertical interdependence. Nations might respond differently to the commercial intercourse between them; factor prices might proceed in different directions; government policy might be inflationary in one case and deflationary in another. In the net there is an amalgam of influences: high horizontal flows tending to produce an equalization of prices; different governmental policies producing divergent prices. Thus, high horizontal interdependence could be consistent with either high or low vertical interdependence. On the other hand high horizontal interdependence is the necessary (but not sufficient) condition of high vertical interdependence. High factor price correlations without a substantial flow of goods, services, capital, and other factors of production between societies could hardly be taken to indicate true interdependence. In the absence of such horizontal flows, parallel changes in factor prices might simply be the result of worldwide economic forces impinging upon economies in similar fashion or of parallel, but independent, policies. Where horizontal flows are high, however, this cannot be the case. The flows themselves are both cause and result of factor price changes.

APPROACHES TO INTERDEPENDENCE

There are at least four different orientations ("schools" is too strong a word) toward contemporary economic interdependence. One, initiated by Deutsch and Eckstein, sees interdependence secularly declining with industrialization.[11] From this standpoint interdependence may have been at a peak in 1913, but has certainly decreased since. A second view, which relates interdependence to the absolute size of the foreign sector, sees interdependence among developed societies increasing more or less continuously since 1945.[12] This view has also been associated with the idea that political modernization forces national governments to recognize and take due account of international economic forces as they impinge upon the domestic electorate. Even if the size of the foreign sector was not continually increasing, there would still be high interdependence because the political significance of world economic trends would be high or growing. Thirdly, there is the view that interdependence is fundamentally a product of an existing political-military regime in world politics. Economic interdependence tends to be high under the aegis of a *Pax Britannica* or *Pax Americana* but to decline when these regimes are challenged or overthrown. Thus, in this view, interdependence among industrial countries was high until shortly before World War I, and was briefly high again after 1945. After some point in the 1960s, however, it has declined with the erosion of the American dominance of world politics.[13]

A potential fourth approach to such relationships would see interdependence increasing with the size of the foreign sector until a point is reached where governments act to reduce its actual or potential impact upon domestic politics. This would represent a second stage in the politicization of economic activity. In most countries, such politicization occurred after World War I and was further increased by the impact of the Depression and World War II. Full employment acts, Beveridge plans, and commitments to domestic growth and welfare abounded after 1945. This did not mean, however, that in any given choice between maintenance of domestic expansion and the preservation of international trade the first would always win out. Bretton Woods, reflecting on the disastrous "beggar thy neighbor" system of the 1930s, instituted new measures of domestic restraint and discipline designed to protect and nourish the international economy. Nations were not supposed to devalue their currencies except in cases of "fundamental disequilibrium." Exchange controls were to be gradually dismantled. Under GATT qualitative and quantitative restrictions on trade were discouraged. The typical means of overcoming a short-term payments crisis was through provision of liquidity. The general assumption of the post–World War II economic era was that nations would continue to exercise the domestic discipline necessary to keep their international positions in equilibrium. Certainly it was not assumed that a nation would simply tailor its international economic policies to protect a domestic "hothouse" environment.

A second stage in the politicization of international interdependence would be reached, then, if nations decided to seek actively to reduce their dependence upon each other or to limit the impact of international forces in order to safeguard or insulate their domestic economies. Even more precisely, a new stage would be attained if nations found means of gradually detaching their domestic economies from foreign pressures without great and obvious harm to the international economic system. Such a change might come if governments decided not to impose cuts in wages or employment in order to meet international obligations. This fourth approach to interdependence would not depend upon a particular pattern of political-military relationships in world politics, but would result from a keener awareness of the limitations placed by domestic economic and political forces upon a nation's participation in an interdependent world.

Each of these approaches has much to commend it in historical and theoretical terms. Nonetheless, since the contentions are partly contradictory, they cannot all be true. According to the first, one would expect to find high vertical and horizontal interdependence before 1913, but a major decline thereafter. The second approach would see a marked increase of interdependence since 1945, proceeding more or less linearly to the present. The third would see high interdependence in the 1890s when the British had hegemony in world politics, and high interdependence again between 1945–1960 when America was dominant. The other periods, however, should be characterized by low or declining interdependence. The fourth approach, largely focused on the contemporary era, would see increases from 1945 to 1960 and a stabilization or decline since.

THE VALIDATION OF POSITIVE INTERDEPENDENCE: THE UNITED STATES' CASE[14]

Is there such a thing as positive interdependence among separate economic and social units? Or do economic societies advance at the expense of one another, with constant or zero-sum relationships among contending participants? Traditional theories of international trade, beginning with Adam Smith and David Ricardo, have contended that all nations can benefit from trade and exchange. If positive interdependence exists, it should first be discerned among the constituent markets of a major nation-state.[15] Since no one would question that the level of integration and interdependence is very high in such a case, the measures of positive interdependence should surely underscore the point. A brief excursion into economic links between separate regional markets in the United States affords a test case for the measures of positive interdependence. If there is no relationship among factor prices in the American case, they can have no validity for relations among nations. If both measures of vertical interdependence are extremely high and stable, on the other hand, a standard of positive interdependence is set to which cases involving individual nation-states can be compared. A brief study of the United States' example is more relevant in that, unlike the economy of Luxembourg or Belgium, there is more than one market and more than one major city. Indeed, the very geographic extent and climatological variation in the United States might be expected to produce some of the same differences among regional markets that are attained between national markets on the continent. The American data, therefore, take on unusual importance.

Interestingly, but not surprisingly, the results in Appendix Tables 1–4 indicate that both relative and absolute measures of vertical interdependence capture the underlying interdependence and integration of US markets. This is especially true of consumer prices where price indices and also changes in such indices are highly correlated. If any result stands out, it is that American markets have become even more integrally related since 1941. Wage and manufacturing data are less related, but even here most relationships are strong. Traditionally, of course, one would expect wages to be less interdependent than say, prices or interest rates, because of labor immobility. The somewhat lower correlations of manufacturing prices may be due to inclusion of different commodities in the bundle of manufactured goods in different markets.

A number of features of the US data should be underscored. First, vertical measures of interdependence appear clearly to have captured the high integration of US regional markets. Both correlation of price indices and correlation of changes in such indices are high. The massive flows of goods, persons, capital, and other factors of production between regional markets does in fact produce significant and positive relationships between factor prices. If such correlations could be observed among national markets at the international level, one could justly claim that they were highly interdependent. Second, the high correlation of factor prices is not found only among indices, but also among change in such indices. This suggests that not only are the general trends moving in the same direction, but also that individual and detailed changes in factor price in one market will bring similar changes in another. Finally, the high economic integration of US regional markets has great political significance. There could be no major economic change in different sections of the country without important political repercussions. This means that interdependence and politicization can occur simultaneously, at least where there is a single decision-making center.

INTERDEPENDENCE BEFORE WORLD WAR I

An intriguing question is whether the high interdependence of markets attained domestically in the United States can ever be approximated internationally. Prima facie one might assume that the coherence of the US national economy depends upon the centralization that is achieved only within the nation-state; between states, therefore, interdependence must perforce be much lower. But any such conclusion is clearly premature. The pre–World War I system demonstrated high interdependence among separate national markets even though these were not held together by a political bond. Many studies have attested to the high horizontal flows of capital and goods between countries.[16] International trade was in general a higher proportion of national income than it is today. Direct and indirect investment was a much larger fraction of Gross National Product than is now the case. The City of London was dominant in the international market, producing a greater financial integration among nations than has been achieved since. Most of the six countries did large shares of their trade with each other, an amount ranging from 30 percent in the case of Germany to 90 percent in the Canadian case. Further, since 1913, only the United States and Germany have reattained the percentile levels of trade reached before World War I with their industrial partners. Wholesale price indicators evince high correlations of both absolute trends and changes in such trends. Consumer prices display a weaker association and are available only for four countries. French prices react differently from the other three, and the strongest relationship appears to be that between the United States and the United Kingdom. (See Appendix Tables 5–6.)

Interest rates indicate a strong interdependence of the European members of our set of six industrial countries. Data gathered include not only a measure of association among indices (the Pearson r) but also a convergence measure used by Hawkins in his study of interest rates within the EEC.[17] The latter is the absolute value of the sum of differences in rates between two countries, divided by the total number of dyads for the period. The lower the convergence statistic, the greater the degree of equalization among rates. Such high convergence is amply demonstrated in the scores for France, Germany, and Britain; even more precisely, one finds high convergences of French and German rates with British. The Canadian financial market is very closely tied to Britain's and thus is also associated with trends in the other European countries.

Correlation measures point to similar interdependencies. The intra-European relationship is very strong, although the US connection with Britain is also marked. It appears, not surprisingly, that London is the link between continental and North American markets. (See Appendix Tables 7-8.) To test for changes in interdependence within the period we have also divided the data into two parts: 1890-1900 and 1901-13. The results (in Appendix Tables 9-10) show no obvious decline in interdependence as World War I approaches. The correlations of absolute indices increase as one moves toward 1913; but the correlations of changes decline.

The pre-World War I international system was highly interdependent in a number of respects. Horizontal flows among states were large; one economy responded very quickly to price changes in another. Wholesale price levels are closely associated. Not only are absolute correlations high; there also is a strong relationship among price changes. In 1913 the United States was being drawn into an association with European countries, and a core of European financial strength was in process of consolidation. The percentage of significant correlations among factor prices and price changes does not approach the very high figures attained in the domestic American case, and one does not want to claim that the same form of structural interdependence has been attained. Strictly speaking, if full interdependence with all states moving in the same direction is achieved, that relationship should become permanent and stable. No state should have an incentive to better its position in respect to any other state. In the real world this ideal interdependence has not yet been approximated. While short of this standard, it remains noteworthy that in 1890-1914 wholesale price relationships among the European three and between the three and the United States are both strong and significant.

There was only limited politicization of economic ties among nations, however, and economic interdependence did not constrain nations from going to war in 1914. The political significance and relevance of economic relationships was not yet fully established. The data from 1890-1914 accord broadly with the Deutsch-Eckstein approach to interdependence, apparently supporting the notion that interdependence would reach a peak relatively early in the process of economic development and fall as nations were able to replace imports with products of their own manufacture. A problem with this approach, however, is that interdependence remains very high as late as 1913, well after the first phase of industrialization in Britain and France. Interdependence also remains high at a stage when British power has declined in relation to Germany and the United States. The *Pax Britannica* is over; yet the halcyon afterglow continues.

INTERDEPENDENCE IN THE INTERWAR PERIOD

The relatively high interdependence attained in 1913 was shattered by the Great War. In order to finance arms programs, economic ministries sold their foreign assets, indulged in wholesale borrowing and in the printing of money. The ensuing inflation caused a dramatic depreciation of currencies against gold. While the international financial mechanism was partly reestablished after the war, Britain no longer had the resources and reserves to be lender to the system. The United States might have filled the gap, but was disinclined to do so.[18] In part this was because the United States wanted its war debts repaid, and did not extend credit to the degree necessary. Ultimately, no single international financial center emerged, and nations held their reserves in Paris and New York as well as London.

The financial rivalry between Paris and London was reinforced by different policies toward Germany. The French, determined that Berlin should pay for the war, demanded immediate fulfillment of reparations obligations. The British and to some degree the Americans recognized that Germany could not pay without being able to borrow and lent considerable sums. But the central core of the international economy—the links between Britain, France, and Germany—was broken by the war. The magnetic power of the continent, drawing the United States and Japan into an essentially Europe-centered system, greatly lessened. America became a mighty financial and trading power in its own right and moved to an independent position.

A second major consequence of the war was the politicization of economic activity. No longer could governments stand aside as international economic forces determined domestic economic welfare. This change had two effects: first, it greatly raised the significance of the external economic sector; second, it spurred finance ministries to find new means of controlling that sector. The first greatly furthered international interdependence by increasing the political saliency and relevance of economic relationships. The second, however, represented a net reduction of interdependence because it meant reshaping international relationships according to national criteria.

Three different phases of the interwar period must be distinguished. In the first, from 1920–29, the German inflation stemming from the war and from the French occupation of the Ruhr, cut the ties with other European economies. Exchange rate manipulations began. Trade fell off both absolutely and relatively. Insecure governments sought to protect themselves against foreign financial and trading competition. France and Germany engaged in economic warfare, while neither power moved in step with its erstwhile British and American colleagues. Both wholesale and consumer price indicators fluctuated irregularly, often in opposed directions as the correlations in Appendix Tables 12–13 demonstrate. Interest rates moved apart, with France closer to the American than to the British market. (See Tables 14–15.)

In the second period, 1930–32, the financial crisis and the onset of the Depression produced a momentary galvanic response that sent all economies in the same direction. The correlations of wholesale and consumer prices returned briefly to high levels, though the relationship of the European three to the United States was stronger than their relationship to each other. The US-Canadian tie was still the primary interdependent bond in world politics. (See Appendix Tables 16–17.) Despite the Franco-German divergence, interest rates began to move in tandem. These short-term links did not inaugurate a new era of economic harmony; they were but the prelude to autarchy and conflict. After 1932 governments sought to insulate their economies from the impact of worldwide Depression, and the resulting patchwork of national policies undermined the structure of homogeneity and interdependence. Between 1933–39 the spurious unanimity of the 1930–32 economic crisis gradually dissolved. The number of significant price correlations fell from 80 percent in the crisis period to 36 percent by 1939. The same change occurred in interest rates. In 1930–32, 30 percent of the correlations were significant. By 1939 the figure had fallen to 14 percent. (See Tables 17–19.)

As vertical interdependence (as measured by the relationship of factor prices) declined, so also did the horizontal flows and investment. Between 1921 and 1938 total world investment decreased by 168 percent.[19] In the decade before 1938 world trade fell by 55 percent.[20] This absolute decrease paralleled a decline in the proportion of its trade that each one of the six countries did with the others. (See Table 11.) Seeking new trading partners, each country did about 10 percent less of its trade with the five others in 1938 than it did in 1913. Perhaps most significant was the breakdown in intra-European trade. By 1938 France, Britain, and Germany were doing about half the percentage trade with each other that they had done in 1913.

The interwar system of international relations thus marks the breakup of the core of interdependence: the European relationship. There is a high politicization of economic activity, but this does not forward interdependence. Horizontal flows of factors of production have greatly declined. The correlation of factor prices has diminished and that of factor price changes is virtually nonexistent. The only period of prima facie interdependence, between 1930–32, is in fact the result of the immediate impact of the financial crisis and Depression. As states fashion individual policies to cope with the economic downturn, they move further and further apart. By 1939 the patterns of economic interdependence mirror the political conflicts that are about to cause World War II.

The decline of interdependence between 1913 and 1939 accords broadly with the Deutsch-Eckstein thesis that the external sector becomes less significant as nations industrialize, though the special circumstances of worldwide depression may offer a spurious confirmation of their findings. One caveat in this conclusion, however, is that if the decline should be greatest immediately after the completion of the first phase of industrialization, one should expect the largest decreases in interdependent relationships to be found in the cases of Germany and Japan. No special circumstances of this sort, however, appear to obtain. The second approach which sees interdependence growing or decreasing with the size of the international sector would of course anticipate a marked decline in interdependence during the thirties; and it certainly occurs. The third argument also holds in this period: there is no political hegemony in world politics, and economic relationships begin to fall apart.

INTERDEPENDENCE AFTER THE SECOND WORLD WAR

The received wisdom of many students and practitioners is that 1945 ushered in a new era of world interdependence.[21] Even if relations with the Soviet bloc and the developing countries were not immediately transformed, the inexorable processes of economic development and transnational communications fashioned a world in which the major democratic and Western industrial nations were clearly interdependent. The size of the international sector grew enormously: trade, investment, and technological advance altogether outstripped their prewar equivalents. Domestic economies became more "sensitive" to international forces. In a number of areas of production, national economies became more dependent upon products from a few suppliers and hence more vulnerable to any interruption in their supply.[22] If anything, the political centrality of economic policy increased and domestic electorates were taught that their economic welfare was partly dependent upon decisions taken in other states. For perhaps the first time, investment of Western developed states seemed to concentrate in each other, increasing their mutual stake in trade and domestic growth.[23]

Trade charted a similar course. While foreign trade as a whole increased by a factor of five since 1945, the percentage trade of the six countries with each other also rose. The most significant increase, somewhat surprisingly, was that for the United States. The US did 33 percent of its trade with the five other countries in 1950, but by 1972 this figure rose to 56.4 percent, exceeding the percentage in 1913. In the case of Britain, France, and Germany marked increases also occurred. (See Appendix Table 20.)

But the question has remained: if worldwide trade and investment flows are increasing, if national economies are more sensitive to one another, and if governments cannot insulate their populations from the impact of the external sector – do these features alone assure high vertical interdependence? The answer to this question is not yet entirely clear, but preliminary data indicate that economies have not uniformly responded to these flows in a fully interdependent manner over the thirty-year period. Indeed, it is impossible to talk of the magnitude or type of interdependence without distinguishing between at least four time periods: 1950–58; 1959–72; 1973–74 (the energy crisis); and 1975 (the post-crisis period).

1. 1950–58

The first period, 1950–58, is marked by a general restoration of international trade under the leadership of the United States. Factor prices and factor price changes mark a new stability in relationships among economies. These do not quite attain the strength of the patterns before 1914, but they are still very significant. The percentage of significant correlations among wholesale prices and price change rises to 73.3 and 46.6 percent respectively. The figures for consumer prices are 80 and 26.6 percent. The homogeneity and stability of interdependence can be seen in the almost complete absence of negative signs. (See Tables 21 and 22.) Trade and factor prices, however, seem to attain normal relationships before interest rates. Partly because of convertibility and other problems, the international financial system remains somewhat disconnected in this period. (See Tables 23 and 24.) The relatively strong financial interdependence of the United States, the United Kingdom, and France does not extend to Japan and Germany. Japanese rates in particular seem to be following an independent path. Wage rate correlations clearly show that the French labor market is distinct from that of other industrial countries. (See Table 25.)

2. 1959–72

The period of the sixties is decisive for many theories of interdependence. Those who argue that interdependence is increasing secularly with the size of the international sector and industrial and political modernization see the 1960s as a period in which the force of economic interdependence tends to overwhelm parochial nationalism.[24] The sixties display the maximum thrust of American foreign investment, and represent the heyday of the multinational corporation. On the other hand, those who believe that high interdependence is linked to a given pattern of political dominance in world politics would expect to see interdependence diminish at the end of the sixties as the American influence declines. Those who are convinced that interdependence declines with industrialization and economic development would also expect a marked decrease in the 1959–72 period. They might have expected that the fifties could show an increase of interdependence as the artificial restraints and blockages occasioned by the Depression and World War II were overcome. But the sixties should, from this point of view at least, demonstrate a renewed decline in interdependence.

The sixties are also critical to the fourth approach to international interdependence. This approach, stressing a renewed politicization of international economic forces, would expect to see a loosening of interdependent ties among nations. This argument would stress the beginning in the early sixties of a greater national willingness to use inflation as a means of escaping the domestic discipline otherwise required to maintain equilibrium in the balance of payments. Instead of taking the domestic contractionist measures to produce a balance of imports and exports, nations regain a formal equilibrium by either exporting their currencies (in the case of the United States) or engaging in devaluation (Britain, France, and other countries). In the US case the demand that nations hold excess dollars in payment for US obligations contributed to the informal dollar glut which eventually forced a formal devaluation in 1971–73. In the case of most other countries, the lack of wage restraint and the political need to maintain full employment eventually required devaluation. But devaluation in its turn brought inflation, and an increase of export prices which could only be remedied by further devaluation. The alternative course – price and wage restraint – appeared to be politically impossible. In the United States, these tendencies were obvious as early as the Kennedy Administration. In Britain they attained dominance between 1964–67, and in France at least by 1968.

We therefore have conflicting theoretical expectations for the sixties: some posit new peaks of interdependence; others a slackening or decline of interdependence. Viewed from these standpoints the data on factor price relationships are remarkably tantalizing, for what we find (in Tables 26 and 27) is a very substantial increase in the relationship among consumer price indices, and a very considerable fall in the relationship among changes in wholesale prices. The consumer price correlations are 100 percent significant. The wholesale price correlations are stronger, if no more significant than those of the previous period. These tendencies would seem to indicate greater interdependence. Economies now seem to be moving generally in the same direction.

As we look at the changes in prices, however, the precise association of the 1950–58 period disappears. The significance of the correlation of price changes either remains the same or falls precipitously. Whereas

46.6 percent of wholesale price change correlations were significant in 1950-58, *none* is significant in the period 1959-72. At the very minimum this would appear to suggest that while in terms of general economic trends the six industrial countries are moving in the same direction, the specific economic policies employed to reach the general goal have become different for different countries.[25] One begins to see the intervention of domestic economic authorities in the international process. The automaticity of the international economic mechanism declines and even partly disappears.

The range or amplitude of international economic change has greatly increased. The pattern of the sixties seems to indicate that price trends can go in one direction, while price changes can go in another. Individual responses to interdependence become less predictable. These ambivalences occur at a time when there is a short period of harmony in international financial markets. Tables 28 and 29 show that during 1959-72 Germany responded to capital flows in much the same way as other members of the international financial system. Only Japan followed an individual course. Tables 30 and 31 which examine the last part of the period in greater detail (1965-72) demonstrate, however, that Japan eventually rejoined the system. By 1965 her financial policies corresponded closely with those of other industrial states. The same period finds the reconsolidation of the European labor market, with very high correlations among wage rates and changes among the European three. (See Table 36.) Canada and the United States seem closely associated with this pattern. Again, only Japan followed a different path.

The sixties therefore can be all things to all men. Individual tendencies both confirm and deny the existence of greater interdependence. The detachment or partial decoupling of individual factor price reactions from general factor price trends, however, would appear to give greatest support to those who see a gradual shift in favor of individual national policies within a context of broad interdependence. This conclusion would seem most congenial to those who underscore the gradual loosening of the American hegemonic grip or who believe that domestic imperatives are gradually gaining ascendancy over international imperatives in the formulation of national economic policy.

3. 1973-74

The ambivalence of the 1959-72 data makes a study of subsequent periods even more important. Perhaps some of the ambiguities of the sixties can be resolved by later information. But the next period, 1973-74, also coincides with the oil crisis. On the basis of the data on 1930-32, one would expect that a major shock to the system would find economies reacting almost in unison. Thus 1973-74 should produce high correlations of factor prices and price changes, temporarily obliterating the effects of separate national policies. This is precisely what happens. As Tables 26 and 27 show, consumer prices remain almost perfectly correlated, and (in contrast to 1959–72) the correlation of wholesale prices and wholesale price changes rises very significantly. The percentages of significant correlations equal or exceed even that of 1950–58. If the oil crisis effects were permanent, one might be tempted to say that a stage of new and higher economic interdependence had been attained among industrial countries.

Unfortunately, however, its effects do not last. Even the interest rate data show how rapidly separate national economic policies can assert themselves. While initially all countries raise their rates, Germany (the strongest nation financially) can afford to reduce them rapidly. Thus for most of the period German rates appear inversely correlated with those of other industrial countries. (See Tables 32–33.) One anticipates, moreover, that these financial divergencies will later manifest themselves in equally contradictory price trends.

4. 1975

This expectation is amply borne out for 1975. While consumer price and price change correlations are even more uniformly significant, the association among wholesale prices is almost completely shattered. Only 20 percent of wholesale price relationships attain significance, the lowest level since 1929. (See Table 27.) Not only Germany but also France have embarked on divergent economic policies. In finance Canada and Britain are unique in stressing high or increasing rates, manifesting trends contrary to those of the other members of the system. (See Tables 34–35.) Relationships among European nations are less close than they were, and the United States no longer cements the system together. The US-Canadian tie in wholesale price relationships is still very strong, with the United Kingdom drawn in via the American market. The system, however, is very mixed with Japan associating with the US, Britain, and Canada in price relationships and with Germany and France in interest rates. But no pattern obtains throughout the data. The harmony of the Franco-German financial market is marred by entirely different wholesale price structures and movements. Most noticeable of all, perhaps, is the decline in the central role of the American capital market. In all previous periods the United States leads other countries in the number of high and positive correlations with other markets. In 1975, however, Germany, Japan, and France produce the strong relationships, and the US is relegated to a peripheral role.

The ambivalence of 1975 is if anything greater than that of 1959–72. The difference between consumer and wholesale price patterns is more marked. In the former period wholesale and consumer price trends were closely linked; the divergence occurred in price changes. In 1975 the price trends themselves diverge. This pattern, of course, cannot continue indefinitely. Wholesale price changes eventually reflect themselves in retail or consumer prices, though with a lag. It seems likely that subsequent data will show a similar change in consumer price trends. If so, it would represent a gradual attenuation of factor price links between industrial countries, and to that degree a decline in economic interdependence. The temporary peaks in association of 1950–58 and (briefly) 1973–74 would then have given way to independent national policies.

CONCLUSIONS AND IMPLICATIONS

A number of conclusions seem warranted from this investigation of interdependence among developed nations. First, factor price relationships do appear to be a sensitive indicator of the degree of interdependence among markets as defined for the purpose of this article. This is evidenced clearly in extremely strong relationships between regional markets in the United States. But it is also shown by the high but less uniform correlations attained before 1914, and the collapse of those relationships by 1939. If the conventional wisdom is correct in concluding that interdependence was high in the 1950s, our measures appear to be valid in pointing to similar conclusions. It thus seems important to claim that such vertical data must accompany horizontal data if we are to ascertain the presence of "positive" interdependence (as opposed to mere "connectedness") among nations.

Second, the pattern of contemporary interdependence is much more mixed than many have believed. The amplitude of economic change has increased, and the response of one economy to another has become more unpredictable. Relationships no longer appear to be stable across time. Interdependence may be becoming unstable.

Third, the four theories of interdependence do not fare equally well in the period 1890–1975. Least supported by our data are those which prescribe either secular increases or declines in interdependence. There is little evidence that interdependence has decreased steadily since 1890–1913. Interdependence in 1950–58 is far higher than that in the twenties or thirties, rivaling even the pre–World War I era. On the other hand, the steady increases in interdependence predicted for the post-1945 period also have not emerged. The 1950s represented a temporary plateau of interdependence, but the experience since has been very uneven. The theory that links interdependence with patterns of hegemony in world politics is partly confirmed by our data in that the highest points of interdependence are reached prior to 1914 and again in the 1950s. The first can be roughly identified with British preeminence, the second with American primacy. In neither case, however, is the relationship exact. Interdependence does not fall off between 1900–14 despite the relative decline in British power. The interdependence of factor price indices (as opposed to factor price changes) remains high in the 1960s even though American influence is declining.[26] The fourth theory, involving a re-politicization of international economic policies after 1960, seems to receive the greatest support from factor price data.

Fourth, data from recent years indicate a gradual and progressive detachment of individual national policies from the general trend toward interdependence. This detachment, if very recent data are to be credited, may even have an effect in altering that trend, reducing the positive and direct relationship among industrial economies. Over time this might or might not reduce general world interdependence. We have seen numerous cases in international relations where consciousness of declining solidarity has been a stimulus to new measures of political and institutional cooperation and interdependence. Setbacks in European integration sometimes bring a *relancement*. It is also possible that the decline in the relationship among industrial countries may reflect a more intimate relationship of these economies with outside states – the oil producers, the developing world, or the Communist nations. In this case a decline in specifically industrial interdependence might assist a broader world interdependence. At the moment, however, one of the unique characteristics of the post–World War II era, the increasing dependence of industrial countries upon each other, seems to have been overborne.

At the very least this casts doubt upon theories of continuing linear increases in interdependence in the post–World War II period. Interdependence appears to have cycled up and down, and to have varied in qualitative aspects. Economic changes have been abrupt and discontinuous, and international relationships have been subject to sudden reversals. Such transformations have occurred when the American hand was weakening on the tiller of world politics, but it is difficult to explain them entirely on this basis. In certain aspects the result is due not only to American weakness, but to the weakness of several industrial countries under pressure from the domestic electorate. Even the movement to flexible exchange rates internationally conforms with this trend: it makes it easier for governments to avoid domestic economic discipline. Balance of payments equilibrium can be found through exchange rate adjustments without a major effort to control prices or wages.

The net result, of course, is international inflation. There is a continuing debate about the seriousness of the problem: whether employment and growth can be stimulated without concern for inflation; or whether inflation (if unchecked) must inevitably set limits upon growth.[27] If a boom with inflation ultimately forces monetary authorities to intervene or causes consumers to stop buying it may be that sustained growth depends upon some control of increases in prices and wages. But this in turn requires political authorities to undertake the unpleasant tasks that they have sought to avoid in the past ten years. If inflation could be restrained in industrial societies, interdependence would almost certainly rise. For what we have seen in the past decade has been differential responses to inflation in one country after another, leading to separate domestic and international economic policies.

It is much too early to say whether such control is possible. Political factors will affect the outcome as much as economic ones. Indeed, political patterns of intervention in the economic process have had a crucial effect on interdependence over the years. One of the reasons for high interdependence among economies before 1914 was the general disinclination to intervene in the relatively free play of the international financial system. Tariffs existed of course. But within very general limits, the flow of goods, persons, and capital was permitted to influence a nation's domestic price levels and employment. Interdependence before 1914 was the interdependence of states largely open to international economic influences. After 1950, in contrast, interdependence occurred partly because national economic planners reacted more or less in unison to international economic forces. Concerted political action under American leadership kept developed economies in line and in touch with one another. Since 1960, however, there has been no automatic and uniform registration of the effects of international flows. The advantages deriving from nineteeth century openness no longer obtain. At the same time, the advantages that might be gained from international coordination and central regulation have not been seized upon. There seems to have been a loosening of the linkage between domestic and international economic policy since the 1950s. The episodic attempts at a reintegration have largely failed. Kingston and the various economic summits have merely transformed the de facto into the de jure. One legitimizes what is already occurring rather than planning a new, cooperative system. Above all, one avoids centralized authority.

The future of interdependence among industrial countries, then, lies open. It is likely to be determined by the structure of political cooperation among states. At the moment, political responses to declining economic interdependence seem inadequate to provide the greater coordination that is manifestly needed. But there is nothing inevitable about this. Nations, facing great problems, have concerted solutions before, and they can do it again.

NOTES

1. The original contentions were those of Raymond Vernon and Charles Kindleberger. For a revised view see C. Fred Bergsten, "Economic Tensions:

America v. the Third World" in R. Rosecrance, ed., *America as an Ordinary Country: U.S. Foreign Policy and the Future* (Ithaca: Cornell University Press, 1976) and the same author, "Let's Avoid a Trade War," *Foreign Policy* 23 (Summer 1976), pp. 24–31.

2. See the definition offered by Edward Morse in "Transnational Economic Processes" in R. Keohane and J. Nye, Jr., *Transnationalism in World Politics* (Cambridge: Harvard University Press, 1972).

3. This is not true of Kenneth Waltz. See his "The Myth of Interdependence" in C. Kindleberger, ed., *The International Corporation* (Cambridge: M.I.T. Press, 1970).

4. It is striking that the literature has made little or no mention of the difference between situations in which interdependence means movement in the same direction and when it means movement in opposed directions. If complete interdependence in the former sense were achieved, nations would have no incentive to seek advantage at the expense of each other.

5. For a summary of argument and current horizontal data see Peter Katzenstein, "International Interdependence: Some Long-Term Trends and Recent Changes," *International Organization* 29 (Autumn 1975), pp. 1024–34.

6. See Alex Inkeles, "The Emerging Social Structure of the World," *World Politics* 27 (July 1975), pp. 477–86.

7. E. Haas argues that this is what, by and large, the United States has done. See his *Tangle of Hopes* (Englewood Cliffs: Prentice-Hall, 1969), pp. 130–31. His argument, however, was completed before the dynamic actions of the United States in August 1971.

8. See particularly R. Tollison and T. Willett, "International Integration and the Interdependence of Economic Variables," *International Organization* (Spring 1973), Richard N. Cooper, *The Economics of Interdependence* (New York: Columbia University Press, 1968), chapter 1, and Bela Balassa, *The Theory of Economic Integration* (Homewood: R. D. Irwin, 1961), passim.

9. The former defines the long-term or secular trend in vertical data while the latter affords a measure of the cyclical or short-term variation. High interdependence should be reflected in high correlations on both measures.

10. Waltz argues that interdependence only exists if nations are vulnerable to any interruption in relations. The interdependent relation is one that is costly to break.

11. The key work here is K. Deutsch and A. Eckstein, "National Industrialization and the Declining Share of the International Economic Sector: 1850–1959," *World Politics* 13 (January 1961), pp. 267–99.

12. Both Morse and Cooper, cited above, incline to this view.

13. This thesis was offered particularly by Robert Gilpin in "The Politics of Transnational Economic Relations" in Keohane and Nye. It has been subjected to partial test in S. Krasner, "State Power and the Structure of International Trade," *World Politics* 28 (April 1976), pp. 314–47.

14. In what follows we first investigate the degree of interdependence of US regional markets and then compare that with interdependence between national markets. For an analogous treatment of domestic and international data see K. W. Deutsch, "Shifts in the Balance of Communication Flows: A Problem of Measurement in International Relations," *Public Opinion Quarterly* 20 (1956), pp. 143–60.

15. For an essential comparison between international and interregional effects see B. Ohlin, *Interregional and International Trade* (Cambridge: Harvard University Press, 1967).

16. See particularly Deutsch and Eckstein, and Waltz. S. Kuznets in *Modern Economic Growth* (New Haven: Yale University Press, 1966) argues that small economies are more dependent upon foreign trade than large. The growth of trade among such economies in the nineteenth century was truly striking. (See pp. 302–10.)

17. See Robert G. Hawkins, "Intra-EEC Capital Movements and Domestic Financial Markets," National Bureau of Economic Research, Conference Series No. 24, *International Mobility and Movement of Capital* (New York: National Bureau of Economic Research, 1972), pp. 51–77.

18. See Leland B. Yeager, *International Monetary Relations* (New York: Harper and Row, 1966), p. 274.

19. Peter Katzenstein, "International Interdependence: Some Long-Term Trends and Recent Changes," *International Organization* 29 (Autumn 1975), pp. 1021–34.

20. *Ibid.*

21. See inter alia Oran Young, "Interdependencies in World Politics," *International Journal* 24 (Autumn 1969), E. Morse, "The Politics of Interdependence," *International Organization* 23 (Spring 1969), pp. 311–26, and R. Cooper.

22. See R. Rosecrance and A. Stein, "Interdependence: Myth or Reality?" *World Politics* 26 (October 1973), pp. 1–27.

23. Recent investment in Europe is one example. While Europe, Oceania, and Africa constituted only about 1.8 percent of long-term direct investment made by Japan between 1951–59, Europe alone comprised 20.1 percent of the Japanese total in 1973. The European share of US direct investment was 14.7 percent in 1950, but had risen to 32.6 percent by 1972. In 1958 only 8 percent of British earning on direct investment came from Europe, but by 1971 the total was 17.7 percent. France and Germany were even more strongly committed to Europe. France had 16.8 percent of its long-term investments in the EEC in 1962; ten years later the total had grown to nearly 25 percent. In 1961 Germany invested 38.6 percent of its long-term funds in Europe; by 1970 the total was nearly 57 percent.

24. See E. Morse, *Foreign Policy and Interdependence in Gaullist France* (Princeton: Princeton University Press, 1973).

25. Such divergence is unlikely to be stable. If price indices converge while changes move in opposite directions, the relationship of price indices themselves would eventually be affected.

26. Stephen Krasner in "State Power and the Structure of International Trade" reaches similar conclusions. He measures the openness of the international trading structure by low tariffs and high ratios of trade to GNP; relative state power is estimated using ratios of economic size, per capita income, and share of world trade. Openness tends to persist even after power ratios have begun to decline.

27. New speculation along these lines is reported in Edwin Dale, Jr., "A New Theory: Inflation Triggers Recession," *New York Times*, July 18, 1976.

APPENDIX TO CHAPTER 7

TABLE 1* NEW YORK CITY

| | CONSUMER PRICES | | | | WAGES | | MANUFACTURING | |
| | 1920-1941 | | 1947-1973 | | 1947-1974 | | 1947-1971 | |
	Index	Deltas	Index	Deltas	Index	Deltas	Index	Deltas
Boston	1.00	.98	1.00	1.00	.07	.94	1.00	.83
Cleveland	.98	.95	1.00	1.00	1.00	-.53	1.00	.87
Chicago	.99	.97	.99	1.00	1.00	.85	1.00	.87
Houston	.97	.98	1.00	1.00	.99	.76	.99	.60
Minneapolis	.97	.97	1.00	1.00	1.00	.94	.99	.77
Kansas City	.96	.95	1.00	1.00	.99	.63	.99	.50
Philadelphia	1.00	.98	1.00	1.00	1.00	.95	.99	.86
Washington	.98	.97	1.00	1.00	1.00	.96	.99	.62
St. Louis	.99	.99	.99	1.00	1.00	.97	1.00	.67
San Francisco	.99	.98	.99	1.00	1.00	.97	1.00	.64
Atlanta	.98	.98	1.00	1.00	.14	.49	.98	.36

INDEX - 100%	100%	82%	100% significant correlations
DELTA - 100%	100%	91%	100% significant correlations

*This and the following tables include Pearson correlations of price indices and correlations of changes in such indices (Deltas). The determination of the threshold at which the adjective "significant" is to be applied is necessarily subjective. The threshold employed should indicate the variation in the data without doing violence to the statistic. Price indices tend (with significant exceptions, for instance, the Depression) to increase monotonically with time. Thus a certain auto-correlation may affect price index relationships. Only very strong relationships should be considered significant. The threshold adopted here is correlations above .75. No such tendency exists in the relationship among price changes. These, in any event, tend to be low. Yet there are apparently stable low level relationships which need to be taken into account. We have therefore decided to regard correlations above .30 as significant. After each table the percentage of significant correlations in each category is given.

Sources: (TABLES 1-4)

International Monetary Fund, International Monetary Statistics (series), Washington.

United States Bureau of Economic Analysis, Survey of Current Business (series), Washington.

TABLE 2 ATLANTA

| | CONSUMER PRICES | | | | WAGES | | MANUFACTURING | |
| | 1920-1941 | | 1947-1973 | | 1947-1974 | | 1947-1971 | |
	Index	Deltas	Index	Deltas	Index	Deltas	Index	Deltas
Boston	.99	.98	1.00	1.00	1.00	.57	.98	.14
Cleveland	.99	.95	1.00	1.00	.04	.40	.99	.56
Chicago	.97	.93	1.00	1.00	.03	.93	.99	.53
Houston	.99	.98	1.00	1.00	.18	.21	.99	.54
Minneapolis	.99	.98	1.00	1.00	.14	.34	.99	.40
Kansas City	.99	.97	1.00	1.00	.11	.49	.98	.56
New York	.98	.98	1.00	1.00	.14	.49	.98	.36
Philadelphia	.98	.97	1.00	1.00	.15	.61	.99	.50
Washington	1.00	.99	1.00	1.00	-.03	.51	.99	.65
St. Louis	.99	.98	1.00	1.00	.09	.51	1.00	.82
San Francisco	.99	.97	.99	1.00	.14	.56	.98	.48

| | INDEX - 100% | 100% | 9% | 100% |
| | DELTA - 100% | 100% | 91% | 91% |

TABLE 3   KANSAS CITY

	CONSUMER PRICES				WAGES		MANUFACTURING	
	1920-1941		1947-1973		1947-1974		1947-1971	
	Index	Deltas	Index	Deltas	Index	Deltas	Index	Deltas
Boston	.97	.96	1.00	1.00	.07	.66	.98	.24
Cleveland	.97	.95	1.00	1.00	.99	-.29	.99	.53
Chicago	.94	.91	1.00	1.00	.99	.76	.99	.49
Houston	.99	.98	1.00	1.00	.98	.44	.99	.61
Minneapolis	.99	.97	1.00	1.00	.99	.66	.99	.62
New York	.96	.95	1.00	1.00	.99	.63	.99	.50
Philadelphia	.96	.94	1.00	1.00	.99	.70	.99	.50
Washington	.99	.97	1.00	1.00	.99	.70	.99	.48
St. Louis	.97	.95	1.00	1.00	.99	.67	.99	.55
San Francisco	.97	.95	1.00	1.00	.99	.56	.99	.69
Atlanta	.99	.97	1.00	1.00	.11	.49	.98	.56

```
         INDEX - 100%        100%        82%        100%
         DELTA - 100%        100%        91%         91%
```

TABLE 4 SAN FRANCISCO

| | CONSUMER PRICES | | | | WAGES | | MANUFACTURING | |
| | 1920-1941 | | 1947-1973 | | 1947-1974 | | 1947-1971 | |
	Index	Deltas	Index	Deltas	Index	Deltas	Index	Deltas
Atlanta	.99	.97	.99	1.00	.14	.56	.98	.48
Boston	.99	.97	1.00	1.00	.07	.95	.99	.52
Cleveland	1.00	.95	1.00	1.00	1.00	-.44	.99	.70
Chicago	.98	.95	1.00	1.00	1.00	.92	.99	.70
Houston	.99	.98	.99	1.00	.99	.72	.99	.76
Minneapolis	.99	.97	1.00	1.00	1.00	.93	.99	.82
Kansas City	.97	.95	1.00	1.00	.99	.74	.99	.69
Philadelphia	.99	.96	1.00	1.00	1.00	.96	.99	.68
Washington	.99	.96	.99	1.00	1.00	.98	.99	.61
St. Louis	1.00	.98	1.00	1.00	1.00	.97	.99	.61
New York	.99	.98	.99	1.00	1.00	.97	1.00	.64

```
INDEX - 100%        100%        91%        100%
DELTA - 100%        100%        91%        100%
```

TABLE 5

WHOLESALE PRICE CORRELATIONS OF INDICES AND DELTAS, 1890-1913

	CAN.		FR.		GER.		JAP.		U.K.	
	INDEX	DELTAS	INDEX	DELTAS	INDEX	DELTAS	INDEX	DELTAS	INDEX	DELTAS
FR.	.81	.49								
GER.	.63	.28	.91	.70						
JAP.	.94	.70	.87	.66	.90	.38				
U.K.	.86	.51	.95	.69	.82	.58	.84	.51		
U.S.	.74	.51	.92	.58	.94	.52	.82	.03	.86	.64

INDEX - 87%
DELTA - 87%

Sources: (Yearly data)

For all countries--Economic Intelligence Service, Statistical Yearbook of the League of Nations (series), Washington.

TABLE 6

CONSUMER PRICE CORRELATIONS OF INDICES AND DELTAS, 1890-1913

	CAN.		FR.		GER.		JAP.		U.K.	
	INDEX	DELTAS	INDEX	DELTAS	INDEX	DELTAS	INDEX	DELTAS	INDEX	DELTAS
FR.										
GER.			.46	.40						
JAP.										
U.K.			.45	.15	.92	.24				
U.S.			.32	.14	.96	-.02			.93	.58

INDEX - 50%
DELTA - 33%

Sources: (Yearly data)

For all countries--Economic Intelligence Service, Statistical Yearbook of the League of Nations (series), Geneva.

TABLE 7   INTEREST RATE CONVERGENCES   1900-1914

	CAN.	FR.	GER.	JAP.	U.K.
FR.	.786				
GER.	.933	1.04			
JAP.	2.803	4.076	3.095		
U.K.	.524	.694	.636	3.459	
U.S.	1.322	2.151	1.322	1.915	1.594

Sources: (TABLES 7 and 8)

    CAN. - M. C. Urquhart and K. A. H. Buckley, eds., Historical Statistics of Canada, Toronto.

    FR., GER., U.K. - Bankers' Insurance Managers' and Agents' Magazine, London.

    U.S. - Report of the Comptroller of the Currency, Washington.

TABLE 8   INTEREST RATE CORRELATION   1900-1914

	CAN.[*]	FR.	GER.	JAP.	U.K.
FR.	.42				
GER.	.27	.73			
JAP.[*]	.13	-.01	-.08		
U.K.	.21	.73	.74	-.09	
U.S.	.09	.56	.52	.15	.74

*Japan and Canada figures based on annual means; all others on monthly rate.

TABLE 9

WHOLESALE PRICE CORRELATIONS OF INDICES AND DELTAS, 1890-1913

	CAN.		FR.		GER.		JAP.		U.K.	
	INDEX	DELTAS	INDEX	DELTAS	INDEX	DELTAS	INDEX	DELTAS	INDEX	DELTAS
FR. 1890-1900	.87	.69								
1901-1913	.82	.27								
GER. 1890-1900	.30	.44	.49	.60						
1901-1913	.86	.01	.96	.77						
JAP. 1890-1900										
1901-1913										
U.K. 1890-1900	.89	.52	.91	.66	.31	.43				
1901-1913	.85	.41	.96	.75	.96	.75				
U.S. 1890-1900	.88	.72	.97	.91	.50	.50			.88	.65
1901-1913	.85	.20	.84	.29	.93	.51			.90	.61

1890-1900 INDEX - 60%   1901-1913 INDEX - 100%
         DELTA - 100%   DELTA - 60%

Sources: See TABLE 5.

TABLE 10

CONSUMER PRICE CORRELATIONS OF INDICES AND DELTAS, 1890-1913

	CAN.		FR.		GER.		JAP.		U.K.	
	INDEX	DELTAS	INDEX	DELTAS	INDEX	DELTAS	INDEX	DELTAS	INDEX	DELTAS
FR. 1890-1900										
1901-1913										
GER. 1890-1900			.48	.59						
1901-1913			.81	.25						
JAP. 1890-1900										
1901-1913										
U.K. 1890-1900			.41	-.21	.70	.26				
1901-1913			.89	.38	.90	.10				
U.S. 1890-1900			-.05	-.45	.70	.06			.73	.60
1901-1913			.82	.17	.94	-.37			.95	.67

1890-1900 INDEX - 0%   1901-1913 INDEX - 100%
         DELTA - 33%   DELTA - 33%

Sources: See TABLE 6.

TABLE 11

PERCENTAGE FOREIGN TRADE OF SIX COUNTRIES WITH EACH OTHER, 1913-1938

			Indicated country's trade as proportion of second country's trade						Total % With 5 Countries	% Change With 5 Countries 1913-1938
			CAN.	FR.	GER.	JAP.	U.K.	U.S.		
	CAN.	1913		1.70	1.70	0.50	30.00	56.00	90.00	
		1929		1.60	2.60	2.10	23.70	51.90	81.90	- 7.90
		1938		0.80	1.30	1.70	29.70	49.70	82.10	
	FR.	1913	0.30		12.70	0.90	16.80	8.60	39.20	
		1929	1.00		10.00	1.00	12.00	10.00	34.00	-13.20
		1938	1.00		7.00	1.00	9.00	9.00	26.00	
	GER.	1913	0.60	6.60		0.80	11.10	11.60	30.70	
		1929	1.40	5.90		2.00	8.10	10.30	27.70	-14.30
		1938	0.90	3.30		1.10	5.90	5.20	16.40	
	JAP.	1913	0.50	4.80	6.00		11.40	22.50	45.30	
		1929	2.20	1.60	3.90		5.00	35.90	48.60	- 5.80
		1938	2.00	0.90	3.80		3.70	26.80	39.50	
	U.K.	1913	4.50	5.90	9.90	1.50		13.50	35.30	
		1929	4.30	4.60	5.60	1.20		12.50	28.10	- 9.80
		1938	7.50	2.90	3.90	0.80		10.30	25.50	
	U.S.	1913	12.50	6.60	12.20	3.50	20.90		55.70	
		1929	14.50	4.50	6.90	7.20	12.20		45.40	-14.30
		1938	14.40	3.70	3.40	7.20	12.60		41.40	

Trade Statistics Sources:

CAN - Dept. of Trade and Commerce, The Canada Yearbook (series), Ottawa
FR - Statistique Generale de la France, Annuaire Statistiques (series)
GER - (Kaiserlichen Statistischen Amte, 1900-1918) (Statistischen Reichsamt, 1919-1940) Statistisches Jahrbuch fur das Deutsche Reich (series), Berlin
JAP - Statistics Bureau of the Prime Ministers Office, Japan Statistical Yearbook (series)
U.K. - Board of Trade, Statistical Abstract for the United Kingdom (series), London
U.S. - U. S. Dept. of Commerce, Statistical Abstract of the United States (series), U. S. Government Printing Office, Washington, D.C.

TABLE 12

WHOLESALE PRICE CORRELATIONS OF INDICES AND DELTAS, 1921-1939

		CAN.		FR.		GER.		JAP.		U.K.	
		INDEX	DELTAS	INDEX	DELTAS	INDEX	DELTAS	INDEX	DELTAS	INDEX	DELTAS
FR.	1921-1929	-.21	.22								
	1930-1932	.96	-.01								
	1933-1939	.59	.23								
GER.	1921-1929	-.02	-.12	-.12	-.07						
	1930-1932	.95	.17	.93	-.10						
	1933-1939	.69	.13	-.56	.10						
JAP.	1921-1929	.50	.17	-.60	.11	.22	-.02				
	1930-1932	.75	.44	.72	.45	.57	.08				
	1933-1939	.62	.51	.97	.26	.64	.03				
U.K.	1921-1929	.59	.39	-.19	.22	.06	-.04	.66	.29		
	1930-1932	.99	.51	.96	-.11	.97	.27	.71	.37		
	1933-1939	.81	.62	.33	.16	.75	.13	.40	.35		
U.S.	1921-1929	.72	.34	-.63	.32	.10	.03	.79	.45	.52	.33
	1930-1932	.97	.68	.92	.10	.87	.27	.83	.53	.94	.31
	1933-1939	.87	.21	.71	-.11	.67	.04	.78	.21	.67	.16

1921-1929	INDEX - 7%	1930-1932	INDEX - 80%	1933-1939	INDEX - 33%
	DELTA - 33%		DELTA - 46%		DELTA - 20%

Sources: (Monthly data)

For all countries--Economic Intelligence Service, op. cit.

TABLE 13

CONSUMER PRICE CORRELATIONS OF INDICES AND DELTAS, 1922-1939[*]

		CAN.		FR.		GER.		JAP.		U.K.	
		INDEX	DELTAS	INDEX	DELTAS	INDEX	DELTAS	INDEX	DELTAS	INDEX	DELTAS
FR.	1922-1929	.58									
	1930-1932	.76									
	1933-1939	.85									
GER.	1922-1929	.03	.00	-.20							
	1930-1932	.98	.22	.84							
	1933-1939	.81	.00	.55							
JAP.	1922-1929	-.49	.06	-.94		.15	-.12				
	1930-1932	.77	-.02	.11		.67	-.27				
	1933-1939	.86	.21	.93		.74	-.29				
U.K.	1922-1929	-.21	.32	-.80		.12	.08	.80	.16		
	1930-1932	.95	.03	.67		.91	.22	.81	.24		
	1933-1939	.95	.48	.82		.77	-.19	.87	.21		
U.S.	1922-1929	.40	.15	.19		.01	.21	.05	.11	.22	.37
	1930-1932	.99		.77		.97		.61		.97	
	1933-1939	.75	.07	.52		.82	-.08	.57	-.02	.69	.10

[*]Missing correlations on deltas indicate time periods where French and U. S. data were available only on a quarterly basis.

1922-1929 INDEX - 7%   1930-1932 INDEX - 73%   1933-1939 INDEX - 66%
           DELTA - 20%   DELTA - 0%   DELTA - 10%

Sources: (Monthly data)

     For all countries--Economic Intelligence Service, op. cit.

TABLE 14   INTEREST RATE CORRELATION - Pearson r
1922-1929

	CAN.*	FR.	GER.	JAP.	U.K.
FR.					
GER.		.38			
JAP.		.01	-.70		
U.K.		.76	.36	-.65	
U.S.		.81	.52	-.36	.26

*No data

Sources: (TABLES 14 and 15) (Monthly data)

CAN., FR., GER., U.K. - League of Nations, Statistical Yearbook (series).

JAP. - Department of Finance, Financial and Economic Annual of Japan (vols. 32, 38), Tokyo.

U.S. - Board of Governors, Federal Reserve System, Banking and Monetary Statistics, Washington.

TABLE 15   INTEREST RATE CONVERGENCES   1922-1929

	CAN.	FR.	GER.	JAP.	U.K.
FR.*					
GER.**		3.484			
JAP.		2.261	1.405		
U.K.		1.633	1.310	2.895	
U.S.		2.159	1.135	2.543	.84

*Data began in 1928.
**Data began in 1926 for German money rates, thus they do not reflect the inflation of 1923-24.

TABLE 16   INTEREST RATE CONVERGENCES   1930-1932

	CAN.	FR.	GER.	JAP.	U.K.
FR.					
GER.		3.508			
JAP.		3.546	.796		
U.K.		.954	2.642	2.230	
U.S.		1.117	2.391	2.363	1.124

Sources: (TABLES 16 and 17) (Quarterly data)

   See TABLES 14 and 15.

TABLE 17   INTEREST RATE CORRELATION - Pearson r
1930-1932

	CAN.	FR.	GER.	JAP.	U.K.
FR.					
GER.		.02			
JAP.		.53	.57		
U.K.		.39	.81	.78	
U.S.		.83	.30	.73	.56

TABLE 18   INTEREST RATE CORRELATION - Pearson r
1933-1939

	CAN.	FR.	GER.	JAP.	U.K.
FR.	-.03				
GER.	-.05	-.32			
JAP.	---	-.22	.75		
U.K.	.36	-.25	-.01	.03	
U.S.	-.05	-.08	.58	.74	.03

Sources: (TABLES 18 and 19) (Monthly data)

See TABLES 14 and 15.

TABLE 19   INTEREST RATE CONVERGENCES   1933-1939

	CAN.*	FR.	GER.	JAP.	U.K.
FR.	2.271				
GER.	2.070	1.101			
JAP.	2.614	1.094	.451		
U.K.	.268	2.251	2.332	2.764	
U.S.	.186	2.12	2.186	2.566	.392

*Canadian rates do not begin until 1935.

TABLE 20

PERCENTAGE FOREIGN TRADE OF SIX COUNTRIES WITH EACH OTHER, 1950-1972

		Indicated country's trade as proportion of second country's trade						Total % With 5 Countries	Total % With 5 Countries 1950-1972
		CAN.	FR.	G.F.R.	JAP.	U.K.	U.S.		
CAN.	1950		0.5	0.3	0.5	13.7	66.3	80.3	+ 0.8
	1969		0.9	2.1	3.7	6.2	68.2	81.1	
FR.	1950	0.6		7.3	0.0	6.5	8.3	22.7	+11.6
	1969	0.9		21.3	0.9	4.2	7.0	34.2	
G.F.R.	1950	0.4	8.3		0.4	4.3	11.0	24.4	+ 6.2
	1969	1.2	13.5		1.5	4.1	10.2	30.6	
JAP.	1950	1.7	0.8	1.0		1.8	33.5	38.7	+ 0.9
	1972	4.3	1.1	3.1		2.8	28.2	39.6	
U.K.	1950	6.4	3.2	1.8	0.2		6.8	18.4	+10.8
	1971	5.2	4.4	6.2	1.9		11.5	29.2	
U.S.	1950	20.6	2.4	2.8	3.1	4.4		33.3	+23.1
	1972	27.0	2.9	7.0	13.9	5.6		56.4	

Second country's trade as proportion of indicated country's trade

Trade Statistics Sources:

For all countries--United Nations, Dept. of Economic and Social Affairs, Yearbook of International Trade Statistics, New York.

TABLE 21

CONSUMER PRICE CORRELATIONS OF INDICES AND DELTAS, 1951-1958

	CAN.		FR.		G.F.R.		JAP.		U.K.	
	INDEX	DELTAS	INDEX	DELTAS	INDEX	DELTAS	INDEX	DELTAS	INDEX	DELTAS
FR.	.87	.15								
G.F.R.	.94	.47	.86	.33						
JAP.	.68	.30	.63	-.06	.57	.05				
U.K.	.85	.10	.84	.06	.82	.34	.89	-.01		
U.S.	.93	.14	.90	.15	.88	.22	.78	.10	.94	.02

INDEX - 80%
DELTA - 27%

Sources: (Monthly data)

For all countries--Organization of Economic and Community Development, Main Economic Indicators (series), Paris.

TABLE 22

WHOLESALE PRICE CORRELATIONS OF INDICES AND DELTAS, 1950-1958

	CAN.		FR.		G.F.R.		JAP.		U.K.	
	INDEX	DELTAS	INDEX	DELTAS	INDEX	DELTAS	INDEX	DELTAS	INDEX	DELTAS
FR.	.68	.19								
G.F.R.	.72	.23	.97	.54						
JAP.	.63	.35	.91	.35	.94	.34				
U.K.	.71	.21	.95	.26	.97	.33	.94	-.04		
U.S.	.83	.37	.84	.23	.86	.28	.84	.34	.89	.17

INDEX - 73%
DELTA - 47%

Sources: (Monthly data)

For all countries--Organization of Economic and Community Development, Main Economic Indicators (series), Paris.

United Nations, Statistical Office, Monthly Bulletin of Statistics (series), Great Neck, N.Y.

TABLE 23   INTEREST RATE CORRELATION - Pearson r
1950-1958

	CAN.	FR.	G.F.R.	JAP.	U.K.
FR.	.25				
G.F.R.	.04	-.50			
JAP.	-.55	-.68	.54		
U.K.	.52	.64	.36	-.69	
U.S.	.71	.44	.05	-.76	.75

Sources: (TABLES 23 and 24) (Monthly data)

1950-1954

   CAN., FR., JAP., U.K., U.S. - International Monetary Fund, International
   Monetary Statistics.

   G. F. R. - Deutsche Bundesbank Monthly Report.

1955-1958

   CAN., U.S. - Federal Reserve Bulletin.

   FR., G.F.R., U.K. - Deutsche Bundesbank Monthly Report.

   JAP. - Bank of Japan, Monthly Statistics of Japan, Nihon Tōkei geppo.

TABLE 24   INTEREST RATE CONVERGENCES   1950-1958

	CAN.	FR.	G.F.R.	JAP.	U.K.
FR.	1.331				
G.F.R.	2.802	2.306			
JAP.	6.317	4.930	3.710		
U.K.	.956	1.496	2.967	6.501	
U.S.	.683	1.797	3.292	6.947	.819

TABLE 25

WAGE RATE CORRELATIONS OF INDICES AND DELTAS, 1955-1958

	CAN.		FR.		G.F.R.		JAP.		U.K.	
	INDEX	DELTAS	INDEX	DELTAS	INDEX	DELTAS	INDEX	DELTAS	INDEX	DELTAS
FR.	-.62	-.07								
G.F.R.	.98	.39	-.62							
JAP.	.55	.08	-.26	.40	.59	.17				
U.K.	.98	.37	-.69	-.26	.98	.00	.61	.12		
U.S.	.98	.32	-.65	-.11	.99	.03	.60	-.11	.99	.13

INDEX - 40%
DELTA - 27%

Sources: (Quarterly data)

    For all countries--Organization of Economic and Community Development, <u>Main Economic Indicators</u> (series), Paris.

TABLE 26

CONSUMER PRICE CORRELATIONS OF INDICES AND DELTAS, 1959-1975

		CAN.		FR.		G.F.R.		JAP.		U.K.	
		INDEX	DELTAS	INDEX	DELTAS	INDEX	DELTAS	INDEX	DELTAS	INDEX	DELTAS
FR.	1959-1972	.99	.13								
	1973-1974	1.00	.09								
	1975	.99	-.64								
G.F.R.	1959-1972	.98	.18	.99	.34						
	1973-1974	.98	-.13	.98	-.39						
	1975	.95	-.45	.97	.76						
JAP.	1959-1972	.98	-.15	1.00	.24	.99	.05				
	1973-1974	.99	-.22	.99	.38	.99	.03				
	1975	.92	-.62	.96	.61	.96	.32				
U.K.	1959-1972	.99	.23	.99	.22	.99	.39	.98	.20		
	1973-1974	.99	.12	1.00	.46	.98	.12	.99	.24		
	1975	.96	-.22	.97	.42	.99	.68	.95	.31		
U.S.	1959-1972	.99	.44	.98	.31	.97	.16	.97	.06	.99	.25
	1973-1974	1.00	.48	.98	.31	.97	.16	.97	.06	.99	.01
	1975	1.00	.61	.99	-.23	.96	-.17	.93	-.24	.96	-.22

1959-1972 INDEX - 100%   1973-1974 INDEX - 100%   1975 INDEX - 100%
         DELTA - 27%   DELTA - 20%   DELTA - 47%

Sources: (Quarterly data)

For all countries--Organization of Economic and Community Development, Main Economic Indicators (series), Paris.

TABLE 27

WHOLESALE PRICE CORRELATIONS OF INDICES AND DELTAS, 1959-1975

	CAN.		FR.		G.F.R.		JAP.		U.K.	
	INDEX	DELTAS	INDEX	DELTAS	INDEX	DELTAS	INDEX	DELTAS	INDEX	DELTAS
FR. 1959-1972	.97	.13								
1973-1974	.95	.35								
1975	-.35	.47								
G.F.R. 1959-1972	.89	.15	.93	.12						
1973-1974	.97	.32	.99	.72						
1975	-.27	-.21	-.57	-.61						
JAP. 1959-1972	.65	.13	.67	-.13	.52	-.13				
1973-1974	.98	.10	.98	.46	.99	.54				
1975	.52	.40	-.24	.10	.04	.51				
U.K. 1959-1972	.97	.10	.98	.04	.90	-.17	.74	.20		
1973-1974	.95	-.05	.93	.24	.97	.42	.96	.26		
1975	.75	-.22	-.86	-.46	.00	.52	.44	.34		
U.S. 1959-1972	.98	.01	.96	.04	.87	.06	.75	.02	.98	-.01
1973-1974	.99	.45	.95	.14	.96	.06	.98	.19	.95	-.03
1975	.97	.62	-.64	.14	-.25	.27	.52	.55	.93	.38

1959-1972 INDEX - 73%   1973-1974 INDEX - 100%   1975 INDEX - 20%
           DELTA - 0%   DELTA - 47%   DELTA - 56%

Sources: (Monthly data)

    For all countries--Organization of Economic and Community Development, Main Economic Indicators (series), Paris.

TABLE 28   INTEREST RATE CORRELATION - Pearson r
1959-1972

	CAN.	FR.	G.F.R.	JAP.	U.K.
FR.	.61				
G.F.R.	.28	.61			
JAP.	-.13	-.29	-.38		
U.K.	.57	.62	.49	-.31	
U.S.	.83	.86	.65	-.36	.74

Sources: (TABLES 28 and 29) (Monthly data)

CAN. - (1959-1966) Federal Reserve Bulletin.
        (1967-1975) Bank of Canada Review.

FR., G.F.R., U.K. - Deutsche Bundesbank Monthly Report.

JAP. - Bank of Japan, Monthly Statistics of Japan, Nihon Tokei geppo.

TABLE 29   INTEREST RATE CONVERGENCES   1959-1972

	CAN.	FR.	G.F.R.	JAP.	U.K.
FR.	1.168				
G.F.R.	1.744	1.185			
JAP.	1.992	1.862	2.083		
U.K.	1.014	1.034	1.347	1.564	
U.S.	.742	.682	1.169	1.846	.797

TABLE 30   INTEREST RATE CORRELATION - Pearson r
1965-1972

	CAN.	FR.	G.F.R.	JAP.	U.K.
FR.	.58				
G.F.R.	.05	.48			
JAP.	.66	.35	.02		
U.K.	.78	.35	.12	.62	
U.S.	.84	.84	.50	.49	.67

Sources: (TABLES 30 and 31) (Monthly data)

See TABLES 28 and 29.

TABLE 31   INTEREST RATE CONVERGENCES   1965-1972

	CAN.	FR.	G.F.R.	JAP.	U.K.
FR.	1.401				
G.F.R.	2.284	1.488			
JAP.	1.056	1.224	1.694		
U.K.	.858	1.59	1.722	.576	
U.S.	.92	.755	1.483	.92	.759

TABLE 32   INTEREST RATE CORRELATION - Pearson r
1973-1974

	CAN.	FR.	G.F.R.	JAP.	U.K.
FR.	.88				
G.F.R.	-.16	-.18			
JAP.	.84	.95	-.08		
U.K.	.37	.55	.10	.53	
U.S.	.92	.77	.13	.77	.38

Sources: (TABLES 32 and 33) (Monthly data)

See TABLES 28 and 29.

TABLE 33   INTEREST RATE CONVERGENCES   1973-1974

	CAN.	FR.	G.F.R.	JAP.	U.K.
FR.	4.259				
G.F.R.	4.375	3.118			
JAP.	.878	3.417	3.566		
U.K.	2.232	2.304	2.474	1.665	
U.S.	2.444	1.967	2.805	1.872	1.460

TABLE 34   INTEREST RATE CORRELATION - Pearson r
1975

	CAN.	FR.	G.F.R.	JAP.	U.K.
FR.	-.81				
G.F.R.	-.81	.97			
JAP.	-.95	.80	.78		
U.K.	.64	-.23	-.22	-.68	
U.S.	-.13	.51	.45	.26	.10

Sources: (TABLES 34 and 35)

See TABLES 28 and 29.

TABLE 35   INTEREST RATE CONVERGENCES 1975

	CAN.	FR.	G.F.R.	JAP.	U.K.
FR.	1.787				
G.F.R.	2.688	3.022			
JAP.	1.663	.673	2.916		
U.K.	1.633	1.633	3.887	1.182	
U.S.	1.327	1.765	1.361	1.625	2.631

TABLE 36

WAGE RATE CORRELATIONS OF INDICES AND DELTAS, 1959-1975

	CAN.		FR.		G.F.R.		JAP.		U.K.	
	INDEX	DELTAS	INDEX	DELTAS	INDEX	DELTAS	INDEX	DELTAS	INDEX	DELTAS
FR. 1959-1971 1973-1974 1975	.99	.23								
G.F.R. 1959-1971 1973-1974 1975	.98	.26	.99	.44						
JAP. 1959-1971 1973-1974	.92 .34 .20	-.01 -.13 -.09	.93	.15	.91	.10				
U.K. 1959-1971 1973-1974 1975	1.00 .97 .95	.42 .01 .07	1.00	.31	.99	.36	.92 .34 .36	-.35 -.46 .11		
U.S. 1959-1971 1973-1974	1.00 .99 .96	.58 .35 .08	1.00	.21	.99	.20	.92 .40 .16	-.22 .02 .22	1.00 .98 .91	.43 .21 -.18

1959-1971 INDEX - 100%   1973-1974 INDEX - 50%   1975 INDEX - 50%
           DELTA - 40%   DELTA - 17%   DELTA - 0%

Sources: (1959-1972, Quarterly data. 1973-1975, Monthly data.)

For all countries--Organization for Economic and Community Development, Main Economic Indicators (series), Paris.

8
The Politics of Transnational Economic Relations

A major tenet of the globalists is that economics generally, and the multinational corporations specifically, undermine the nation-state by integrating the world economy. Gilpin challenges that theory. According to his thinking, "There is little evidence to substantiate . . . that the multinational corporation as an independent actor has had a significant impact on international politics." Indeed, he argues that transnational economic actors reflect the policies of their home governments. To support this contention, Gilpin traces the development of the British empire and America's economic relations with Japan and Europe.

The international corporations have evidently declared ideological war on the "antiquated" nation state. . . . The charge that materialism, modernization and internationalism is the new liberal creed of corporate capitalism is a valid one. The implication is clear: the nation state as a political unit of democratic decision-making must, in the interest of "progress," yield control to the new mercantile mini-powers.
— Kari Levitt, "The Hinterland Economy,"
Canadian Forum, July-August 1970 (Vol. 50, Nos. 594–595), p. 163.

While the structure of the multinational corporation is a modern concept, designed to meet the requirements of a modern age, the nation state is a very old-fashioned idea and badly adapted to serve the needs of our present complex world.
— George W. Ball, "The Promise of the Multinational
Corporation," *Fortune,* June 1, 1967 (Vol. 75, No. 6), p. 80.

I

These two statements – the first by a Canadian nationalist, the second by a former United States undersecretary of state – express a dominant theme of contemporary writings on international relations. International society, we are told, is increasingly rent between its economic and its political organization. On the one hand, powerful economic and technical forces are creating a highly integrated transnational economy, blurring the traditional significance of national boundaries. On the other hand, the nation-state continues to command men's loyalties and to be the basic unit of political decision. As one writer has put the issue, "The conflict of our era is between ethnocentric nationalism and geocentric technology."[1]

George W. Ball and Kari Levitt represent two contending positions with respect to the political implications of contemporary economic and technical forces and especially of their primary agent, the multinational corporation. Whereas Ball advocates the diminution of the powers of the nation-state in order to give full rein to the productive potentialities of the multinational corporation, Levitt argues for a powerful Canadian nationalism which could counterbalance American economic domination. What appears to one as the logical and desirable consequence of economic rationality seems to the other to be an effort on the part of American imperialism to eliminate all contending centers of power.

The issues raised by these contrasting positions are central to any evaluation of the impressive growth of transnational economic relations since the end of the Second World War. In specific terms the issue is whether the multinational corporation has become or will become an important actor in international affairs, supplanting, at least in part, the nation-state. If the multinational corporation is indeed an increasingly important and independent international actor, what are the factors that have enabled it to break the political monopoly of the nation-state? What is the relationship of these two sets of political actors, and what are the implications of the multinational corporation for international relations? Finally, what about the future? If the contemporary role of the multinational corporation is the result of a peculiar configuration of political and economic factors, can one foresee the continuation of its important role into the future?

Fundamental to these rather specific issues is a more general one raised by the growing contradiction between the economic and political organization of contemporary international society. This is the relationship between economic and political activities. While the advent of the multinational corporation puts it in a new guise, the issue is an old one. It was, for example, the issue which in the nineteenth century divided classical liberals like John Stuart Mill and the German Historical School represented by Georg Friedrich List. Whereas the former gave primacy to economics and the production of wealth, the latter emphasized the political determination of economic relations.[2] As this issue is central to the contemporary debate on the implications of the multinational corporation for international relations, I would like to discuss it in brief outline.

The classical position was, of course, first set forth by Adam Smith in *The Wealth of Nations.*[3] While Smith appreciated the importance of power, his purpose was to inquire into the nature and causes of wealth. Economic growth, Smith argued, is primarily a function of the extent of the division of labor which in turn is dependent upon the scale of the market. Much of his attack, therefore, was directed at the barriers erected by feudal principalities and mercantilist states against the free exchange of goods and the enlargement of markets. If men are to multiply their wealth, Smith argued, the contradiction between political organization and economic rationality had to be resolved in favor of the latter.

Marxism, the rebellious ideological child of classical liberalism, erected the concept of the contradiction between economic and political relations into a historical law. Whereas classical liberalism held that the requirements of economic rationality *ought* to determine political relations, the Marxist position was that the mode of production *does* determine the superstructure of political relations. History can be understood as the product of the dialectical process—the contradiction between evolving economic forces and the sociopolitical system.

Although Karl Marx and Friedrich Engels wrote amazingly little on the subject of international economics, Engels in his famous polemic, *Anti-Dühring,* dealt explicitly with the question of whether economics or politics was primary in determining the structure of international relations.[4] Karl Dühring's anti-Marxist theory maintained that property relations resulted less from the economic logic of capitalism than from extraeconomic political factors. Engels, on the other hand, using the example of the unification of Germany in his attack on Dühring, argued that economic factors were primary.

Engels argued that when contradictions arise between economic and political structures, political power adapts itself to changes in the balance of economic forces and yields to the dictates of economic development. Thus, in the case of nineteenth-century Germany, the requirements of industrial production had become incompatible with feudal, politically fragmented Germany. Though political reaction was victorious in 1815 and again in 1848, it was unable to prevent the growth of large-scale industry in Germany and the growing participation of Ger-

man commerce in the world market.[5] In summary, Engels argued that
"German unity had become an economic necessity."[6]

In the view of both Smith and Engels the nation-state represented a
progressive stage in human development because it enlarged the
political realm of economic activity. In each successive economic epoch
the advancing technology and scale of production necessitates an
enlargement of political organization. Because the city-state and
feudalism were below the optimum for the scale of production and the
division of labor required by the Industrial Revolution, they prevented
the efficient utilization of resources and were superseded by larger
political units. Smith considered this to be a desirable objective; for
Engels it was a historical necessity.

In our era this Marxist emphasis on the historical law of development
has been made by many writers—Marxists and non-Marxists—in
discussing the contemporary contradiction between the nation-state and
the multinational corporation. This position that economic forces are
determining the structure of international relations has been put most
forcibly by the economist Stephen Hymer. In an intriguing article entitled "The Multinational Corporation and the Law of Uneven Development" Hymer has argued that contemporary international relations are
rapidly being reshaped by "two laws of economic development: the Law
of Increasing Firm Size and the Law of Uneven Development."[7]

The law of increasing firm size, Hymer argues, is the tendency since
the Industrial Revolution for firms to increase in size "from the *workshop*
to the *factory* to the *national corporation* to the *multi-divisional corporation*
and now to the *multinational corporation.*"[8] The law of uneven development, he continues, is the tendency of the international economy to
produce poverty as well as wealth, underdevelopment as well as development. Together these two economic laws will produce the following
consequence:

> A regime of North Atlantic Multinational Corporations would tend to
> produce a hierarchical division of labor between geographical regions cor-
> responding to the vertical division of labor within the firm. It would tend to
> centralize high-level decision-making occupations in a few key cities in the
> advanced countries, surrounded by a number of regional sub-capitals, and
> confine the rest of the world to lower levels of activity and income, i.e., to
> the status of towns and villages in a new Imperial system. Income, status,
> authority, and consumption patterns would radiate out from these centers
> along a declining curve, and the existing pattern of inequality and
> dependency would be perpetuated. The pattern would be complex, just as
> the structure of the corporation is complex, but the basic relationship be-
> tween different countries would be one of superior and subordinate, head
> office and branch office.[9]

In contrast to the position of liberals and Marxists alike who stress the primacy of economic relations, nationalists and the so-called realist school of political science have emphasized the primacy of politics. Whereas the liberal or Marxist emphasizes the production of wealth as the basic determinant of social and political organization, the realist stresses power, security, and national sentiment. Thus, whereas Ball predicted to a session of the Canadian House of Commons that economic logic would lead to the eventual total integration of Canada and the United States, Levitt and other Canadian nationalists prefer national independence to a higher standard of living.

Although himself a proponent of economic liberalism, the late Jacob Viner made one of the best analyses of the relationship of economic and political factors in determining the structure of international relations and concluded that political and security considerations are primary. In his classic study, *The Customs Union Issue,* Viner analyzed all known cases of economic and political unification from the perspective of whether the basic motivation was political or economic.[10] Thus, whereas Engels interpreted the formation of the Zollverein as a response to the industrialization of Germany and the economic necessity of larger markets, Viner argued "that Prussia engineered the customs union primarily for political reasons, in order to gain hegemony or at least influence over the lesser German states. It was largely in order to make certain that the hegemony should be Prussian and not Austrian that Prussia continually opposed Austrian entry into the Union, either openly or by pressing for a customs union tariff lower than highly protectionist Austria could stomach."[11] In pursuit of this strategic interest it was "Prussian might, rather than a common zeal for political unification arising out of economic partnership, [that] had played the major role."[12]

Whereas liberalism and Marxism foresee economic factors leading to the decline of political boundaries and eventually to political unification, Viner argued that economic and political boundaries need not coincide and may actually be incompatible with one another. The tendency today, he pointed out, to take the identity of political and economic frontiers for granted is in fact a quite modern phenomenon and is even now not universal. With respect to tariffs, the concern of his study, the general rule until recently was that political unification was greater than the area of economic unification. Furthermore, any attempt to further economic unification might undermine political unification; this was the case with respect to the American Civil War and is the case today in Canada.[13]

Viner concluded his argument that economic factors are of secondary importance to political unification with the following observation which is highly relevant for the concerns of this essay:

The power of nationalist sentiment can override all other considerations; it can dominate the minds of a people, and dictate the policies of government, even when in every possible way and to every conceivable degree it is in sharp conflict with what seem to be and are in fact the basic economic interests of the people in question. To accept as obviously true the notion that the bonds of allegiance must necessarily be largely economic in character to be strong, or to accept unhesitatingly the notion that where economic entanglements are artificially or naturally strong the political affections will also necessarily become strong, is to reject whatever lessons past experience has for us in this field.[14]

The contemporary argument that interstate relations will recede in face of contemporary technological developments and will be replaced by transnational relations between large multinational corporations was anticipated in the 1930s by Eugene Staley. In a fascinating book, *World Economy in Transition,* Staley posed the issue which is our main concern: "A conflict rages between technology and politics. Economics, so closely linked to both, has become the major battlefield. Stability and peace will reign in the world economy only when, somehow, the forces on the side of technology and the forces on the side of politics have once more been accommodated to each other."[15]

While Staley believed, along with many present-day writers, that politics and technology must ultimately adjust to one another, he emphasized, in contrast to contemporary writers, that it was not inevitable that politics adjust to technology. Reflecting the intense economic nationalism of the 1930s, Staley pointed out that the adjustment may very well be the other way around. As he reminds us, in his own time and in early periods economics has had to adjust to political realities: "In the 'Dark Ages' following the collapse of the Roman Empire, technology adjusted itself to politics. The magnificent Roman roads fell into disrepair, the baths and aqueducts and amphitheatres and villas into ruins. Society lapsed back to localism in production and distribution, forgot much of the learning and the technology and the governmental systems of earlier days."[16]

II

This rather lengthy discussion of the relationship between economics and politics argues the point that, although the economic and technical substructure partially determines and interacts with the political superstructure, political values and security interests are crucial determinants of international economic relations. Politics determines the framework of economic activity and channels it in directions which tend to serve the political objectives of dominant political groups and organizations. Throughout history each successive hegemonic power has organized economic space in terms of its own interests and purposes.

Following in this vein, the thesis of this essay is that transnational actors and processes are dependent upon peculiar patterns of interstate relations. Whether one is talking about the merchant adventurers of the sixteenth century, nineteenth-century finance capitalists, or twentieth-century multinational corporations, transnational actors have been able to play an important role in world affairs because it has been in the interest of the predominant power(s) for them to do so. As political circumstances have changed due to the rise and decline of nation-states, transnational processes have also been altered or ceased altogether. Thus, as the French economist François Perroux has observed, the world economy did not develop as a result of competition between equal partners but through the emergence and influence of great national economies that successively became dominant.[17]

From this perspective the multinational corporation exists as a transnational actor today because it is consistent with the political interest of the world's dominant power, the United States. This argument does not deny the analyses of economists who argue that the multinational corporation is a response to contemporary technological and economic developments. The argument is rather that these economic and technological factors have been able to exercise their profound effects because the United States—sometimes with the cooperation of other states and sometimes over their opposition—has created the necessary political framework. By implication, a diminution of the Pax Americana and the rise of powers hostile to the global activities of multinational corporations would bring their reign over international economic relations to an end.

The basic point was made some years ago by E. H. Carr when he wrote that "the science of economics presupposes a given political order, and cannot be profitably studied in isolation from politics."[18] An international economy based on free trade, Carr sought to convince his fellow Englishmen, was not a natural and inevitable state of affairs but reflected the economic and political interests of Great Britain. The regime of free trade had come into existence and was maintained by the exercise of British economic and military power. With the rise after 1880 of new industrial and military powers with contrasting economic interests, namely, Germany, Japan, and the United States, an international economy based on free trade and British power became less and less viable. A proponent of appeasement, Carr advocated in defense of the Munich Pact that England work with these challenging powers, particularly Germany, to create a new international system which reflected the changed balance of economic and military power and interests in the world.

Perhaps the most effective way to defend the thesis that the pattern of international economic relations is dependent upon the structure of the international political system is to review the origins of the Pax Britannica, its demise with the First World War, and the eventual rise of a Pax Americana after the Second World War. What this history clearly reveals is that transnational economic processes are not unique to our own age and that the pattern of international economic activity reflects the global balance of economic and military power.

Each successive international system that the world has known is the consequence of the territorial, diplomatic, and military realignments that have followed history's great wars. The origins of the Pax Britannica lie in the complicated series of negotiations that followed the great upheavals of the Napoleonic wars. The essential features of the system which were put into place at that time provided the general framework of international economic relations until the collapse of the system under the impact of the First World War.

The first essential feature of the Pax Britannica was the territorial settlement and the achievement of a balance of power among the five Great Powers.[19] This territorial realignment can be divided into two parts. In the first place, on the continent of Europe the territorial realignments checked the ambitions of Russia in the east and France in the west. Second, the overseas conquests of the continental powers were reduced at the same time that Great Britain acquired a number of important strategic overseas bases. As a result the four major powers on the Continent were kept in check by their own rivalries and by offshore Britain which played a balancing and mediating role.

British naval power, the second essential feature of the Pax Britannica, was able to exercise a powerful and pervasive influence over global politics due to a fortunate juncture of circumstances. Great Britain's geographical position directly off the coast of continental Europe and its possession of several strategic naval bases enabled it to control Europe's access to the outside world and to deny overseas colonies to continental governments. As a consequence, from 1825 when Great Britain warned France not to take advantage of the revolt of the Spanish colonies in America to the latter part of the century, the greater part of the non-European world was either independent or under British rule. Moreover, the maintenance of this global military hegemony was remarkably inexpensive; it thus permitted Great Britain to utilize its wealth and energies in the task of economic development.

Third, using primarily the instruments of free trade and foreign investment in this political-strategic framework, Great Britain was able, in effect, to restructure the international economy and to exercise great influence over the course of international affairs. As the world's first industrial nation, Great Britain fashioned an international division of labor which favored its own industrial strengths at the same time that it brought great benefits to the world at large. Exchanging manufactured goods for the food and raw materials of other nations, Great Britain was the industrial and financial center of a highly interdependent international economy.

One may reasonably argue, I believe, that in certain respects the regime of the Pax Britannica was the Golden Age of transnationalism. The activities of private financiers and capitalists enmeshed the nations in a web of interdependencies which certainly influenced the course of international relations. In contrast to our own era, in which the role of the multinational corporation in international economic relations is unprecedented, the private institutions of the City of London under the gold standard and the regime of free trade had a strategic and central place in world affairs unmatched by any transnational organization today. Prior to 1914 the focus of much of international relations was the City of London and the private individuals who managed the world's gold, traded in commodities, and floated foreign loans. Though this interdependence differs radically in kind from the internationalization of production and the immense trade in manufactured goods which characterize our own more industrialized world economy, this earlier great age of transnationalism should not be overlooked. In exaggerated acknowledgment of the political importance of the transnational actors which dominated this age J. A. Hobson in his book on imperialism asked rhetorically whether "a great war could be undertaken by any European State, or a great State loan subscribed, if the house of Rothschild and its connexions set their face against it."[20]

The foundations underlying the Pax Britannica and the transnational processes it fostered began to erode in the latter part of the nineteenth century. On the Continent the industrialization and unification of Germany profoundly altered the European balance of power. France, too, industrialized and began to challenge Great Britain's global supremacy. Overseas developments of equal or potentially greater magnitude were taking place. The rapid industrialization of Japan and the United States and their subsequent creation of powerful navies ended British control of the seas. No longer could Great Britain use its naval power to deny rivals access to the globe. With the decline of British supremacy the imperial struggle for the division of Africa and Asia began, leading eventually to the outbreak of the First World War.

The war completed the destruction of the pre-1914 system. As a consequence of the duration and intensity of the conflict one sector after another of economic life was nationalized and brought into the service of the state. The role of the state in economic affairs became pervasive, and economic nationalism largely replaced the laissez faire traditions upon which so much of prewar transnationalism had rested. Not until the Second World War would political relations favor the reemergence of extensive transnational activity.

The failure to revive the international economy after the First World War was due to many causes: the policies of economic revenge against Germany; the ill-conceived attempt to reestablish the gold standard; the nationalistic "beggar-my-neighbor" policies pursued by most states, etc. In terms of our primary concern in this essay one factor in particular needs to be stressed, namely, the failure of the United States to assume leadership of the world economy, a role Great Britain could no longer perform. Whereas before the war the City of London provided order and coordinated international economic activities, now London was unable and New York was unwilling to restructure the international economy disrupted by the First World War. The result was a leadership vacuum which contributed in part to the onset of the Great Depression and eventually the Second World War.

For our purposes two developments during this interwar period hold significance. The first was the Ottawa Agreement of 1932 which created the sterling area of imperial preference and reversed Great Britain's traditional commitment to multilateral free trade. The purpose of the agreement between Great Britain and the Commonwealth, an action whose intellectual roots went back to the nineteenth century, was to establish a regional trading bloc effectively isolated from the rest of the world economy. Germany in central Europe and Japan in Asia followed suit, organizing under their hegemonies the neighboring areas of strategic and economic importance. "This development of trading blocs led by great powers," one authority writes, "was the most significant economic development of the years immediately preceding the Second World War. As always the breakdown of international law and economic order gave opportunity to the ruthless rather than to the strong."[21] Such a system of law and order the international gold standard had provided. Under this system transnational actors could operate with little state interference. With its collapse nation-states struggled to create exclusive spheres of influence, and trade relations became instruments of economic warfare.

The second important development from the perspective of this essay was the passage of the Reciprocal Trade Agreements Act in June 1934. The purpose of this act was to enable the United States government to negotiate reductions in tariff barriers. Followed in 1936 by the Tripartite Monetary Agreement, the act not only reflected the transformation of the United States into a major industrial power but also represented the first step by the United States to assert its leadership of the world economy. Furthermore, it demonstrated the potential of bilateral negotiation as a method to achieve the expansion of multinational trade even though the immediate impact of the act was relatively minor. World trade continued to be dominated by preference systems, especially the sterling area, from which the United States was excluded. The importance of this prewar situation and the determination of the United States to overcome this discrimination cannot be too greatly emphasized. The reorganization of the world economy was to be the keynote of American postwar planning.

III

American plans for the postwar world were based on several important assumptions. In the first place, American leadership tended to see the origins of the Second World War as largely economic.[22] The failure to revive the international economy after the First World War and the subsequent rise of rival trading blocs were regarded as the underlying causes of the conflict. Second, it was assumed that peace would be best promoted by the establishment of a system of multinational trade relations which guaranteed to all states equal access to the world's resources and markets. Third, the main obstacles to the achievement of such a universal system, Americans believed, were the nationalistic and discriminatory measures adopted in the 1930s by various European countries—trade preferences, exchange controls, quantitative restrictions, competitive currency depreciations, etc.

The importance of economic considerations in American postwar planning has led in recent years to a spate of writings by revisionist historians who interpret these efforts as part of a large imperial design.[23] While this literature does serve to correct the simple-minded orthodox position that the cold war originated as a Communist plot to achieve world domination, it goes much too far and distorts the picture in another direction.

There is no question that the creation of a system of multilateral trade relations was in the interests of the United States. Preference systems ran directly counter to American basic interests as the world's dominant economic power and a major trading nation. It does not follow from this fact, however, that American efforts to achieve such a system were solely self-serving and unmotivated by the sincere belief that economic nationalism and competition were at the root of the Second World War. Nor does it follow that what is good for the United States is contrary to the general welfare of other nations.

The American emphasis on postwar economic relations represented a long tradition in American thought on international relations. The American liberal ideal since the founding of the Republic has been the substitution of commercial for political relations between states.[24] In the best free trade tradition trade relations between nations are considered to be a force for peace. Furthermore, as a nation which felt it had been discriminated against by the more powerful European states, the United States wanted a world in which it would have equal access to markets. Universal equality of opportunity, not imperial domination, was the motif of American postwar foreign economic planning.

This naive American faith in the beneficial effects of economic intercourse was reflected in the almost complete absence of attention to strategic matters in American postwar plans. In contrast to the prodigious energies devoted to the restructuring of the international economy little effort was given to the strategic and territorial balance of the postwar world. This neglect is explicable in large part, however, by the prevailing American assumption that a universal system based on an integrated world economy and on the United Nations would replace the traditional emphasis on spheres of influence and the balance of power.

If one accepts the revisionist argument that imperial ambition underlay American postwar plans, then the cold war should have been between the United States and Western Europe, particularly the United Kingdom, rather than between the Union of Soviet Socialist Republics and the United States. The bête noir of American planners was European discrimination and especially the imperial preference which encompassed a high percentage of world trade and exercised considerable discrimination against American goods. American plans for the postwar era were directed against the British in particular. Beginning with the framing of the Atlantic Charter in 1941 and continuing through the negotiation of the Lend-Lease Act (1941), the Bretton Woods Agreement (1944), and the British loan (1945), the thrust of American policy was directed against Commonwealth discrimination.

In light of the intensity of these American efforts to force the United Kingdom and other European countries to accept a multilateral system it is important to appreciate that they were abandoned in response to growth of Soviet-American hostility. As American leadership came to accept the Soviet diplomatic-military challenge as the major postwar problem, the United States' attitude toward international economic relations underwent a drastic reversal. In contrast to earlier emphases on multilateralism and nondiscrimination the United States accepted discrimination in the interest of rebuilding the shattered West European economy.

The retort of revisionists to this argument is that the American-Soviet struggle originated in the American desire to incorporate Eastern Europe, particularly Poland, into the American scheme for a global empire. This effort, it is claimed, clashed with the legitimate security concerns of the Soviet Union, and the cold war evolved as the Soviet defensive response to the American effort to expand economically into the Soviet sphere of influence. If the United States had not been driven by the greed of its corporations, American and Soviet interests could easily have been accommodated.

There are sufficient grounds for this interpretation to give it some plausibility. Certainly, American efforts to incorporate Eastern Europe and even the Soviet Union into the world capitalistic economy raised Soviet suspicions. Although the American view was that the withdrawal of the Soviet Union from the world economy following the Bolshevik Revolution had been a contributing factor to the outbreak of the Second World War and that a peaceful world required Soviet reintegration, the Russians could easily interpret these efforts as an attempt to undermine communism. No doubt in part they were. But it is a long jump from these American efforts to trade in an area of little historical interest to the United States to a conflict so intense and durable that it has on several occasions taken the world to the brink of thermonuclear holocaust.

A more realistic interpretation, I believe, is that the origins of the cold war lie in the unanticipated consequences of the Second World War. The collapse of German power in Europe and of Japanese power in Asia created a power vacuum which both the United States and the Soviet Union sought to fill to their own advantage. One need not even posit aggressive designs on either side to defend this interpretation, although my own position is that the Soviet Union desired (and still desires) to extend its sphere of influence far beyond the glacis of Eastern Europe. To support this political interpretation of the cold war it is sufficient to argue that the power vacuums in Central Europe and the northwestern Pacific created a security dilemma for both powers. In terms of its own security neither power could afford to permit the other to fill this vacuum, and the efforts of each to prevent this only increased the insecurity of the other, causing it to redouble its own efforts. Each in response to the other organized its own bloc, freezing the lines of division established by the victorious armies and wartime conferences.

One cannot understand, however, the pattern of the cold war and its significance for international economic relations unless one appreciates the asymmetric situations of the United States and the Soviet Union. Whereas the Soviet Union is a massive land power directly abutting Western Europe and the northwestern Pacific (primarily Korea and Japan), the United States is principally a naval and air power separated from the zones of contention by two vast oceans. As a consequence, while the Soviet Union has been able with relative ease to bring its influence to bear on its periphery at relatively much less cost in terms of its balance of payments, the United States has had to organize a global system of bases and alliances involving an immense drain on its balance of payments. Moreover, while the Soviet system has been held together largely through the exercise of Soviet military power, economic relations have been an important cement holding the American bloc together.

These economic and strategic differences between the two blocs have been crucial determinants of the postwar international economy and the patterns of transnational relations which have emerged. For this reason some attention must be given to the interplay of economic and political factors in the evolution of relations between the three major components of the contemporary international economy: the United States, Western Europe, and Japan.

Contrary to the hopes of the postwar economic planners who met at Bretton Woods in 1944, the achievement of a system of multilateral trade was soon realized to be an impossibility. The United Kingdom's experience with currency convertibility, which had been forced upon it by the United States, had proven to be a disaster. The United Kingdom and the rest of Europe were simply too weak and short of dollars to engage in a free market. A further weakening of their economies threatened to drive them into the arms of the Soviet Union. In the interest of preventing this the United States in cooperation with Western Europe had to rebuild the world economy in a way not envisaged by the postwar planners.

The reconstruction of the West European economy involved the solution of three problems. In the first place, Europe was desperately short of the dollars required to meet immediate needs and to replenish its capital stock. Second, the prewar European economies had been oriented toward colonial markets. Now the colonies were in revolt, and the United States strongly opposed the revival of a world economy based on a colonial preference system. Third, the practices of economic nationalism and closed preference systems between European states and their overseas colonies had completely fragmented the European economy.

The problem of rehabilitating the economy of the Federal Republic of Germany (West Germany) was particularly difficult. The major trading nation on the Continent, its division into Soviet and Western zones and the Soviet occupation of Eastern Europe had cut industrial West Germany off from its natural trading partners in the agricultural German Democratic Republic (East Germany) and the East. The task therefore was to integrate the industrial Western zones into a larger West European economy comprising agricultural France and Italy. The failure to reintegrate industrial Germany into the larger world economy was regarded to have been one of the tragic errors after World War I. A repetition of this error would force West Germany into the Soviet camp.

The American response to this challenge is well known. Through the

Marshall Plan, the Organization for European Economic Cooperation (OEEC), and the European Coal and Steel Community (ECSC), the European economy was revived and radically transformed. For our purposes one point is significant. In the interest of security the United States tolerated, and in fact promoted, the creation of a preference area in Western Europe which discriminated against American goods. At first the mechanism of discrimination was the nonconvertibility of European currencies; then, after the establishment of the European Economic Community (EEC) in 1958, discrimination took the form of one common external tariff.

The economic impact of economic regionalism in Western Europe was not, however, completely detrimental to United States–European trade. One can in fact argue that regionalism gave Europe the courage and security to depart from traditions of economic nationalism and colonialism. The establishment of a large trading area in Europe turned out to be more trade-creating than trade-diverting. As a consequence American and European economic ties increased and the United States continued to enjoy a favorable balance of trade with its European partners.

With respect to Japan the United States faced a situation similar to that presented by West Germany. Although Japan was not severely damaged by the war, it was a densely populated major trading nation exceptionally dependent upon foreign sources of raw materials, technology, and agricultural products. With the victory of the Communists on the Chinese mainland Japan's major prewar trading partner came under the control of the Soviet bloc. Furthermore, Japan suffered from discrimination by other industrialized states both in their home markets and in their overseas colonial empires. The exclusion of the Japanese from South and Southeast Asia practiced by the Dutch, French, and British had been a major cause of Japan's military aggression, and the continued existence of these preference systems threatened its economic well-being. Separated from the Soviet Union by a small body of water and economically isolated, Japan's situation was a highly precarious one.

As in the case of West Germany the task of American foreign policy was to integrate Japan into the larger world economy and lessen the attraction of markets controlled by the Communist bloc. While this history of American efforts to restructure Japan's role in the world economy is less well known than is the history of its European counterpart, the basic aspects deserve to be emphasized. In the first place, the United States brought pressures to bear against Dutch, French, and British colonialism in South and Southeast Asia and encouraged the integration of these areas into a larger framework of multilateral trade. Second, over the strong opposition of Western Europe the United States sponsored Japanese membership in the International Monetary Fund (IMF), the

General Agreement on Tariffs and Trade (GATT), and other international organizations.[25] Third, and most significant, the United States in the negotiations leading to the Treaty of Peace with Japan granted Japan privileged access to the American home market.[26]

At the same time that these developments in the economic realm were taking place, through the instrumentalities of the North Atlantic Treaty Organization (NATO) and the Treaty of Peace with Japan, Western Europe and Japan were brought under the protection of the American nuclear umbrella. In Europe, Japan, and around the periphery of the Soviet Union and the People's Republic of China (Communist China) the United States erected a base system by which to counter the Soviet advantage of geographical proximity. Thus, with their security guaranteed by this Pax Americana, Japan, Western Europe, and, to a lesser extent, the United States have been able to devote the better part of their energies to the achievement of high rates of economic growth within the framework of a highly interdependent transnational economy.

Just as the Pax Britannica provided the security and political framework for the expansion of transnational economic activity in the nineteenth century, so this Pax Americana has fulfilled a similar function in the mid–twentieth century. Under American leadership the various rounds of GATT negotiations have enabled trade to expand at an unprecedented rate, far faster than the growth of gross national product in the United States and Western Europe. The United States dollar has become the basis of the international monetary system, and, with the rise of the Eurodollar market, governments have lost almost all control over a large segment of the transnational economy. Finally, the multinational corporation has found the global political environment a highly congenial one and has been able to integrate production across national boundaries.

The corollary of this argument is, of course, that just as a particular array of political interests and relations permitted this system of transnational economic relations to come into being, so changes in these political factors can profoundly alter the system and even bring it to an end. If, as numerous writers argue, there is a growing contradiction between the nation-state and transnational activities, the resolution may very well be in favor of the nation-state or, more likely, of regional arrangements centered on the dominant industrial powers: Japan, the United States, and Western Europe.

IV

This argument that contemporary transnational processes rest on a peculiar set of political relationships can be substantiated, I believe, if one analyzes the two most crucial relationships which underlie the contemporary international economy. The first is the relationship between the United States and West Germany, the second is that between the United States and Japan.

While the American–West German special relationship is based on a number of factors including that of mutual economic advantage, from the perspective of transnational activities one factor is of crucial importance. In simplest terms this is the exchange of American protection of West Germany against the Soviet Union for guaranteed access to EEC markets for American products and direct investment. In both agricultural commodities and manufactured goods the United States continues to enjoy a very favorable trade balance with Western Europe. With respect to direct investment the subsidiaries of American corporations have been able to establish a very powerful position in Western Europe since the beginning of the EEC in 1958.

Without this overall favorable trade balance with Western Europe and West German willingness to hold dollars, the American balance-of-payments situation might, the West Germans fear, force the United States to reduce its troop strength in West Germany. As such a move could lessen the credibility of the American nuclear deterrent, the West Germans are very reluctant to make any moves which would weaken the American presence in Western Europe. Consequently, while the significance of American direct investment in Europe for the American balance of payments is unclear, the West Germans are unwilling to take any action regarding this investment which might alienate American opinion and lessen the American commitment to Western Europe.

The importance of the military dependence of West Germany on the United States for continued access to EEC markets for subsidiaries of American corporations was revealed several years ago. In the early 1960s President Charles de Gaulle of France launched an offensive against increasing American economic penetration of Western Europe. While the major part of this effort was directed against "the hegemony of the dollar," a parallel attempt was made to arrest and possibly reverse the flow of American direct investment in Western Europe.[27]

The initial move of the French government was to prevent further American direct investment in France. This effort, however, soon proved to be self-defeating. Denied permission to establish or purchase subsidiaries in France, American corporations were welcomed into one of France's partners in the EEC and thus still had access to the French market. That France acting alone could not solve the problem was driven home to the French when General Motors Corporation, denied permission to locate in France, established one of the largest automobile assembly plants in Western Europe across the border in Belgium.

In response to this situation de Gaulle sought to obtain West German cooperation against American investment in EEC countries. Together these two most powerful of the six could dictate a policy which the others would be forced to accept. Through the instrumentality of the Franco-German Friendship Treaty of 1963, therefore, de Gaulle sought to form a Bonn-Paris axis directed against American hegemony in Western Europe. While the terms of this treaty go beyond our immediate concerns, two aspects are important. In the first place, de Gaulle wanted West Germany to join France in taking a stand against American investment. Second, he wanted to see joint West German–French cooperative efforts in science, technology, and industry in order to lessen European dependence upon the United States in these areas.

Although there was sentiment in West Germany favorable to taking measures to limit the rapidly growing role of American subsidiaries in EEC countries, the West German government refused to take any action which might weaken the American commitment to defend Western Europe. The United States government not only reminded the West Germans that a continued American military presence was dependent upon West German support of measures to lessen the American balance-of-payments deficit, West Germany was also pressured to increase its military purchases from the United States and to avoid competitive arrangements with France. Largely as a result of these American pressures the Friendship Treaty was in effect aborted and the first serious counteroffensive of the nation-state against the multinational corporation collapsed. It is clear, however, that the outcome of this tale would have been altogether different if West Germany had desired greater military and economic independence from the United States.

Turning to the other pillar of the contemporary transnational economy, the American-Japanese special relationship, mutual economic interest is an important bond, but the primary factor in this relationship has been the security issue. In contrast to the American–West German situation, however, this relationship involves American protection and a special position for the Japanese in the American market in exchange for United States bases in Japan and Okinawa. The asymmetry of this relationship compared with that between the United States and West Germany reflects the differences in the economic and military situations.

As mentioned earlier the basic problem for American foreign policy with respect to Japan was how to reintegrate this highly industrialized and heavily populated country into the world economy. Given Communist control of mainland Asia and the opposition of European countries to opening their markets to the Japanese this meant throwing open the American economy to Japanese exports. As a consequence of this favored treatment the Japanese have enjoyed an exceptionally favorable balance of trade with the United States. For security reasons the United States has not only tolerated this situation but, with a few exceptions, has not restricted Japanese imports or forced the Japanese to open their economy to American direct investment.

In contrast to the situation prevailing in Europe the purpose of American military base structure in Japan is not merely to deter local aggression against the Japanese; rather, it is essential for the maintenance of American power and influence throughout the western Pacific and Southeast Asia. Without access to Japanese bases the United States could not have fought two wars in Asia over the past two decades and could not continue its present role in the area. Largely because of this dependence upon Japanese bases for its strategic position around the periphery of Communist China, the United States has been willing to tolerate in a period of balance-of-payments deficit the $1.5 billion annual trade surplus Japan enjoys vis-à-vis the United States.

In the case of both the American-European and the American-Japanese relationships new forces are now at work which threaten to undermine the foundations of contemporary transnational relations. In the case of United States–European relations the most dramatic change is the decreased fear of the Soviet Union by both partners. As a consequence both Americans and Europeans are less tolerant of the price they have to pay for their special relationship. The Europeans feel less dependent upon the United States for their security and are more concerned with the detrimental aspects of close economic, military, and diplomatic ties with the United States. The United States, for its part, is increasingly sensitive to European discrimination against American exports and feels threatened by EEC moves toward the creation of a preference system encompassing much of Western Europe, the Middle East, and Africa. As the Mansfield amendment to reduce United States military forces in Europe reveals, Americans, too, are less willing to pay the cost of maintaining a large military force abroad.[28]

With respect to the relationship of Japan to the United States, strategic and economic changes are undermining the foundations of transnationalism. At the same time that Communist China is receding as a security threat to the United States and Japan, economic strains are beginning to aggravate relations between the two countries. In the eyes of the United States Japan's economy is no longer weak and vulnerable, necessitating special consideration by the United States. As a consequence the demands of American interests for import curbs against Japanese goods and for the liberalization of Japanese policies on foreign direct investment are beginning to take precedence over foreign policy and strategic considerations. Nor does the United States continue to accept the fact that the defense burden should rest so heavily on it alone.

Underlying the Nixon Doctrine of American retrenchment in Asia is the appreciation that a greater Japanese military effort would not only reduce American defense costs but would also cause the Japanese to divert resources from their export economy and relieve Japanese pressures in the American market.

The Japanese for their part resent the fact that they are almost totally dependent upon the United States for their security and economic well-being. While they of course want to maintain a strong position in the American market and feel particularly threatened by protectionist sentiment in the United States, they are growing increasingly concerned about the price they must pay for their close association with the United States. Moreover, they feel especially vulnerable to American economic pressures such as those that have been exerted to induce Japan to permit direct investment by American corporations. But the dominant new factor is the Japanese desire to play a more independent role in the world and to enjoy the prestige that is commensurate with their powerful and expanding economy.

In the cases of both American-European and American-Japanese relations new strains have appeared which threaten to undermine the political framework of transnational economic activity. Diplomatic and military bonds tying Europe and Japan to the United States have weakened at the same time that economic conflicts have intensified and have become less tolerable to all three major parties. As a result the favorable political factors that have facilitated the rapid expansion of transnational processes over the past several decades are receding. In their stead new political forces have come into play that are tending to isolate the United States and to favor a more regional organization of the international economy.

On the other hand, one must readily acknowledge that the multinational corporation and transnational processes have achieved tremendous momentum. It is not without good reason that numerous authorities have predicted the demise of the nation-state and the complete reordering of international life by 200 or 300 "megafirms."[29] Perhaps, as these authorities argue, the multinational corporation as an institution has sufficiently taken root in the vested interests of all major parties that it can survive the vicissitudes of political change. History, however, does not provide much comfort for this train of thought. As Staley and Viner have suggested, the contradiction between the economic and political organization of society is not always resolved in favor of economic rationality. Moreover, whatever the outcome – the preservation of multilateral transnational processes, a reversion to economic nationalism, or the division of the globe by economic regionalism – the determining consideration will be the diplomatic and strategic interests of the dominant powers.

V

Prior to concluding this essay one crucial question remains to be treated: What, after all, has been the impact of transnational economic activities, especially the multinational corporation, on international politics? In answer to this question both Marxists and what one might call the transnational ideologists see these transnational processes and actors as having had a profound impact on international relations. Some go much further. By breaking the monopoly of the nation-state over international economic relations the multinational corporation is claimed to have altered the very nature of international relations.

Under certain circumstances and in relation to particular states there can be little doubt that the multinational corporation has, and can exercise, considerable influence over domestic and international relations. One could mention in this connection the international petroleum companies, for example. But in general there is little evidence to substantiate the argument that the multinational corporation as an independent actor has had a significant impact on international politics. As Staley has convincingly shown in his study of foreign investment prior to World War II, where business corporations have exercised an influence over political developments they have tended to do so as instruments of their home governments rather than as independent actors.[30]

Contemporary studies on the multinational corporation indicate that Staley's conclusion continues to hold true. While the evidence is indisputable that the multinational corporation is profoundly important in the realm of international economic relations, its political significance is largely confined to its impact on domestic politics where it is an irritant to nationalistic sentiments. In part the resentment has been due to the unwarranted interference by foreign-owned corporations in domestic affairs; this has especially been the case in less developed countries. More frequently, nationalistic feelings have been aroused by the predominant positions multinational corporations may hold in the overall economy or in particularly sensitive sectors.

Despite all the polemics against multinational corporations there is little evidence to support the view that they have been very successful in replacing the nation-state as the primary actor in international politics. Where these business enterprises have influenced international political relations, they have done so, like any other interest group, by influencing the policies of their home governments. Where they have tried to influence the foreign and economic policies of host governments, they have most frequently been acting in response to the laws of their home countries and as agents of their home governments. In defense of this argument it should be noted that a Canadian study of American direct investment in Canada focused its concern almost exclusively on the extraterritorial application of American law (antitrust laws, the Trading with the Enemy Act, and balance-of-payments regulations).[31] As Canada has a higher percentage of foreign ownership than any other industrialized country and as this study was one of the most thorough which any government has conducted on foreign direct investment, its conclusions are especially significant.

Contrary to the argument that the multinational corporation will somehow supplant the nation-state, I think it is closer to the truth to argue that the role of the nation-state in economic as well as in political life is increasing and that the multinational corporation is actually a stimulant to the further extension of state power in the economic realm. One should not forget that the multinational corporation is largely an American phenomenon and that in response to this American challenge other governments are increasingly intervening in their domestic economies in order to counterbalance the power of American corporations and to create domestic rivals of equal size and competence.

The paradox of the contemporary situation is that the increasing interdependence among national economies, for which the multinational corporation is partially responsible, is accompanied by increased governmental interference in economic affairs. What this neo-mercantilism constitutes, of course, is one response to the basic contradiction between the economic and political organization of contemporary international society. But in contrast to the opinion of a George Ball who sees this conflict resolved in favor of transnational processes, the internationalization of production, and actors like the multinational corporation, nationalists in Canada, Western Europe, and the less developed world favor upholding more powerful states to counterbalance large multinational corporations.

Similarly, the impetus today behind the EEC, Japan's effort to build an economic base less dependent on the United States, and other moves toward regionalism reflect in part a desire to lessen the weight of American economic power; in effect, these regional undertakings are essentially economic alliances between sovereign governments. Although they are altering the political framework within which economic forces will increasingly have to operate, the basic unit is and will remain the nation-state. For better or for worse it continues to be the most powerful object of man's loyalty and affection.

NOTES

1. Sidney Rolfe, "Updating Adam Smith," *Interplay*, 4 (November 1968), p. 15.
2. An analysis of the argument is provided by Edmund Silberner, *The Problem*

of War in Nineteenth Century Economic Thought, trans. Alexander H. Krappe (Princeton: Princeton University Press, 1946).

3. Adam Smith, *An Inquiry into the Nature and Causes of the Wealth of Nations,* ed. Edwin Cannan (New York: Modern Library, 1937).

4. The relevant sections appear in Ernst Wangermann, ed., *The Role of Force in History: A Study of Bismarck's Policy of Blood and Iron,* trans. Jack Cohen (New York: International Publishers, 1968). The best exposition of Marxist theories of economic relations is P.J.D. Wiles, *Communist International Economics* (New York: Frederick A. Praeger, 1969).

5. Wangermann, p. 13.

6. Ibid., p. 14.

7. The article appears in J. N. Bhagwati, ed., *Economics and World Order* (New York: World Law Fund, 1970).

8. Ibid., p. 1.

9. Ibid., pp. 2–3.

10. Jacob Viner, *The Customs Union Issue* (Studies in the Administration of International Law and Organization, No. 10) (New York: Carnegie Endowment for International Peace, 1950).

11. Ibid., pp. 98–99.

12. Ibid., p. 101.

13. Ibid., pp. 95–101.

14. Ibid., p. 105.

15. Eugene Staley, *World Economy in Transition: Technology vs. Politics, Laissez Faire vs. Planning, Power vs. Welfare* (Publications of the Council on Foreign Relations) (New York: Council on Foreign Relations [Under the auspices of the American Coordinating Committee for International Studies], 1939), pp. 51–52.

16. Ibid., p. 52.

17. Perroux's theory of the dominant economy is set forth in his "Esquisse d'une theorie de l'économie dominante," *Économie appliquée,* 1 (April–September 1948), pp. 243–300.

18. Edward Hallett Carr, *The Twenty Years' Crisis, 1919–1939: An Introduction to the Study of International Politics* (2nd ed.; New York: St. Martin's Press, 1954), p. 117.

19. Albert H. Imlah, *Economic Elements in the Pax Britannica: Studies in British Foreign Trade in the Nineteenth Century* (Cambridge: Harvard University Press, 1958), chapter I.

20. J. A. Hobson, *Imperialism: A Study* (3rd rev. ed.; London: G. Allen & Unwin, 1938), p. 57.

21. J. B. Condliffe, *The Commerce of Nations* (New York: W. W. Norton & Co., 1950), p. 502.

22. The basic source for this period is Richard N. Gardner, *Sterling-Dollar Diplomacy: The Origins and Prospects of Our International Economic Order* (expd. ed.; New York: McGraw-Hill Book Co., 1969).

23. The most ambitious statement of this thesis is Gabriel Kolko, *The Politics of War: The World and the United States Foreign Policy, 1943–1945* (New York: Random House, 1968).

24. See the study by Felix Gilbert, *To the Farewell Address: Ideas of Early American Foreign Policy* (Princeton: Princeton University Press, 1961).

25. For the history of these efforts see Gardner Patterson, *Discrimination in International Trade: The Policy Issues, 1945–1965* (Princeton: Princeton University Press, 1966), chapter 6.

26. Frederick S. Dunn, in collaboration with Annemarie Shimoney, Percy E. Corbett, and Bernard C. Cohen, *Peace-Making and the Settlement with Japan* (Princeton: Princeton University Press, 1963), chapter 7.

27. For this history see Robert Gilpin, *France in the Age of the Scientific State* (Princeton: Princeton University Press [for the Center of International Studies, Princeton University], 1968), chapter 3.

28. United States, Congress, House, *Amending the Military Selective Service Act of 1967 to Increase Military Pay; To Authorize Military Active Duty Strengths for Fiscal Year 1972; And for Other Purposes,* H.R. 6531, 92nd Cong., 1st sess., 1971, Amendment No. 86.

29. Howard V. Perlmutter, "Some Management Problems in Spaceship Earth: The Megafirm and the Global Industrial Estate," *Academy of Management Proceedings, 29th Annual Meeting, Chicago, August 24–27, 1969,* pp. 59–93.

30. Eugene Staley, *War and the Private Investor: A Study in the Relations of International Politics and International Private Investment* (Garden City: Doubleday, Doran & Co., 1935).

31. *Foreign Ownership and the Structure of Canadian Industry,* Report of the Task Force on the Structure of Canadian Industry (Ottawa: Queen's Printer, January 1968).

9
Transnationalism, Power Politics, and the Realities of the Present System

In this selection Sullivan critically examines contentions pertaining to the transformation of world politics in terms of actors, issues, interdependence, and force. While acknowledging change and the importance of continuing re-evaluation of the makeup of the contemporary world, Sullivan suggests that world affairs today are characterized more by continuity than by discontinuity.

INTRODUCTION

Beginning in the late 1960s and early 1970s, assumptions about the basic structure of the international system once again came under scrutiny. The state-centric "realist" image, some argued, was becoming more irrelevant to the contemporary international system as that system became dominated by new actors, increased interdependence, and the emergence of new issues.[1] In essence, it was said, the international system had been transformed to such a degree that traditional paradigms for understanding international politics were to one degree or another either outmoded or severely flawed, and new paradigms were needed.

This chapter, part of a larger work on transformation in the contemporary system, investigates the issue by reviewing some empirical evidence on the makeup of the present system. It will begin by contrasting the traditional "realist" model with what – for want of a better term – will be described here as a transnationalist view. Such an enterprise, condensing an extensive literature into one label, is always hazardous. In the present case, "transnationalism" covers a very broad and diverse group of scholars and policymakers. Some may see this as an over-simplification that perhaps creates a "straw man"; nonetheless, the perusal of a rather extensive academic literature and existing policy statements[2] strongly suggests that this grouping does in fact have validity. Although there have been some critiques of this school of thought recently,[3] and some of the ideas outlined below have been either rejected or changed since they were first presented, the characterization still represents an accurate portrait of a continuing body of literature. Moreover, these contrasting positions have a long history of tension with each other, so this analysis has relevance beyond the 1960s and 1970s.

The realist perspective is well known. Nation-states and their decision-makers are the most important actors. Each nation-state is sovereign in international politics; it is an independent entity. International relations is both a struggle for power and an attempt to attain peace; the major – or perhaps only – issue is the military security of the sovereign nation. The ultimate recourse a nation has in defense of its sovereignty is, of course, war.

> The key insight underlying these assumptions relates to the realist under-
> standing of power. Nation-states are seen as the critical actors, because
> they alone are sovereign and can marshal the necessary resources to wield
> power.[4]

The broad characteristics of the "transnationalist" perspectives can be outlined briefly. First, the role and function of the nation-state in international politics has changed. New actors, such as multinational corporations, international organizations, cartels, terrorists, and hijackers, have emerged. Traditional models do not take these non-state actors sufficiently into account.[5] Second, non-military and non-security issues, such as population, pollution, distribution of food, depletion of natural resources, dependency of Third World countries on the more developed countries, and use of the oceans and outer space, have come to the forefront.

The third characteristic is an increase in interdependence: trade, technology transfer, investment, travel, migration, student exchanges, and other transactions have all multiplied. Even when hard evidence may not clearly *show* that interdependence is increasing, there seems to be an underlying faith that it is there:

> Though many of the relevant factors do not show up clearly in an enumera-
> tion of iterative transactions, there can be little doubt that political
> decision-makers in any given part of the system are more sensitive to
> events occurring in other parts of the world than was the case in the past.[6]

The fourth characteristic is that war is no longer a major option for foreign policy decision-makers, and the more powerful the nation, the less viable war becomes. Weapons of massive destruction have drastically changed the nature of warfare. "We are moving to an era dominated by economic power – an era in which war between major states may virtually disappear."[7]

Although scholars have tackled these factors singly,[8] few have focused on all four or on their relationship to the broader question of the models we use to study international politics. The next four sections of this chapter present some data relevant to these "views" of the world. Underlying this exercise, of course, is the epistemological assumption that a real world exists and that we can know it. At the same time, no empirical analysis can demonstrate definitively that one view of the world is more accurate than another. One reason for this, as we shall see, is that the realist and transnationalist views, although differing markedly in several respects, nonetheless bear some similarities. These similarities should raise questions about the uniqueness and utility of the "new" paradigm. The transnationalists *have* highlighted some phenomena ignored by more traditional analysis, but one of the implications of this study will be that, rather than concluding that a new framework is needed, we should investigate *how much* change has taken place and whether that change itself might not be subjected to realist concepts. The concluding section presents some further implications concerning our understanding of the recent, and possibly future, transformations of the international system.

ACTORS IN INTERNATIONAL POLITICS

Admittedly, the nation-state is unlikely to exist forever; nonetheless, its decline has been heralded before – witness the surge of "internationalism" after both world wars. Questions about the viability or usefulness of the nation-state are not new. But perhaps, it is argued, things are different now. This section presents first some evidence in agreement with that contention, and then some opposing evidence.

One of the few projects to investigate this question empirically can be used as an illustration. The Non-State Actor Project (NOSTAC) contended that the state-centric model had become "obsolete."[9] Using "events data," this project showed that from 1948 to 1972 non-state actors *were* involved in international interactions. For example, in the Middle East the United Nations was the fourth most frequent initiator of actions and the third most frequent target. Of the twenty most frequent actors, seven were non-state; six of twenty targets were non-state. In Latin America, thirteen of twenty targets were non-state. In Western Europe, non-state actors were less important, but nonetheless eleven of twenty initiators and ten of the twenty most frequent targets were non-state. The investigators concluded that "of all the dyadic interactions in the three regions for twenty-five years, under half involved nation-states simultaneously as actors and targets, and over 11 percent involved non-state actors exclusively."[10]

Other evidence also illustrates this view. Intergovernmental organizations (IGOs) have ballooned, especially since 1940. Starting at less than 25 in 1820, their number remained steady until just after 1900; it jumped to almost 75 in 1920, to 80 in 1940, and to over 175 in 1960. In Asia IGOs grew from 1 in 1950 to 25 in 1975. Asian memberships in regional IGOs grew from 6 in 1950–1953 to 180 in 1970–1971; professional staff grew from 7 to 357; and IGO budgets grew from $850,000 in 1955–1956 to $16 million in 1970–1971.[11] The number of international non-governmental organizations (INGOs) grew from about 10 in 1855 to over 300 in 1950. Even in more recent years, the number of "active" INGOs (as opposed to many that become defunct) increased on an average 4.7 percent each year from 1954 to 1968; from 1962 to 1968, the average annual increase was 6.2 percent.[12]

Multinational corporations (MNCs) have generated popular controversy. Although much of the conflict is ideological, there is no doubt that MNCs are economically important. If it is accurate to compare nations' gross national products with multinational corporations' gross annual sales, as many analysts do, it is clear that such corporations can be potent actors. Combining nations and multinational corporations into one list by ranking GNPs and annual sales shows that forty of the top ninety-nine members are corporations.[13] General Motors ranks twenty-third, Standard Oil of New Jersey twenty-seventh, Ford twenty-ninth, and Royal Dutch/Shell thirty-sixth; all have higher annual sales than the gross national products of Finland, Iran, South Korea, New Zealand, Cuba, and Saudi Arabia.

In conclusion, actors *other than* nations are involved in international politics. Further evidence will be presented shortly, but here let us consider the *interpretation* of some of these data and their implication for international relations theory. For instance, another way of reading the NOSTAC data mentioned above is to note that 44 percent of all events from 1948 to 1972 still had a nation-state as *both* actor *and* target, while only 11 percent had a non-state actor as both actor and target. Moreover, nation-states were the *initiators* in over 63 percent of *all* actions and were *targets* in almost 70 percent. Although the conclusions of the NOSTAC investigators were quite clear, they were aware that "nation-states through their governments are still the primary actors involved in global politics if we take "involvement" to mean the appearance of a given actor as *either* the actor or target in a dyad."[14] Perhaps more important, from 1948 to 1972 there was actually a decline from 32 percent to 18 percent in events in which some non-state actor was involved.

This latter finding leads to the next set of evidence, which also supports the contention of the transnationalists, if only to an extent. The World Event Interaction Survey (WEIS) data showed an overall 17 percent reading for non-state behavior for the 1966–1975 period; but again it is more interesting to observe the changes in this non-state behavior. The range of such involvement is from 12 percent to 23 percent. There is a clear increase from 1966 (12 percent) to 1970 (23 percent), mostly accounted for by the Viet Cong and the National Liberation Front in South Vietnam; then the percentages drop for the next two years, increase for one year, and drop to 14 percent by 1975. Thus just as there was an overall *decrease* shown in the NOSTAC data, here we see a rather marked *increase* followed by a return to about the level of a decade earlier. We will come back to this evidence below in considering more specifically terrorist activity.

To return to the NOSTAC data for a moment, the obvious methodological problem is equating each action, as reported by the media, of an IGO, INGO, MNC, political party, individual, terrorist group, or nation-state. Although a single terrorist act, such as a threat to blow up a loaded passenger plane, may have more impact than an action of a small nation, there is certainly a question of which actor is more important in the aggregate. This problem is partly illustrated in a study of U.S.–West German relations,[15] in which the authors showed that in regard to conflict and cooperation, nine of the ten most conflictual actors were non-state.[16] But those ten actors account for only 184 of 2598 actions, or 7 percent. Moreover, to view as important the fact that 100 percent of Arab behavior was conflictual compared to 20 percent of U.S. behavior disregards the fact that Arab conflict consisted of 18 acts compared to 200 for the United States.

A related problem arises when considering the possibility of one other type of new actor in the contemporary system. Richard W. Mansbach and John A. Vasquez used the "bureaucratic politics" model[17] to argue that the traditional notion of nation-states acting as single units is outmoded. They found that although the United States, treated as a single, unitary actor, exhibited 20.7 percent conflictual behavior, the U.S. Department of Commerce and U.S. "central decision-makers" showed 57.1 percent and 11.6 percent conflict, respectively. They concluded that "to ignore such differences is to provide a map that may be of little utility" and this would be "a particularly egregious omission if bureaucratic action tended to specialize in certain types of issues and interacted only with certain types of targets."[18] However, their own data show that 92 percent of all U.S. actions were initiated by "governmental" or "central" decision-makers, whereas the Department of Commerce accounted for only .7 percent of the total.

William D. Coplin and his coauthors also argued that sub-national actors must be considered.[19] By looking at each bureaucratic actor's position on the issue, its level of power, and the salience of the issue to it, they came to a more refined prediction concerning the case of the United States' agreement with the twelve-mile rule than they could have by considering the United States as one unified actor. However, they were only studying a single, limited issue; they noted that they were unconcerned with whether their method became universally accepted, or with the effect that acceptance – or non-acceptance – would have on international politics as a whole, or with any other dependent variable. The implication, therefore, is *not* that nations must be broken down into their respective bureaucracies in order to understand all foreign policies, but that the more narrow the international behavior we focus upon, the more we may need to disaggregate the actors.

So far we have seen that there are new, non-state actors, and that in some cases there have been increases in such actors; at the same time, we have seen that the evidence is not quite as easy to interpret in terms of drawing implications for understanding international politics. Going somewhat beyond these questions, James M. McCormick and Young W. Kihl looked at the *role* of one type of non-state actor, namely IGOs. In the realist view, they argued, the role of IGOs should be limited; for realists, nations should constitute the primary actors, and therefore IGOs should only be used for relatively less important matters, that is, for non-core values outside the military area, and more powerful countries should use them less.[20] On the other hand, McCormick and Kihl stated, the "complex interdependence" model[21] contends that since military security issues are losing their primacy, states will turn more and more to IGOs rather than to bilateral diplomacy, there will be high use of IGOs by nations, and IGOs will be used for many issues.

McCormick and Kihl concluded that the realist perspective is generally supported by the evidence.[22] Although the use of international organizations is greater than realists might expect, about 54 percent of the behavior occurring inside as opposed to outside international organizations, 92 percent of the behavior initiated within IGOs is for *routine* as opposed to *crisis* situations. Compared to the 8 percent of IGO behavior devoted to crisis situations, 40.5 percent of the behavior outside IGOs was devoted to crises. More powerful states used IGOs less, more symbolic ("verbal") as opposed to tangible ("deeds") behavior occurred within IGOs, and, within crises, the more powerful states, when they acted in IGOs, used less tangible and more symbolic behavior. Finally, only in 1964 and 1968 were there increases over the previous years in the use of "low politics" (economic or functional) as opposed to "high politics" (political) IGOs; in 1968 there was a 25 percent usage of low politics IGOs, compared to 35 percent in 1959. In sum, while neither the realist nor the transnationalist model is "confirmed" as correct, behavior we would expect given the transnationalist assumptions does not clearly appear.

Returning now to the question of terrorist activity mentioned earlier, two additional sources confirm the WEIS data patterns:[23] from relatively infrequent terrorist activity from 1960 to 1968, all three sources show drastic increases in 1969-1970, followed by a decline in 1971-1972, another increase in 1973 (one source showing a further increase in 1974), and declines in 1974-1975. One of the sources shows that the percentage of terrorist acts went from about 1.5 percent of all events in 1967 to 13 percent in 1970 and back to about 4 percent in 1975.

The three sets of data are not uniform, the peaks and valleys are not simultaneous, but the overall trends are similar. But three other points deserve mention here. First, perhaps it is not so important to note the increase in such non-state behavior as to try to *account for* such increases; in other words, what brought them about? Second, what accounts for the fluctuations, with terrorist behavior high in some years and low in others? Third and equally important is the observation that terrorist activity decreased by 1975.[24]

In other words, we should be as interested in *explaining* the changes as in simply pointing them out. Perhaps system transformation itself is a cause of such changes, and the fact that several different *types* of non-state behavior fluctuated together might suggest some contagion explanation. Finally, some thrust is taken out of the argument that a "new system" has emerged if in fact in some dimensions—such as terrorist activity—the system has reverted to previous levels of activity.

Hence, we come to an unsurprising conclusion: non-state actors exist but nation-states are still important in international affairs. However, given the existence and in some cases increase in non-state actors in international politics, two theoretical questions must still be asked: "In what way does an analysis of non-state actors help us better to understand patterns of international politics? Exactly how much, what types, and what domains of international politics are now made amenable to understanding?" The tendency has been to focus on the first question to the neglect of the second; we will return to this point in the concluding section.

THE ISSUES IN INTERNATIONAL POLITICS

The second component of the transnationalist view is that the issues in world politics have changed. Because traditional issues focused on military might, force, violence, and the ultimate resort to war—all based on "power"—the emergence of new concerns means that the importance of "power" has waned. It certainly seems to be the case that world leaders have focused in recent years on different issues. Traditional concerns—the ongoing SALT talks, periodic international crises in the Middle East and Asia—are still present; nonetheless, through much of the 1970s there appeared to be a new agenda: the Law of the Sea, increased interest in trade negotiations, concerns over international drug-trafficking and airline hijacking, the actions of economic cartels, and so on.

But, as with the question of actors, there are really several different areas of concern. In addition to whether "new" issues are present, we should ask whether we need distinguish among different types of "issue-areas." Further, does the emergence of new issues mean that resolution of conflicts over these issues will be different than resolution of conflicts over more traditional issues? In other words, does the emergence of seemingly "non-power" issues mean that power will no longer play a role in resolving them, and what exactly is gained by disaggregating issues?

In regard to the first question, the NOSTAC project found that issues did change from 1948 to 1972,[25] and the authors argued that an accurate description of the politics in the Middle East, Latin America, and Western Europe can be garnered only through the realization of a substantial issue change. In a later study, Mansbach and Vasquez, in looking at U.S.–West German relations from 1949 to 1975, concluded that the amount of conflict and cooperation across different issues differs. In their aggregated data, spanning a number of countries and seventy-eight issues, 14.3 percent of the events were conflictual and 60 percent cooperative (with the rest falling into a residual category). Yet for the issue of World War II conferences, for instance, 39 percent of the behavior was conflictual and 28.8 percent cooperative; on the Western commitment to Berlin, 11.4 percent of the behavior was conflictual and 33.6 percent was cooperative, and on the international monetary issue only 2.6 percent was conflictual and 89.9 percent was cooperative. Restricting their analysis solely to the U.S.–West German dyad, they found that although in total there was 13.9 percent conflictual behavior from the United States to West Germany, there was 40 percent on the U.S.-European trade issue, 66.7 percent on Nazi-related questions, and only 8.3 percent on the issue of German reunification. Similar differences emerged in West German behavior toward the United States.

But again the interpretation of these data is not necessarily straightforward. For one thing, an investigation of the three periods in the NOSTAC report shows that the rank orders of the issues across all three time periods for the three regions are remarkably similar: of the nine resulting correlations, seven are positive and only two are negative; five of the seven positive correlations are substantial (.40 to .79), but only one of the negative ones reaches that level. In other words, while issues did change, there was substantial similarity across the three time periods.

Further, concerning Mansbach and Vasquez's data, which cover a twenty-six-year period, legitimate questions can be raised about what has been accomplished by breaking down the issues. For the U.S.-West German dyad, fifty-four of the seventy-eight issues had fewer than 5 interactions in either direction. Of the remaining twenty-four issues, nineteen had less than 20 actions in either direction. Moreover, of the total sample of 3,399 actions, the events in these twenty-four most discussed issues amount to only 364, or just over 10 percent. Such disaggregation of issues, therefore, rather than resulting in either substantive or theoretical advances, may simply produce instability in the data.

Likewise, Coplin and his coauthors, in their PRINCE framework, argue that combined conflict-cooperation indexes may obscure what is occurring in specific issue-areas.[26] For instance, they investigated the actions of four dyads—U.S.-North Korea, U.S.-Egypt, U.S.-People's Republic of China, and Israel-Egypt—on six different issues. In several cases, the overall conflict-cooperation score differs from the score by issue-area. However, of the twenty-four possibilities (four dyads and six issue-areas), half led to two acts or less, making average scores meaningless. For the remaining twelve possibilities, seven of the mean scores within issue-areas were significantly different from the aggregated conflict-cooperation scores. Thus, half of all possible breakdowns by issue had so few actions they could not be analyzed (suggesting again that these data might be unstable); and less than 30 percent of all the possible combinations were statistically different from the overall assessment of conflict-cooperation.[27]

There is no arguing with the position that scholars and policymakers seem to be focusing on different specific issues, but it has not been made clear how the emergence of these specific—and perhaps sometimes fleeting—issues substantially affects our understanding of world politics. More important, the emergence of such new issues becomes less vital if, in fact, the outbreak, process, and resolution of conflicts surrounding them follow traditional patterns. In other words, resolution of such issues as control of the oceans and outer space, international trade disputes, the pricing of oil, and so on may be subject to traditional factors or may lend themselves to different success rates in different types of international systems, such as bipolar, multipolar, concentrated, or dispersed.

One final observation comes from William C. Potter's review of the research on issue-areas in foreign policy analysis. He notes that to date this research has not "provided plausible hypotheses (or any hypotheses in some cases) that relate issue content to foreign policy behavior" and that the actual data analyses that he reviewed "have yielded very ambiguous results." But his final conclusion is perhaps the most interesting:

> Under these circumstances adoption of the method of focused comparison, such as that used by Keohane and Nye, may be the best means to explore the potential explanatory power of process-oriented issue typologies and to identify substantive issue areas which can be linked theoretically to foreign policy processes and/or outcomes.[28]

What this means is that to answer certain questions there must be a return to case study analysis, a venerable and helpful methodology but one not particularly geared to general theory-building. It would seem, then – and we will return to this conclusion later – that part of the transnationalist thrust has been to ask questions that can be best answered by case studies and not by general hypothesis formulation and testing.

INTERNATIONAL INTERDEPENDENCE

There is certainly much evidence that interdependence is high and in some instances increasing, a perception fostered at least partly by highly visible increases in international communication, travel, and trade. As Peter J. Katzenstein points out, from 1954 to 1961, world trade flow increased 63 percent, and in the subsequent seven years increased another 86 percent. Likewise, the flow of world capital during the 1950s increased 83.3 percent. Migration, foreign students, tourism, mail flow, telegram flow, telephone calls: all appear to be increasing, and in some cases the increases are drastic.[29]

In terms of vertical interdependence (percent changes over time as opposed to straight trends), between 1959 and 1967 there were strong relations between fluctuations in United States Treasury Bill rates and fluctuations in the rates of Eurodollars, and there was also a convergence toward a common rate.[30] The range across countries from the highest to the lowest interest rates on these bills in 1958 was 7 percent, and by 1967 the rates had converged within a range of less than two percentage points. Implications for state-centric policy are clear: "To the extent that integration of money and capital markets does occur, national monetary and credit policies are weakened."[31]

In what is perhaps the most extensive and systematic analysis in recent years, Richard Rosecrance and his colleagues investigated five different economic dimensions – wholesale prices, consumer prices, wage rates, interest rates, and interest rate convergences – among six industrialized countries from 1890 to 1975. They found increases in almost all five indicators.[32] At the same time, their conclusions were not uniform. For instance, although there were a number of significant correlations in wholesale prices from 1921-1974, there was a substantially higher percentage in 1890-1913, and the year 1975 proved to have the lowest percentage, except for 1921-1929. Going by the de-trended data, the 1959-1972 period was lower than any preceding period.

For consumer prices, with the exception of 1901-1913, the post-1951 era has significantly moved toward greater interdependence, if trend data is considered. Again, however, using the change data, and with the exception of 1975, the 1951-1975 period does not indicate any shift toward greater interdependence. In wage rates, given only for 1955-1975, 1959-1971 was the highest period of interdependence, in both the index and the change data. Since 1971 there has been a decline in the percentage of significant correlations.

For interest rates, the average correlation ranged between .45 and .56 (with the exception of the two prewar periods), but there is no trend in more recent years toward higher correlations. However, since 1965, there has been a lack of negative correlations. In four earlier periods – the latest being 1959-1972 – usually about a third of the correlations were negative, and several were rather high. This indicates that interest rate fluctuations more recently have moved in the same, not opposite, directions. Finally, there is certainly no trend toward interest rate convergence. Surprisingly, the period that many argue was the one of great interdependence – 1950-1958 – in Rosecrance's data shows the lowest amount of interest rate convergence; the period with the second lowest amount was 1973-1974.

Certainly one problem with these data is that new interdependencies may have emerged between these developed countries and smaller, developing, exporting countries (such as OPEC nations), so that interdependencies may be occurring in other dimensions. But if that is true, we would expect to find evidence of these new interdependencies spilling over into the dimensions Rosecrance investigated.

Katzenstein's data, referred to above, showed generally high and increasing levels of interdependence. At the same time, for world capital flows, the 1950s showed just about the same amount of increase, in terms of growth per decade, as the 1890/1900-1900/1913 period. Likewise, 1961-1966 showed the highest increase in migration since 1846; still, in terms of foreign student exchange and tourism, the 1960s showed a smaller percent of increase than the 1950s. The same pattern occurred with international communication (mail, telegrams, telephone calls): in the 1961-1969 period it increased 19.7 percent, but this growth was smaller than the 143 percent and 151.4 percent increases of 1885/1893–1912 and 1952–1961.

Another way of looking at this evidence is to inspect the average growth rate of transactions per decade in percentages. Even allowing for the increase in population and in the number of states, the percentage increase in trade and capital flow as well as in total communications was in every case higher (ranging from 74.7 percent to 85.6 percent) than the increase in population (20.9 percent) or the number of states (43.6 percent). But if we compare these data since World War II to the data from 1890/1893 to 1912/1913, and adjust for increases in population in both cases, the average growth rate of the previous era was substantially higher than that since World War II. Admittedly some of these figures are affected by the smaller base of the earlier data; nonetheless, some differences between earlier and later periods are so great that it is unlikely that they are entirely explained by that methodological factor.

As for the other types of interdependencies mentioned earlier, we find once again that they are not new. According to Oskar Morgenstern, there was a fairly high correlation and agreement between pairs of countries in short-term interest rates in the periods 1871–1914 and 1925–1938.[33] Philip Klein cites numerous studies showing common business cycles in many nations going as far back as 1790, cycles that lasted – according to one study – for over 130 years. He also cites a study by G. H. Moore that found a "consensus international cycle" of 4½ years on average, the "same length Ilse Mintz found for her world import cycles during the period from 1879 to 1959."[34] Interestingly enough, the years from 1962 to 1966 showed poor correspondence in these dimensions.

Finally, although there is some substantial evidence that European "integration" – or interdependence – has been increasing, it is of more than passing note that one possibly significant dimension does not corroborate that impression. Konrad Kressley reports that the volume of international broadcasting has grown in Europe (through the Eurovision network) in terms of licenses and hours of TV viewing, but that relative to the domestic ability to receive – namely, the number of TV sets – there was a decline during the period from 1962 to 1972:

> While the sheer volume of international broadcasting has grown, it is shrinking in comparison to locally produced program materials. This supports Deutsch's contention that the dominant forces in today's nation states continue to predispose societal closure despite availability of integrative technology.[35]

These bits of evidence add up to a rather complex picture. One conclusion is certain: interdependence does exist, but current levels of interdependence in some dimensions are not necessarily higher than those of earlier eras. Additionally, one can question whether there is necessarily a continuing trend toward higher levels of interdependence. In other words, as Rosecrance concluded, the most recent data in his study indicate "a gradual and progressive detachment of individual national policies from the general trend toward interdependence."[36]

However, to raise again a point already touched upon, there are substantive as well as theoretical issues involved. The substantive issue is whether interdependence exists and has increased, and the answer we have provided here is certainly a mixed one. The theoretical issue is what implication could be drawn from high levels or increases in interdependence. We will address this latter issue in the concluding section of this chapter; suffice it here to note that a fairly standard implication—that of growing cooperation—is not a confirmed hypothesis.

WAR AND INTENSE CONFLICT

The final characteristic of the transnationalist view is that war has become an anachronism in the contemporary international system, an option no longer available for many foreign policy decision-makers. The use of modern weapons, including nuclear arsenals, is viewed as so irrational and counterproductive that it would of course never happen. There is also the economic argument. Michael Hudson contends that now, unlike in previous eras when war could be used to attain booty and secure international wealth, the costs of war are so great that it is unreasonable. It adversely affects international foreign exchanges, borrowing, and many other economic factors. But Hudson concludes:

> Do these considerations mean that there will be no more war? Not necessarily. . . . Many believed that World War I could not last more than a few months because the Allied and Central Powers would soon run out of funds (as well as physical resources). In one respect these observers were correct: the belligerent powers could not afford the war. But they carried on anyway, even at the cost of deranging and finally bankrupting their economies.[37]

Moreover, this attitude toward war in the modern era has been expounded largely by Americans, and that may say something about the validity of the view. There is certainly a feeling among some Americans that the Vietnam War may have been the country's "last" war, a feeling no doubt made more intense because the war was such a negative experience. But there is also suggestive evidence that American foreign policy may alternate between two different "moods" that are roughly correlated with expansionary (i.e., warlike) and nonexpansionary periods.[38]

These moods have been called "introversion" and "extraversion," the first characterized by withdrawal from foreign involvement and the second by greater foreign involvement. The alternating periods are not fixed, but they tend to run roughly from twenty-two to twenty-seven years. The last American period of introversion may have commenced near the end of the Vietnam War, somewhere between 1968 and 1972,[39] hence, the perception of war as futile and outmoded may reflect a shift to a more introverted U.S. foreign policy stance.

To broaden the question further to include evidence on war in the contemporary period, the conclusions we draw – not surprisingly – depend on the type of question asked and the time perspective utilized. There is some evidence, for instance, that during the 1945–1970 period, war was *not* decreasing in the international system. The Conflict and Peace Data Bank (COPDAB) shows that warlike behavior continued to increase until about the 1963–1967 period and then began to decline for small-country involvement; it remained relatively steady throughout the period for the middle powers and superpowers.[40] It is impossible to tell whether the surge in small-power war involvement in the 1963–1967 period represented a true peak and whether the shift downward to 1970 is representative of current trends. Steven J. Rosen and Walter S. Jones also present evidence of a very steady number of wars through the 1945–1972 period, fluctuating from none to four a year, with no indication into the early 1970s that any downward shift had occurred.[41]

On the other hand, over a longer time period there is evidence supporting the contention that the present era has been much less war-filled than previous eras. J. David Singer and Melvin Small's Correlates of War Project isolated seven periods from 1816 to 1977, the two most recent being 1946–1965 and 1966–1977. On six of eight "normalized" indicators of war (adjusted to allow for number of years in each period and number of nations), the two most recent periods rank lowest and next to lowest in warlike violence.[42] Combining the eight indicators into an overall index shows that the last period, 1966–1977, is the least conflictual, and 1946–1965 is the fifth least conflictual.

However, comparing the current era with previous eras also suggests that there might be some cycle-like changes in the prevalence of war. Singer and Small reported finding periodicity in the number of nation-months of war "with dominant peaks about 20 years apart," and concluded that, "with *some* level of such violence almost always present, there are distinct and periodic fluctuations in the amount of violence."[43]

In their later work Singer and Small pull back from this conclusion:

> If we define periodicity in terms of peaks and valleys of approximate magnitude, occurring at more or less equal intervals, we find no evidence

for such a claim. Even using spectral analysis methods, which are explicitly designed to *find,* no less confirm, any clear cyclical patterns, we turned up nothing of significance.[44]

Yet they also conclude, in the text of their article, that there seems to be a "rather rough, but visible, periodicity in these data over the entire 160-odd years":

> It will be recalled that on many of the indicators, the relative peacefulness of the Concert period gave way to the extreme violence of the 1850s and 1860s, followed by a general decline in martial activities in the 1870s and 1880s. Then we experienced general increases in those activities through World War I, a decline during the inter-war years, and increases again after World War II. Finally, we have the relative decline that we have already described.[45]

This conclusion is shared by others. Frank H. Denton and Warren Phillips, writing a decade prior to Singer and Small and using evidence on war from 1481 to 1900, found support for the hypothesis that "an upswing in violence occurs about once every generation to a generation and a half, if one assumes some change in life spans making up a 'generation'."[46] Although over the period of their study the twenty-five-year cycle fit the best, "the data support such a general trend with 20 years providing a 'best' fit prior to 1680 and about 30 years thereafter."[47]

But what about the possibility that nuclear weapons have entirely transformed the system? Charles Ostrom and John Aldrich have concluded, on somewhat preliminary evidence, that such is not the case:

> During the previous 111 years there were 33 years in which a major power war occurred (29.7 percent), while for the 15 post–World War II years there are four years in which a major power war occurred (26.7 percent). In terms of the aggregate frequency of war, it appears that the presence of nuclear weapons has had no effect on the probability of war. . . . The data . . . indicate that nuclear weapons have had little impact on the probability of a major power war in the international system – war is just as probable before the appearance of nuclear weapons as after.[48]

Some proponents of the "war-is-dead" argument have recently begun to reverse themselves. Klaus Knorr, writing in 1977, concluded that he was no longer as sure that the utility of force had diminished as he had been a decade earlier. The 1964–1975 period had "witnessed plenty of military clashes even if one ignores civil wars in which other countries did not intervene with forces of their own."[49] Knorr argued that "the historical record does not support, or even suggest, the assumption that growing interdependence discourages the generation of divisive vital issues or breeds a dependable aversion to violence."[50]

In the wake of certain events in the late 1970s – the hostage-taking in Iran and the Russian invasion of Afghanistan in 1979 come to mind – taking on the "war-is-dead" argument may seem akin to beating a dead horse. But though some, such as Knorr, have come to question this argument, it remains a popular one. Even in the early 1980s, Werner Levi repeated, in his book *The Coming End of War*,[51] most of the arguments outlined above: war is outmoded because of the internationalization of national interests, its gains are unlike those of the past, nuclear power makes war more dangerous, and the overall changes that have taken place in the international system make it unlikely. Yet this section has suggested that although there is less war now than ten years ago, and certainly less than in some previous eras, extrapolating from that evidence at this time might prove grossly incorrect.

IMPLICATIONS

This work was occasioned by a feeling that some recent perceptions of transformations in international politics may not be quite accurate. Edward L. Morse contends, for instance, that the Treaty of Westphalia, outlining the concept of sovereignty of independent nation-states, is now outmoded in the contemporary system: "The changes that we have examined in this essay make it clear that international politics no longer conforms to the rhetoric and vocabulary of Westphalia, even though our capacity to describe and explain international events remains burdened by its outdated concepts."[52]

But perhaps one of the problems is that the "rhetoric" of Westphalia may have been just that: language that in reality did not describe the international system, at that time or at any time since. Non-state actors and interdependencies have always existed, issues are constantly in flux, and war is periodically viewed as no longer an option. Kenneth Waltz's conclusion about interdependence can be expanded to apply to the other three factors analyzed here:

> It is surprising, then, that so much recent writing about interdependence reads as though it were written at the turn of the century. Economists and political scientists, like others, make free use of the cliches of our day: spaceship earth, the shrinking planet, our global village, international interdependence.[53]

Empirical transformations may be observed that do not necessarily call for a complete overhauling of our theoretical analysis and understanding of important phenomena. Thus, over and above the question of whether evidence exists to support the transnationalist argument, our evaluation of the changes that have occurred depends on whether these changes seriously disrupt our theoretical formulations.

In other words, much work has focused on *describing* the contemporary system and illustrating that in one way or another it differs from previous systems. Description, however, is only one step in the process of understanding international politics. To present a description of the contemporary international system that is at variance with descriptions of past systems only addresses the question of description. To illustrate, breaking down the "actors" within a nation is simply another way of describing what is transpiring when a nation participates in foreign affairs. For some issues, such a breakdown might be important, even crucial; for others, it might not only be unimportant, but it might actually get in the way of answering meaningful questions. An analysis of U.S.-Soviet relations from 1950 to the present can still be very profitably carried out without regarding the sub-national actors in both nations; in fact, to focus on the latter may reveal more of the "trees" in the "forest" than necessary and may get in the way of answering certain types of questions. A study of U.S.-Soviet *trade* conflicts, on the other hand, could more profitably – and perhaps best – be carried out by focusing on the specific sub-national actors involved in that issue. The same distinction applies to the breakdown of issues: nations always interact over issues but it is not always necessary to break down nation-state interactions into these respective issues. For some research questions that technique may be essential, but not necessarily for all.

Coplin, one of the earliest to focus on issue-areas, agrees. The "power politics" framework, he notes, provides a "grand theory perspective" while the issue politics view provides a "middle-range theoretical orientation." However, Coplin is only partly correct when he argues that "the power politics framework brings a grand order to the analysis of international politics, but it ignores those international issues that cannot be directly related to major power struggles."[54] As suggested at several points throughout this chapter, one of the inferences we can draw from an analysis of some of this empirical data is that realist concepts and hypotheses might in fact be applicable to many more issues than simply "major power struggles." The converse, of course, is that it also is possible that issue-area analysis can in fact be related to major power struggles. One of the crucial issue distinctions made by Mansbach and Vasquez[55] is along James Rosenau's tangible-intangible dimension. But distinguishing issues along this dimension is not at all incompatible with understanding great power struggles. Research on the escalation and de-escalation of the Vietnam War suggested that the pattern of war was related to whether American decision-makers viewed the war "symbolically" or "non-symbolically"—or, in other words, as an intangible or a tangible issue.[56] But because the type of issue is important in understanding the escalation and de-escalation of the Vietnam War does not mean it can serve as the underpinning of an entire paradigm for understanding international politics.

Similarly, the utility in some cases of breaking down the actors or the issues does not necessarily imply that the behavior of a nation as a whole or a nation's stance in relation to numerous issues is no longer important. Understanding world politics does not mean drawing a complete picture of all possible behavior at all possible levels. In fact, as noted already, the move toward issue and actor specification represents a move away from general understanding and general theory-building. It would certainly be unfortunate if the emergence of each new set of actors or issues were seen as reason to dump general formulations that should be applicable to a wide range of foreign policy behaviors and issues across different time periods.

In sum, an important component of some recent research is *changing the questions to be asked.* Changes in the international system may affect both ways of understanding the system and proposed policies for dealing with international problems; nonetheless, we first must establish *what* the important problems are and then make sure that the changes in the system really do affect them. To change the questions and then to conclude that models designed to answer other questions are outmoded is neither substantively nor theoretically sound.

A second precaution is to be wary of "old wine in new bottles." As we have noted already, even some who propose a new model based on non-state actors admit that the nation-state remains the major actor in international politics. Others, although arguing that the "military-security" paradigm is no longer appropriate and that conflicting pursuits between states ought not to receive the attention they have in the past, agree that "government-to-government interaction in the 1970s remains the most prominent, conspicuous, and far-reaching in impact among the many different kinds of interaction in the world system."[57]

There is continuing talk, even in discussing "new" economic issues, of the hegemonic power of the United States, the changes in U.S. power, and the power relations or distributions within the system—even though admittedly the discussion of power is no longer solely along military lines. Moreover, hypotheses utilizing the traditional "power" variable are still proposed: "In a system of eroding hegemony, as in the present . . . conflict becomes more likely as weaker states are increasingly able and willing to oppose the wishes of the leading power."[58]

Changing power dimensions are also viewed as affecting behavior in the system:

The result as of 1972 is that power relations in the oil system seem strikingly incongruent with power relations in world politics generally. When we pass onto the oil chessboard, the pawns of world politics suddenly become queens, or at least rooks, with the capacity – at least within the rules of the game as now played – for coordinated and decisive action. Yet insofar as power is fungible, such a situation seems unstable: the analyst is immediately led to ask about developments that could alter the incongruity in one way or another.[59]

Richard Sterling's *Macropolitics,* a central text espousing a globalist or transnationalist view, takes the position that balance-of-power politics should not be the only rational way to play the "game" of international politics. Yet he admits that the "balance of power is a recurrent and very frequent pattern of political behavior, both domestically and internationally" and "it must always be taken into account in political calculations."[60]

Even Morse, who contends that the Treaty of Westphalia and all that goes with it are outmoded, concludes that there is a "paradox" in the contemporary system, in which, "at a time when the nation-state has appeared to be functionally obsolete, it has been reaffirmed by the same processes which would call for its transcendence."[61] He cites Pierre Hassner as noting that "in some respects the nation-state is flourishing and in others it is dying; it can no longer fulfill some of the most important traditional functions, yet it constantly assumes new ones which it alone seems to be able to fulfill."[62] Likewise, Mansbach and Vasquez's "new paradigm for global politics" – formulated in a work in which Chapter 1 announces the "decay of an old paradigm" – contains a model in which nation-state similarity and status, as well as nation-state resources, appear to be the crucial independent variables in a flow chart for the onset of war,[63] and at least one hypothesis sounds familiar to anyone acquainted with realist quantitative research of the last generation: "Relatively equal status produces competition and is threatening; and rapid change in relative status is destabilizing."[64]

In sum, it seems fairly clear that despite the calls for new models and new paradigms because of a "new" international system, there is a fair amount of reliance on at least some traditional concepts and hypotheses. It is not entirely certain, therefore, at least at this point, that the system has changed so drastically that the intellectual paraphernalia for understanding international politics must be completely overhauled.

A third implication also relates to the link between substantive descriptions of the system and propositions implied by those descriptions. For instance, many see interdependence as almost automatically producing greater cooperation; there *must* be more participation and negotiation in this new global system. Interdependence should produce positive benefits: "Whenever the intermeshing of societies across nation-state lines occurs without coercion, it is likely that disputes between the involved nations will be inhibited from escalating to war."[65]

But this hypothesis has not received solid empirical confirmation, and there is a new alternative view emerging: increasing interdependence may produce *negative* outcomes. It has been suggested that foreign investment is "an infringement on national sovereignty," and one observer believes that the United States must formulate the economic equivalent of the Monroe Doctrine – "a national policy that clearly prohibits foreign governments or their intermediaries from making controlling investments in corporate America."[66]

Interdependence arising from technology transfers can also produce negative results. Since one of the principal reasons for importing technology is to enhance technological self-sufficiency, then

> to the extent a technology importer succeeds in building his export capacity, his exports may displace another country's exporter from the same market. Even more clearly, domestic consumption of his product may reduce another state's exports. These are not incontrovertible cases, then, of interdependence growth.[67]

Kal Holsti, in his recent study of U.S.-Canadian relations, concluded that disintegration and fragmentation may be *responses* to asymmetrical integration, and that fragmentation may be a reaction by those who see

> greater interconnectedness not in terms of greater opportunities or benefits, but rather as resulting in inequitable distribution of rewards or as posing threats to national, ethnic, language or religious identity. In brief, the "shrinking world" may result not in greater consensus and internationalism, but in heightened nationalism and drives to extend or protect autonomy.[68]

We find in some contemporary literature more wish and hope for a changed international system than empirical proof. Robert E. Hunter, for example, argues in one essay that the "old symbiotic relationship between power and peace is changing," and that it might be possible to separate the requirements of peace from "their dependence on a particular distribution of power among nations." Yet he admits, in a statement that appears between the above two, that such an outcome would occur "provided that armed conflict between major countries is avoided."[69]

A fourth implication has been raised at numerous points in this chapter. Put briefly, it may be that those who call for "new" paradigms, "new" models, and "new" approaches because of the changes they see in the international system fail to realize that it may be those very changes that merit inquiry. To conclude that structural changes have occurred and that therefore we are required to rethink our approaches to world politics may be missing the point. If multiple issues are now the focus of attention or if new actors have moved onto the world stage, those facts themselves may not call so much for reorientation as for recognition that something has happened in the system to *produce* those changes. It becomes important, then, not merely to describe those changes but to account for them.

This is not to say that changes that have occurred, or that may occur in the future, will not require a complete reorientation of thinking. Certainly in other areas, such as astronomy and physics, there have emerged in recent years physical phenomena that could not be accounted for by previous models and theories. But until such changes have clearly taken place, a search for new models may be premature. This conclusion is further prompted by two other reasons, already mentioned, that are unrelated to the accuracy of the transnationalist view. First, many traditional concepts and hypotheses emerge in the transnationalist literature, which seriously calls into question the uniqueness of the new approach. Second, the call for new paradigms has been partly facilitated and encouraged by changing the basic research questions.

A final inference also relates to the broader study of international politics in general. All areas of study undergo changes. In international relations, Hans J. Morgenthau's paradigm dominated the late 1940s and much of the 1950s and has had influence since. But during the 1950s, "decision-making" analysis attempted to move from that power-centered paradigm to focus on individuals. At the same time, Morton Kaplan's system-level approach used many of Morgenthau's ideas, although in a somewhat more precise manner. During this period the "behavioral revolution" emerged, introducing the use of quantitative techniques to the student of international relations. During the 1960s the focus on individuals continued, with an interest in quantitative content analysis of perceptions of decision-makers and actions of nations. Then there was a turn toward the domestic sources of foreign policy, and large-scale quantitative aggregate studies began to emerge, with an emphasis on "comparative foreign policy." In the late 1960s and early 1970s decision-making studies again became prominent, with bureaucratic and organizational factors coming to the fore.

It was at about that time that the transnationalist literature began to appear. Some of this literature was a part of the "post-behavioral revolution," which argued that traditional models, many generated prior to the behavioral movement and later subjected to testing by behavioral techniques, were becoming more irrelevant because they had so little empirical confirmation.[70] Thus, there was a turn to a somewhat more traditional, non-quantitative, case study orientation. In other words, the call for "new" models *in part* reflects a reaction to general theory-building and aggregated, quantitative system-level analysis, illustrated by the actor-specific and issue-specific approach of some of the transnationalist literature.

CONCLUSION

The issues raised here are not trivial, for they directly affect the view that scholars and policymakers have of the contemporary world and therefore dictate what important issues of world affairs are addressed and what policies are proposed to solve them. As stated already, although events in Iran and Afghanistan at the end of the 1970s took part of the luster off the transnationalist view, that position remains a potent one. While some may feel that the "debate" outlined here is outdated, it should be noted that Rosenau, writing in 1979, noted that "one still has to contend with the declining capacity of governments, the rise of new issues and the advent of new actors, and the many interactive effects that derive from mounting interdependence in an increasingly fragmented world."[71] There must, of course, be a continuing re-evaluation of the makeup of the contemporary world and of how it differs from previous systems. But some of the changes that have been the focus of much recent interest and speculation, in both the academic and the policymaking communities, may not be quite as significant as many in both communities would have us believe. Or, if they are, it is for reasons that for the most part have remained untouched.

NOTES

This chapter was originally presented at the International Studies Association West–Western Political Science Association meeting, Portland, Oregon, March, 1979. I appreciate comments on an earlier draft by Suresht Bald, Donald Crone, Harold Guetzkow, Ron Sherwin, several anonymous reviewers, and the editors of *International Studies Quarterly*.

1. Seyom Brown, *New Forces in World Politics* (Washington, D.C.: Brookings Institution, 1974); Robert E. Hunter, "Power and Peace," *Foreign Policy* 9 (Winter 1972–1973), pp. 37–54; John R. Handleman, John A. Vasquez, Michael K. O'Leary, and William D. Coplin, "Color It Morgenthau: A Data-Based Assessment of Quantitative International Relations Research," PRINCE Research Studies, Paper No. 11, mimeographed, 1973; Richard W. Mansbach, Yale E. Ferguson, and Donald E. Lampert, *The Web of World Politics: Non-State Actors in the Global System* (Englewood Cliffs, N.J.: Prentice-Hall, 1976); Robert C. Keohane and Joseph S. Nye, *Power and Interdependence: World Politics in Transition* (Boston: Little, Brown, 1977); Oran Young, "Interdependencies in World Politics," *International Journal* 24 (Autumn 1969), pp. 726–50; James N. Rosenau, "Muddling, Meddling, and Modelling: Alternative Approaches to the Study of World Politics in an Era of Rapid Change," *Millennium: Journal of International Studies* 8 (Autumn 1979), pp. 130–44; Richard W. Mansbach and John A. Vasquez, *In Search of Theory: A New Paradigm for Global Politics* (New York: Columbia University Press, 1981).

2. Michael P. Sullivan, "Competing Frameworks and the Study of Contemporary International Politics," *Millenium: Journal of International Studies* 7 (Autumn 1978), pp. 93–100.

3. Kal Holsti, "A New International Politics? Diplomacy in Complex Interdependence," *International Organization* 32 (Spring 1978), pp. 513–30.

4. Mansbach and Vasquez, *In Search of Theory*, p. 5.

5. Mansbach, et al., *The Web of World Politics*; Mansbach and Vasquez, *ibid.*; Rosenau, "Muddling, Meddling, and Modelling," p. 132.

6. Young, "Interdependencies in World Politics," p. 734.

7. Hunter, "Power and Peace," p. 381.

8. Kenneth Waltz, *Theory of International Politics* (Reading, MA: Addison-Wesley, 1979).

9. Mansbach et al., *The Web of World Politics*, p. 273.

10. *Ibid.*, p. 275.

11. James N. Schubert, "Toward a 'Working Peace System' in Asia: Organizational Growth and State Participation in Asian Regionalism," *International Organization* 32 (Spring 1978), p. 427.

12. Kjell Skjelsbaek, "The Growth of Nongovernmental Organizations in the Twentieth Century," *International Organization* 25 (Summer 1971), pp. 422–42.

13. D. George Kousalas, *On Government and Politics*, 3d ed. (North Scituate, MA: Duxbury Press, 1975), p. 233.

14. Mansbach et al., *The Web of World Politics*, p. 276.

15. Mansbach and Vasquez, *In Search of Theory*; Richard Mansbach and John A. Vasquez, "The Effect of Issues on Global Conflict-Cooperation: American–West German Foreign Relations, 1959–1975," presented at the annual meeting of the International Studies Association, St. Louis, March, 1977.

16. Mansbach and Vasquez, "The Effect of Issues," p. 18.

17. Graham T. Allison, *Essence of Decision: Explaining the Cuban Missile Crisis* (Boston: Little, Brown, 1971); Morton H. Halperin, *Bureaucratic Politics and Foreign Policy* (Washington, DC: Brookings Institution, 1974).

18. Mansbach and Vasquez, "The Effects of Issues," p. 22.

19. William D. Coplin, Stephen L. Mills, and Michael K. O'Leary, "The PRINCE Concept and the Study of Foreign Policy," in Patrick J. McGowan, ed., *Sage International Yearbook of Foreign Policy Studies,* Vol. 1 (Beverly Hills, CA: Sage Publications, 1973).

20. James M. McCormick and Young W. Kihl, "IGOs and Nation-Behavior: Routine or Salient?", prepared for delivery at the annual meeting of the International Studies Association, Washington, February, 1978, p. 3.

21. Keohane and Nye, *Power and Interdependence.*

22. McCormick and Kihl, "IGOs and Nation-Behavior," p. 11. These data are taken from the Comparative Research on the Events of Nations project (CREON) at Ohio State University, which collected these foreign policy events of thirty-five nations for randomly selected quarters from 1959 to 1968.

23. Edward F. Mickolus, "An Events Data Base for Analysis of Transnational Terrorism," in Richard J. Heuer, Jr., ed., *Quantitative Approaches to Political Intelligence: The CIA Experience* (Boulder, CO: Westview Press, 1978); Brian M. Jenkins and Janera Johnson, "International Terrorism: A Chronology, 1968–1974," prepared for the Department of State and the Defense Advanced Research Projects Agency, Rand Corporation, March, 1975; Brian M. Jenkins and Janera A. Johnson, "International Terrorism: A Chronology (1974 Supplement)."

24. This is not the case with one very narrowly defined type of terrorist activity, namely assassination attempts; see Thomas H. Snitch, "Assassinations and Political Violence, 1968–1978: An Events Data Approach," presented at the annual meeting of the International Studies Association, Los Angeles, March, 1980. These data show minor fluctuations from 1956 to the early 1970s, followed by a dramatic increase; the data through 1978 showed no such decline as outlined here.

25. For instance, in the Middle East the Arab-Israeli issue gave way to "inter-Arab" issues and then regained prominence along with the colonial issue. In Latin America, regime stability was most prominent in all three periods, but democracy-dictatorship gave way to Castroism in the second period and security in the third period.

26. Coplin et al., "The PRINCE Concept."

27. The same observation applies to their critique of William Gamson and Andre Modigliani's work on East-West cooperation and conflict. Coplin et al., showed that if Gamson and Modigliani's data are broken down by region, different patterns of East-West relations emerge, but the frequencies of actions are severely distorted; for instance, breaking out USSR data for Latin America for 1960 means focusing on only one action – out of five major actions that occurred that year. See William Gamson and Andre Modigliani, *Untangling the Cold War: A Strategy for Testing Rival Theories* (Boston: Little, Brown, 1971).

28. William C. Potter, "Issue Area and Foreign Policy Analysis," *International Organization* 34 (Summer 1980), p. 427.

29. Peter J. Katzenstein, "International Interdependence: Some Long-Term Trends and Recent Changes," *International Organization* 29 (Autumn 1975), pp. 1021–34.

30. Richard N. Cooper, *The Economics of Interdependence* (New York: McGraw-Hill, 1968), pp. 120 and 140.

31. *Ibid.,* p. 14.

32. Richard A. Rosecrance et al., "Whither Interdependence?" *International Organization* 31 (Summer 1977), pp. 425–72. One way of sumarizing this evidence is to use the percentage of "significant" correlations; for Rosecrance, a "significant" correlation is one exceeding .75 in trend data and .30 in de-trended (percentage change) data.

33. Oskar Morgenstern, *International Financial Transactions and Busines Cycles* (Princeton: Princeton University Press, 1959), pp. 102, 106, and 109. Six of the twelve pairs of countries had Z scores high enough to reject the null hypothesis of no agreement at the 5 percent level; only two of the twelve showed no correspondence. Six of the correlation coefficients were higher than .60, eight were .40 or higher; only one was below .30.

34. Philip Klein, *Business Cycles in the Post War World: Some Reflections on Recent Research* (Washington, DC: American Enterprise Institute, Domestic Affairs Study No. 42, February, 1976), p. 42.

35. Konrad M. Kressley, "Integrated Television in Europe: A Note on the Eurovision Network," *International Organization* 32 (Autumn 1978), pp. 470–71.

36. Rosecrance et al., "Whither Interdependence?" p. 442.

37. Michael Hudson, *Global Fracture: The New International Economic Order* (New York: Harper and Row, 1977), p. 219.

38. Frank L. Klingberg, "The Historical Alternation of Moods in American Foreign Policy," *World Politics* 4 (January 1952), pp. 239–73; Frank L. Klingberg, "Cyclical Trends in American Foreign Policy Moods and Their Policy Implications," in Charles W. Kegley, Jr., and Patrick J. McGowan, eds., *Challenges to America: United States Foreign Policy in the 1980s* (Beverly Hills, CA: Sage Publications, 1979), pp. 37–56; Michael Roskin, "From Pearl Harbor to Vietnam: Shifting Generational Paradigms and Foreign Policy," *Political Science Quarterly* 89 (Fall 1974), pp. 563–88; Jack E. Holmes, "The Mood/Interest Theory of American Foreign Policy," mimeographed, 1977; Michael P. Sullivan, "The Vietnam War and American Foreign Policy: Some Perspectives," presented at the annual meeting of the International Studies Association/West, Los Angeles, April, 1977.

39. Holmes; "The Mood/Interest Theory"; Sullivan, "The Vietnam War and American Foreign Policy."

40. Edward Azar, *Probe for Peace: Small-State Hostilities* (Minneapolis: Burgess Publishing, 1973), p. 4.

41. Steven J. Rosen and Walter S. Jones, *The Logic of International Relations* (Cambridge, MA: Winthrop Publishers, 1974), p. 156.

42. Melvin Small and J. David Singer, "Conflict in the International System, 1816–1977: Historical Trends and Policy Futures," in Kegley and McGowan, eds., *Challenges to America,* p. 104.

43. J. David Singer and Melvin Small, *The Wages of War, 1816–1965: A Statistical Handbook* (New York: John Wiley and Sons, 1972), p. 215.

44. Small and Singer, "Conflict in the International System," p. 114, footnote 5.

45. *Ibid.,* p. 107.

46. Frank H. Denton and Warren Phillips, "Some Patterns in the History of Violence," *Journal of Conflict Resolution* 12 (June 1968), p. 190.

47. *Ibid.,* p. 193.

48. Charles W. Ostrom, Jr., and John H. Aldrich, "The Relationship Between Size and Stability in the Major Power International System," *American Journal of Political Science* 22 (November 1978), pp. 769–70.

49. Klaus Knorr, "Is International Coercion Waning or Rising?", *International Security* 1 (Spring 1977), p. 93.

50. *Ibid.*, pp. 99–100.

51. Werner Levi, *The Coming End of War* (Beverly Hills, CA: Sage Publications, 1981).

52. Edward L. Morse, *Modernization and the Transformation of International Relations* (New York: Free Press, 1976), p. 178.

53. Waltz, *Theory of International Politics,* p. 140.

54. William D. Coplin, "Power Politics Versus Issue Politics: Paradigmatic Conflict, Levels of Analysis, and Theoretical Integration," presented at the annual meeting of the International Studies Association, Toronto, March, 1979, pp. 6, 8–9.

55. Mansbach and Vasquez, *In Search of Theory.*

56. Michael P. Sullivan, "Symbolic Commitment as a Correlate of Escalation: The Vietnam Case," in Bruce Russett, ed., *Peace, War, and Numbers* (Beverly Hills, CA: Sage Publications, 1972); Michael P. Sullivan, "Foreign Policy Articulations and U.S. Conflict Behavior," in J. David Singer and Michael D. Wallace, eds., *To Augur Well: Early Warning Indicators in World Politics* (Beverly Hills, CA: Sage Publications, 1979).

57. Donald Puchala and Stuart Fagan, "International Politics in the 1970s: The Search for a Perspective," *International Organization* 28 (Spring 1974), pp. 251–52.

58. C. Fred Bergsten, Robert E. Keohane, and Joseph S. Nye, "International Economics and International Politics: A Framework for Analysis," *International Organization* 29 (Winter 1975), p. 23.

59. Robert O. Keohane and Joseph S. Nye, "World Politics and the International Economic System," in C. Fred Bergsten, ed., *The Future of the International Economic Order: An Agenda for Research* (Lexington, MA: Lexington Books, 1973), p. 147.

60. Richard W. Sterling, *Macropolitics: International Politics in a Global Society* (New York: Knopf, 1974), p. 65.

61. Morse, *Modernization and Transformation,* p. 179.

62. *Ibid.*, citing Pierre Hassner, "The Nation-State in the Nuclear Age," *Survey* 67 (April 1968), p. 3.

63. Mansbach and Vasquez, *In Search of Theory,* p. 310.

64. *Ibid.*, p. 407.

65. Brown, *New Forces in World Politics,* p. 196.

66. Kenneth C. Crowe, "Selling America," *Arizona Daily Star,* December 7, 1978.

67. R. D. McLaurin, "Interdependence and Technology Transfer: Some Preliminary Thoughts," presented at the annual meeting of the Midwest Political Science Association, Chicago, April, 1979, p. 19–20.

68. Kal J. Holsti, "Change in the International System: Interdependence, In-

tegration, and Fragmentation," in Ole R. Holsti, Randolph M. Silverson, and Alexander L. George, eds., *Change in the International System* (Boulder, CO: Westview Press, 1980), p. 33.

69. Hunter, "Power and Peace," pp. 38, 46–47.
70. Handleman et al., "Color It Morgenthau."
71. Rosenau, "Muddling, Meddling, and Modelling," p. 132.

RAY MAGHROORI
BENNETT RAMBERG

10
Globalism Versus Realism: A Reconciliation

THE HISTORICAL CONTEXT

The aphorism that the more things change the more they remain the same applies to the globalist-realist debate in historical context. One finds echoes of the first idealist-realist debate of the 1920s and 1930s. The position of the realists remains essentially the same, but today's globalists echo some of the idealist values.

Any comparison of inter-world war realists to contemporary realists shows that the two are almost identical. Both generations see the state as the main actor and maintain that power and the struggle for it determine world affairs. Neither has faith in international law or international organizations as ordering devices. Both maintain distinctions between domestic and foreign policy. They recognize that moral concerns have a definite place in domestic politics but share the view that universal moral principles cannot be applied to the actions of states.

Idealist premises were embedded in the doctrine of harmony of interests and differed sharply from the realist point of view. Rooted in the utopianism of the eighteenth century, the idealists held that an organic relationship existed between the highest interests of individuals and the highest interest of the community. They assumed that all states had common goals and that all nations were affected similarly by disturbances in the international system. Actors were equally devoted to the preservation of international peace and security. Woodrow Wilson, an ardent idealist, best expressed these views when he argued:

> We are participants, whether we would or not, in the life of the world. The interests of all nations are our own also. We are partners with the rest. What affects mankind is inevitably our affair.
>
> We believe that all nations are equally interested in the political stability of free peoples and equally responsible for their maintenance.[1]

Furthermore, many idealists believed that World War I irrefutably demonstrated the uselessness of war, and that "an intellectual grasp of this fact was all that was necessary to induce the nations to keep the peace in the future."[2] The idealists interpreted the political rhetoric of the interwar period as empirical confirmation of their views.[3]

Idealists contended that harmony of interests played a role in coordinating the world economy for the common good. They criticized economic nationalism as antithetical to the interests of the international community. In the words of the 1927 League of Nations conference of economic experts:

> Any strictly nationalist policy is harmful not only to the nation which practices it but also to the others, and therefore defeats its own end, and if it be desired that the new state of mind revealed by the Conference should lead rapidly to practical results, any program of execution must include, as an essential factor, the principle of *parallel* or *concerted* action by the different nations.[4]

Idealists also saw such international organizations as the League of Nations as vehicles for peace and security. They believed that collective security was superior to a balance of power, the inadequacy of which World War I had demonstrated.

The harmony of interest doctrine, which incorporated a desire for peace, a belief that force no longer had utility, and a faith that international organization was a sound mechanism for resolving conflict, inspired the concept of interdependence. In the words of Woodrow Wilson, "The whole world had already become a single vicinage; each part had become neighbor to all the rest. No nation could live any longer to itself . . . duties of neighborhood being what they were."[5]

Globalists hold similar assumptions. They believe that the nation-state is no longer the main actor on the world stage, that force has limited utility, and that international organizations and transnational actors are important agents compelling interdependence in such areas as the treatment of common welfare problems. As Lester Brown notes:

> We live in an age when problems are increasingly worldwide – the world food problem, world environmental crisis, world monetary crisis, world drug problems and so forth. Few, if any, of mankind's more pressing problems have purely national solutions. They can be solved only through multinational or global cooperation.[6]

At the same time, there are distinctions between the idealist and the globalist perspectives. In the main these differences pertain to the forces that compel global integration. The idealists prescribed transformation through such institutions as the League of Nations. Although the world today is not without groups encouraging greater global harmony – the Institute for World Order in New York comes to mind – globalists usually are not crusaders but reporters. And what they report is that several forces are inducing integration and cooperation. These forces include the fear of nuclear war and economic and functional necessities.

RECONCILING REALISM AND GLOBALISM

Contending globalist (Brown, Puchala and Fagan, and Young), realist (Waltz, Gilpin, and Sullivan), and cyclical (Rosecrance and colleagues) conceptualizations of the world today provide stimulating points of departure to understand events. However, the opposition of these views is troubling. As Rosecrance and his coauthors argue in a related context, they cannot all be correct. Or can they? Must the world be conceived in dichotomous globalist-realist terms? We believe it is a misrepresentation of reality to think of the world this way. We would argue that the world is more complex than either globalists or realists usually admit and that perhaps both models as well as others may be applicable to the same historical era. Indeed, Puchala and Fagan hint at this possibility when they recommend defining the world as a collection of subsystems.

Proceeding from this assumption, we have put together several "pretheoretical" subsystemic matrices that progressively grade the complexity of world politics and demonstrate different ways of looking at the globe. Our use of "pretheory" draws on James Rosenau's definition of the term: "[B]oth an early step toward explanation of specific empirical events and a general orientation toward all events, a point of view or philosophy about the way the world is."[7] "Subsystemic" refers to a level of analysis that falls between a single state's foreign policy and "systemic" generalizations of global behavior. States and actors are grouped by their distinct behavior. At issue in applying any conceptualization is the extent to which a nation's sovereignty is compromised by outside forces.

Matrix I presents a simple yet important characterization of the world that can be called the Cold War model. It reflects only U.S.-Soviet competition; other events are interpreted in the context of that relationship. Although détente in the 1970s resulted in trade expansion and arms control, relations between these two actors still clearly center on competition for power, as in the realist model. Secretary of State Alexander Haig articulated this conceptualization in the following terms:

> A major focus of American policy must be the Soviet Union not because of ideological preoccupation but simply because Moscow is the greatest source of international insecurity today. Let us be plain about it: Soviet pro-

MATRIX I

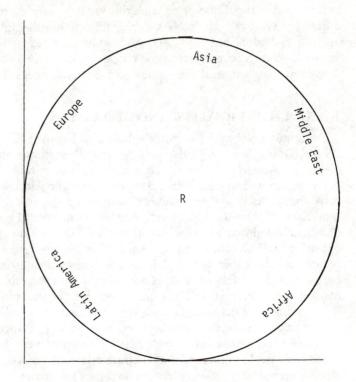

Soviet Union

United States

Key:

R = Realism

motion of violence as the instrument of change constitutes the greatest danger to world peace.

The differences between the United States and the Soviet Union concern the very principles of international action. We believe in peaceful change. . . . In contrast, Soviet policy seeks to exploit aspirations for change in order to create conflict justifying the use of force and even invasion. . . . Our objective must be to restore the prospects for peaceful resolution of conflict. . . . Only the United States has the pivotal strength to convince the Soviets—and their proxies—that violence will not advance their cause.[8]

MATRIX II

	Active	Passive
Active	1 R	3 R
Passive	2 R	4 COL LI

Key

    R   = Realist

    COL = Collaborative

    LI = Limited Interaction

Contemporary realists often define world politics simply in terms of the U.S-Soviet competition. However, realism clearly applies to other contexts as well. Matrix II takes this into account, defining actors generically as "active" and "passive." Active nations use force or the threat of force to undermine, maintain, or otherwise influence strongly another state's political system. Passive actors do not initiate such behavior. Because activists by definition seek power, the realist model can encompass an active-active nexus. Many events in the Middle East result from such interactions. Likewise, realism can explain active-passive relations, such as Vietnam's subjugation of Laos and Cambodia. However, realism cannot define relations between passive nations; for these interactions, other conceptualizations must be found. For example, ties between Argentina and Thailand or Australia and the Ivory Coast, to the extent that they exist, may be best defined in terms of a limited-interactive model (LI). Relations between the membership of the European Economic Community might be understood best as collaborative (COL). Square 4 in Matrix II notes these models. Matrix II might at first appear to be a tautology, but the conclusions it leads to are not well represented in the previous chapters of this book.

Matrix III is a richer representation of world politics. Actors include the twenty-three-nation Organization for Economic Cooperation and Development (OECD) of basically market economies and democratic institutions,[9] Communist states, and developing non-Communist nations as defined by the United Nations.[10] Globalism alone, depicted in square 1, accounts only for relations within the OECD. This interaction is characterized by a voluntary compromise of national sovereignty in several areas. One is trade. Imports—largely from OECD members—average 20 percent of the gross domestic product.[11] Among most of these countries direct investment via multinational corporations is expanding rapidly.[12] The European Economic Community creates further integration among many West European states, as does NATO in the military sphere. Expanding communication links and tourism add ties. Nevertheless, this is not a subsystem without borders. Nations retain juridical, fiscal, and social authority over their subjects, and nationalism remains a major divisive force. Still, relations in this case come closest to the globalist paradigm and are so designated in square 1.

Different conceptualizations apply to ties between Communist states and the remainder of the world, and among Communist nations. To be sure, many of the factors that define U.S.-Soviet relations in Matrix I also apply to most Communist-OECD relations—namely, state-to-state contacts dominated by strategic concerns. The Soviet Union and its allies pose a military threat to Western Europe, manifested in an armed force posture heavily backed up by offensive weapons, such as tanks. The West in turn has responded with its own military buildup. Clearly the realist model applies to these relations, as is shown in squares 2 and 4. At the same time, it would be too simple to suggest that realism is the only model that explains them. Over the last twenty years Communist states increasingly have turned to the West for technological assistance, capital, and foodstuffs. In turn Western Europe and Japan have sought Soviet energy resources. Thus, some interdependencies, i.e., significant

MATRIX III

	OECD	Communist	Developing
OECD	1 G	4 R, i	7 R, D Interdep. Intercon.
Communist	2 R, i	5 R, g Intercon.	8 R Intercon.
Developing	3 R, D Interdep. Intercon.	6 R Intercon.	9 D Intercon. R

Key

G	= Globalist
R	= Realist
g	= tending toward globalism
interdep.	= interdependence
intercon.	= interconnectedness
D	= dependence
i	= elements of interdependence

reciprocal dependencies, have been generated. They do not extend, however, beyond economic intercourse[13] to the appreciably closer political, social, or cultural contacts that a globalist conceptualization entails. Still, because important economic interdependencies are developing, squares 2 and 4 indicate them as well.

Yet another *set* of conceptualizations defines inter-Communist relations. In Europe both realist and globalist models apply. From the Soviet perspective, power politics, strategic issues, and ideology compel Soviet compromise of East Europe's sovereignty, save in Albania and Yugoslavia. Therefore, the realist conceptualization applies. Strategic concerns in Sino-Soviet and Chinese-Vietnamese relations further suggest the realist model. From another perspective, Soviet strategic concerns in Europe compel a unique degree of economic and political integration to the point where globalism best characterizes relations. But this globalism is distinct from globalism within the OECD in that it has not occurred naturally but rather has been imposed by the Russians. Reflecting this difference, square 5 is marked "tending toward globalism." At the same time, this limited globalism does not define relations between Yugoslavia and Albania and other European Communist states. Neither of these countries is a member of the Warsaw Pact and both pursue independent foreign policies. However, they are not totally isolated; they trade with the Soviet bloc and participate in Communist party congresses. To reflect these distinctive ties we introduce a new term, "interconnectedness." Keohane and Nye distinguish interconnectedness from interdependence by the insignificance of relations in terms of costs or benefits.[14]

A less complicated set of conceptualizations characterizes Communist ties to the developing world. In the main, Communist nations view the less developed countries (LDCs) in the Cold War context of competition between themselves and the United States and its allies.[15] Thus, relations fit the realist model. Communist invasions of Afghanistan, Laos, and Cambodia and the presence of Communist advisors and troops in other countries reinforce the applicability of realism. However, there are cases of peaceful commerce and other exchanges. These tend to be relatively insignificant.[16] Still, they are noted in the matrix as another illustration of interconnectedness.

Relations between OECD countries and the developing world are more complicated than Communist-LDC contacts. They reflect realism, interconnectedness, dependence, and interdependence. Realism derives from the superpower competition. For example, some OECD members, notably the United States and France, have sent arms, advisors, and regular combat units to prevent Communist revolutions.[17] However, it would be unfair to characterize the West's interaction with the developing world solely or even primarily in realist terms. Trading relations reflect both dependence, i.e., "a state of being determined or significantly affected by external forces,"[18] and interdependence. Dependence is manifested in OECD reliance on OPEC oil and LDC reliance on Western capital and managerial skills. Saudi Arabia's supply of much of the West's oil and simultaneous reliance on Western military equipment and training and on a strong monetary system that will not depreciate the value of oil demonstrates interdependence. Clearly this interdependence is limited, so the classic globalist model does not apply. Certain North-South relations simply show interconnectedness. An illustration is U.S.-Burmese relations.

Dependence and interconnectedness explain most relations among developing nations, although there are some cases in which the realist model applies. LDCs, like the OECD, rely on OPEC for energy. In other ways inter-LDC commerce is likely to be limited. Developing countries usually import from and export to developed market economies. And although cultural and social ties are likely to occur among LDCs in geographic proximity, as is cooperation among them in international political and economic forums, more often than not interconnectedness defines contacts. However, in South Asia, where tense relations have at times characterized Indo-Pakistani relations, and in the Middle East, where there has been strife among Arab states and between the rest of the Arab world and Iran, the realist model would be appropriate.

Matrix III suggests that the world is more complex than the typical globalist or realist conceptualizations would lead us to believe. Recognizing that models have more than academic import, Keohane and Nye suggest that ill-conceived images of world politics can result in inappropriate or "disastrous" national policies.

> During the 1960s, many otherwise keen observers who accepted realist approaches were slow to perceive the development of new issues that did not center on military-security concerns. The same dominant image in the . . . 1980s would be likely to lead to even more unrealistic expectations. Yet to exchange it for an equally simple view – for instance, that military force is obsolete and economic interdependence benign – would condemn one to equally grave though different errors.[19]

We believe Matrix III supports this judgment.

NOTES

1. Woodrow Wilson, cited in Inis L. Claude, Jr., *Power and International Relations* (New York: Random House, 1962), p. 135.

2. Edward Hallet Carr, *The Twenty Years' Crisis, 1919–1939: An Introduction to the Study of International Relations* (New York: Harper Torchbooks, 1964), p. 52.

3. *Ibid.,* p. 53.

4. *Ibid.,* p. 55.

5. Harley Notter, *The Origins of the Foreign Policy of Woodrow Wilson* (New York: Russell and Russell, 1965), p. 114.

6. Lester R. Brown, *World Without Borders* (New York: Vintage Books, 1973), p. 11.

7. James N. Rosenau, "Pre-Theories and Theories of Foreign Policy," in R. Barry Farrell, ed., *Approaches to Comparative and International Politics* (Evanston, IL: Northwestern University Press, 1966), p. 41.

8. Alexander Haig, "New Direction in U.S. Foreign Policy," *Department of State Bulletin* 81 (June 1981), p. 6.

9. The OECD includes Australia, Austria, Belgium, Canada, Denmark, Finland, France, Germany, Greece, Iceland, Italy, Japan, Luxembourg, the Netherlands, New Zealand, Norway, Portugal, Spain, Sweden, Switzerland, Turkey, the United Kingdom, and the United States.

10. United Nations, *1979 Yearbook of International Trade Statistics* (New York: United Nations, 1980), pp. 160–68.

11. Organization for Economic Cooperation and Development, *OECD Observer* 109 (March 1981), pp. 20–23.

12. Joan Edelman Spero, *The Politics of International Economic Relations* (New York: St. Martin's Press, 1981), p. 107.

13. United Nations, *1979 Yearbook.*

14. Robert O. Keohane and Joseph S. Nye, *Power and Interdependence* (Boston: Little, Brown, 1977), p. 9.

15. For an illustrative review in the Latin American context see Robert S. Leiken, "Eastern Winds in Latin America," *Foreign Policy* 42 (Spring 1981), pp. 94–113.

16. United Nations, *1979 Yearbook.*

17. For a review of French activity in this regard see Pierre Lelouche and Dominique Moisi, "French Policy in Africa: A Lonely Battle," *International Security* 3 (Spring 1979), pp. 108–33.

18. Keohane and Nye, p. 8.

19. *Ibid.,* p. 5.

About the Contributors

EDITORS

Ray Maghroori is a lecturer in the Department of Political Science, University of California, Riverside. His publications include *The Yom Kippur War: A Case Study in Crisis Decision-Making in American Foreign Policy*, with Stephen M. Gorman (1981).

Bennett Ramberg is a research associate at the Center for International and Strategic Affairs, University of California, Los Angeles. His publications include *Destruction of Nuclear Energy Facilities in War: The Problem and the Implications* (1980) and *The Seabed Arms Control Negotiations: A Study of Multilateral Arms Control Conference Diplomacy* (1978).

CONTRIBUTORS

Seyom Brown is Professor of Political Science, Brandeis University. His publications include *Crisis of Power* (1979).

Stuart I. Fagan is the author of *Central American Economic Integration: The Politics of Unequal Benefits* (1970).

Robert Gilpin is Professor of Political Science, Princeton University. His publications include *War and Change in World Politics* (1981).

Donald J. Puchala is Professor of Political Science, Columbia University. His publications include *Global Food Interdependence: Challenge to American Foreign Policy*, with Raymond F. Hopkins (1980).

Richard Rosecrance is Professor of Government, Cornell University. His publications include *International Relations: Peace or War* (1972).

James N. Rosenau is Director of the Institute for Transnational Studies at the University of Southern California. Among his most recent works is *The Study of Political Adaptation* (1981).

Arthur Stein is Assistant Professor of Political Science, University of California, Los Angeles. His publications include *The Nation at War* (1980).

Michael P. Sullivan is Associate Professor of Political Science, University of Arizona. His publications include *International Relations: Theory and Evidence* (1976).

Kenneth Waltz is Professor of Political Science, University of California, Berkeley. His publications include *Theory of International Politics* (1979).

Oran R. Young is Professor of Political Science, University of Maryland. His publications include *Compliance and Public Authority: A Theory with International Applications* (1979).

At the time Chapter 7 was written, **Alan Alexandroff, Wallace Koehler, John Kroll, Shlomit Lacqueur,** and **John Stocker** were students at Cornell University, working under the direction of Richard Rosecrance.

Index